W9-AQC-609

DECORATIVE ARTS

A Handbook of the Collections of the J. Paul Getty Museum

DECORATIVE ARTS

A Handbook of the Collections of the J. Paul Getty Museum

Adrian Sassoon & Gillian Wilson

THE J. PAUL GETTY MUSEUM

MALIBU · CALIFORNIA

1986

17985 Pacific Coast Highway
Malibu, California 90265
(213) 459-7611

Sandra Knudsen Morgan, managing editor
Lynne Dean, manuscript editor
Patrick Dooley, designer
Karen Schmidt, production coordinator
Elizabeth C. Burke, photograph coordinator
Donald Hull, Stephenie Blakemore, Thomas Paul Moon, Penelope Potter, and Jack Ross, photographers

Typography and production by Mondo Typo, Santa Monica, California
Printed by Gardner/Fulmer Lithograph, Buena Park, California

Front cover left to right: Bust of Louix XV, French (Mennecy), ca. 1750–1755 (No. 157); Ewer and basin, French (Sèvres), 1757 (No. 163); Ewer, Chinese, Kangxi, 1662–1722, and French mounts, ca. 1700–1710 (No. 184); Lidded vase from a garniture, German (Meissen), ca. 1730 (No. 243); One of a pair of lidded tureens, liners and stands by Thomas Germain, French (Paris), 1744–1750 (No. 150). The pieces stand on a commode attributed to Joseph Baumhauer, French (Paris) ca. 1750 (No. 29); in the background is a tapestry from the *Story of the Emperor of China* series, *The Emperor on a Journey,* French (Beauvais), ca. 1690–1705 (No. 213).

Back cover: Italian micromosaic roundel from one of a pair of cabinets attributed to Adam Weisweiler, French (Paris), ca. 1785 (No. 16).

Library of Congress Cataloging-in-Publication Data

J. Paul Getty Museum.
Decorative arts : a handbook of the collections of the J. Paul Getty Museum, 1984.

Bibliography: p.
Includes indexes.
1. Decorative arts—California—Malibu—Catalogs.
2. J. Paul Getty Museum—Catalogs. I. Sassoon, Adrian, 1961– . II. Wilson, Gillian, 1941– III. Title.
NK460.M35J25 1986 745'.074'019493 85-24171
ISBN 0-89236-073-9

CONTENTS

Preface vi
Acknowledgments vii
Abbreviations viii

French Decorative Arts

- Cabinets 1
- Commodes 9
- Corner Cupboards 15
- Desks 19
- *Secrétaires* 20
- Tables 25
- Clocks 36
- Seat Furniture 43
- Carved Tables 49
- Supports 50
- Paneling 51
- Lighting 55
  - Candelabra 55
  - Candlesticks 56
  - Chandeliers 57
  - Wall Lights 58
- Firedogs 63
- Inkstands 64
- Silver 65
- Ceramics 70
  - Chantilly Manufactory 70
  - Mennecy Manufactory 71
  - Vincennes Manufactory 71
  - Sèvres Manufactory 73
- Mounted Oriental Porcelain 87
- Mounted Hardstones 94
- Textiles 96
- Tapestries 99
- Carpets 108
- Decorative Carvings 110
- Decorative Drawings 110

German Decorative Arts

- Cabinet 113
- Commodes 113
- Desk 114
- *Secrétaire* 114
- *Torchères* 115
- Floor 115
- Ceramics 116
  - Meissen Manufactory 116

Italian Decorative Arts

- Cabinets 119
- Commode 120
- Tables 120
- Seat Furniture 121

Chinese Decorative Arts

- Ceramics 123

English Decorative Arts

- Cabinets 125
- Seat Furniture 126
- Mirror 126
- Silver 127
- Irish Silver 136

Persian and Indian Decorative Arts

- Persian Carpets 137
- Indian Carpets 139

Index of Makers 141
Index of Owners 145

PREFACE

This handbook contains entries on all of the objects acquired by the J. Paul Getty Museum's Department of Decorative Arts up to 1984. The entries have been grouped by country of origin and then arranged chronologically within categories determined by form.

Each object is illustrated. Where appropriate and available, the following information has also been supplied: place of manufacture, date, maker, materials, description of marks, measurements, accession number, provenance, exhibition history, bibliography, and commentary. Two indexes are provided: the first lists makers with their dates and relevant biographical data; the second, previous owners and named residences.

Catalogues of the collection are being prepared, and it is hoped that in the interim this book will be of use as a survey to scholars in the field. The majority of the objects included are on display, and most of the pieces in storage can be made accessible to students and scholars by appointment.

Gillian Wilson
Curator
Department of Decorative Arts

ACKNOWLEDGMENTS

This handbook is based on files accumulated since 1971 by Gillian Wilson, Curator of Decorative Arts, The J. Paul Getty Museum. The information was compiled by Adrian Sassoon, Assistant Curator of Decorative Arts, and enlarged upon by Gillian Wilson.

Many people within the Museum assisted in the book's production. Charissa Bremer-David, Curatorial Assistant, Department of Decorative Arts, provided much essential information and supervised the gathering and organization of photographs. Barbara Roberts, Conservator of Decorative Arts, and Brian Considine, Assistant Conservator of Decorative Arts, supplied information concerning materials and the manufacture of objects. The many photographs are the work of Donald Hull and Penelope Potter.

A number of colleagues outside of the Museum have offered much important information. We have repeatedly received invaluable assistance from Geoffrey de Bellaigue, Surveyor of the Queen's Works of Art, London; Theodore Dell, New York; Rosalind Savill, Wallace Collection, London; and Sir Francis Watson, formerly Director of the Wallace Collection and Surveyor of the Queen's Works of Art, London. Colin Streeter, New York, corrected the manuscript and the Index of Owners.

We also wish to acknowledge the contributions of the following:

Daniel Alcouffe, Musée du Louvre, Paris
Jean-Dominique Augarde, Paris
Rotraud Bauer, Kunsthistorisches Museum, Vienna
Christian Baulez, Château de Versailles
Frances Buckland, London
Andrew Ciechanowiecki, Heim Gallery, London
Timothy Clarke, Kent
David Cohen, The J. Paul Getty Center for the History of Art and the Humanities, Los Angeles
Anthony Derham, Christie's, New York
David DuBon, Philadelphia Museum of Art
Winthrop Edey, New York
Svend Eriksen, Copenhagen
Ronald Freyberger, New York
Alvar Gonzalez-Palacios, Rome
Arthur Grimwade, Christie's, London
Leslie Harris, Curator, Kedleston Hall, Derbyshire
Henry Hawley, The Cleveland Museum of Art
Guy Kuraszewski, Château de Versailles
Clare Le Corbeiller, The Metropolitan Museum of Art, New York
Roland de L'Espée, Paris
John McKee, Wallace Collection, London
Jessie McNab, The Metropolitan Museum of Art, New York
Bozenna Majewska-Maszkowska, Royal Castle, Warsaw
Stanley Margolis, Davis, California
Daniel Meyer, Château de Versailles
Maria Leonor d'Orey, Museu Nacional de Arte Antiga, Lisbon
James Parker, The Metropolitan Museum of Art, New York
Bruno Pons, Paris
Alexandre Pradère, Sotheby's, Paris
Tamara Préaud, Manufacture Nationale de Sèvres
Peter Pröschel, Munich
Béatrix Saule, Château de Versailles
Anna Somers-Cocks, Victoria and Albert Museum, London
Edith Standen, The Metropolitan Museum of Art, New York
Pierre Verlet, formerly of the Musée du Louvre, Paris

We are grateful to Theodore Dell for assisting in the correcting of proofs, and we would like to thank Lynne Dean for her fine editing and admirable patience.

ABBREVIATIONS

The following abbreviations have been employed in referring to frequently cited works.

"Acquisitions 1982"
Gillian Wilson, Adrian Sassoon, and Charissa Bremer-David, "Acquisitions Made by the Department of Decorative Arts in 1982," *The J. Paul Getty Museum Journal* 11, 1983, pp. 13–66.

"Acquisitions 1983"
Gillian Wilson, Adrian Sassoon, and Charissa Bremer-David, "Acquisitions Made by the Department of Decorative Arts in 1983," *The J. Paul Getty Museum Journal* 12, 1984, pp. 173–224.

"Acquisitions 1984"
Gillian Wilson, Charissa Bremer-David, and C. Gay Nieda, "Selected Acquisitions Made by the Department of Decorative Arts in 1984," *The J. Paul Getty Museum Journal* 13, 1985, pp. 67–88.

Badin, *Beauvais*
Jules Badin, *La Manufacture de tapisseries de Beauvais depuis ses origines jusqu'à nos jours*, 1909.

Ballot, *Cressent*
Marie-Juliette Ballot, *Charles Cressent: Sculpteur, ébéniste, collectionneur,* Archives de l'art français 10, 1919.

Fenaille, *Gobelins*
Maurice Fenaille, *Etat général des tapisseries de la Manufacture des Gobelins depuis son origine jusqu'à nos jours*, 6 vols., 1903–1923.

Göbel, *Wanteppiche*
Heinrich Göbel, *Die Wanteppiche,* vol. 1, pt. 2, 1928.

Hunter, *Tapestries*
George L. Hunter, *The Practical Book of Tapestries*, 1925.

Jarry, "Boucher Tapestries"
Madeleine Jarry, "A Wealth of Boucher Tapestries in American Museums," *Antiques*, August 1972, pp. 222–231.

Meuvret, *Les Ebénistes*
Jean Meuvret and Claude Frégnac, *Les Ebénistes du XVIIIe siècle français*, 1963.

Molinier, *Le Mobilier*
Emile Molinier, *Histoire générale des arts appliqués à l'industrie du Ve à la fin du XVIIIe siècle,* vol. 3, *Le Mobilier au XVIIe et au XVIIIe siècle*, 1896.

Scheurleer, *Porzellan*
D. F. Lunsingh Scheurleer, *Chinesisches und japanisches Porzellan in europäischen Fassungen,* 1980.

Stürmer, *Möbelkunst*
Michael Stürmer, *Handwerk und höfische Kultur: Europäische Möbelkunst im 18. Jahrhundert*, 1982.

Verlet, *Meubles français*
Pierre Verlet, *Les Meubles français du XVIIIe siècle,* 2nd ed., 1982.

Verlet, *Waddesdon*
Pierre Verlet, *The Savonnerie,* The James A. de Rothschild Collection at Waddesdon Manor, 1982.

Watson, *Louis XVI Furniture*
F. J. B. Watson, *Louis XVI Furniture,* 1960.

Wilson, "Acquisitions 1977 to mid 1979"
Gillian Wilson, "Acquisitions Made by the Department of Decorative Arts, 1977 to mid 1979," *The J. Paul Getty Museum Journal* 6/7, 1978/79, pp. 37–52.

Wilson, "Acquisitions 1979 to mid 1980"
Gillian Wilson, "Acquisitions Made by the Department of Decorative Arts, 1979 to mid 1980," *The J. Paul Getty Museum Journal* 8, 1980, pp. 1–22.

Wilson, "Acquisitions 1981"
Gillian Wilson, "Acquisitions Made by the Department of Decorative Arts, 1981," *The J. Paul Getty Museum Journal* 10, 1982, pp. 63–86.

Wilson, *Clocks*
Gillian Wilson, *French Eighteenth-Century Clocks in The J. Paul Getty Museum,* 1976.

Wilson, *Selections*
Gillian Wilson, *Selections from the Decorative Arts in The J. Paul Getty Museum,* 1983.

Wilson, "Sèvres"
Gillian Wilson, "Sèvres Porcelain at The J. Paul Getty Museum," *The J. Paul Getty Museum Journal* 4, 1977, pp. 5–24.

Wilson et al., *Mounted Oriental Porcelain*
Gillian Wilson, F. J. B. Watson, and Anthony Derham, *Mounted Oriental Porcelain in The J. Paul Getty Museum,* 1982.

FRENCH
Decorative Arts

1

CABINETS

1 CHEST
French, late fifteenth century
Maker unknown
Walnut
No marks
Height: 3′1⅜″ (94.9 cm); Width: 6′10¼″ (208.9 cm); Depth: 2′3″ (68.6 cm)
Accession number 78.DA.108

PROVENANCE

Ugo Bardini, Florence, 1960.

Purchased by J. Paul Getty, 1960.

EXHIBITIONS

Woodside, California. Filoli, on loan, 1983–present.

2 COFFER
French, circa 1550–1600
Maker unknown
Oak; iron
No marks
Height: 3′1¾″ (95.9 cm); Width: 5′10¾″ (179.7 cm); Depth: 2′5⅝″ (75.2 cm)
Accession number 78.DA.124

PROVENANCE

O.V. Watney, Cornbury Park, Oxfordshire. Sold, Christie's, Cornbury Park, May 22, 1967, lot 93.

Purchased at that sale by J. Paul Getty.

EXHIBITIONS

Woodside, California. Filoli, on loan, 1983–present.

2

3

3 CABINET
Burgundy, circa 1580, with mid-nineteenth-century elements
Maker unknown
Walnut; set with painted panels
Painted *1580* on one of front panels.
Height: 10′2″ (309.9 cm); Width: 5′5″ (165.1 cm); Depth: 1′10½″ (57.1 cm)
Accession number 71.DA.89

PROVENANCE

Baron Achille Seillière, Château de Mello, Oise. Sold, Paris, May 1890.

Gauthiot d'Anchier, Governor of Besançon.

Duveen Brothers, New York.

Norton Simon. Sold, Parke Bernet, New York, May 7, 1971, lot 193.

Purchased at that sale by J. Paul Getty.

EXHIBITIONS

Boston. Museum of Fine Arts, on loan, 1965–1971.

Philadelphia. Philadelphia Museum of Art, on loan, 1984–present.

BIBLIOGRAPHY

Edmond Bonaffé, "Le Meuble en France au XVIe siècle," *Gazette des beaux-arts*, 1886, pp. 60–63, illus.

Edmond Bonaffé, *Le Meuble en France au XVIe siècle*, 1887, pp. 84–85, 166–167, illus.

Charles Mannheim, *Catalogue of Objects of Art and Rich Furniture from the Collection of Baron Achille Seillière*, 1890, no. 540, illus.

Georg Hirth, *L'Art pratique*, French ed. of *Formenschatz*, 1891, illus. pl. 7.

Alfred de Champeaux, *Le Meuble*, 1906, vol. 1, pp. 198–199, illus. p. 194.

4

4 CABINET ON STAND

Paris, circa 1675–1680
Attributed to the Gobelins Manufactory; medallions after Jean Varin
Oak veneered with ebony, tortoiseshell, pewter, brass, ivory, horn, and stained and natural woods; lignum vitae drawers; gilt-bronze mounts
No marks
Height: 7′6½″ (230.0 cm); Width: 4′11½″ (151.2 cm); Depth: 2′2¼″ (66.7 cm)
Accession number 77.DA.1

PROVENANCE

(?) William Humble, 11th Baron Ward (created 1st Earl of Dudley, 1860), Witley Court, Worcestershire. House acquired with contents in 1838 from Lord Foley.

(?) William Humble, 2nd Earl of Dudley, Witley Court, circa 1920. Sold with the house to Sir Herbert Smith.

Sir Herbert Smith, Witley Court. Sold, Jackson Stops and Staff, Witley Court, September 29, 1938, lot 582.

Violet van der Elst, Harlaxton Manor, Lincolnshire. Sold, Christie's, London, April 8, 1948, lot 142.

John, 6th Viscount Gort, Hamsterley Hall, County Durham. Sold by his heirs, 1976.

Purchased by the J. Paul Getty Museum, 1976.

EXHIBITIONS

Barnard Castle, County Durham. The Bowes Museum, on loan, 1950's.

London. Victoria and Albert Museum, on loan, August 1978–February 1979.

BIBLIOGRAPHY

Stéphane Faniel et al., *Le XVIIe Siècle français,* Collection connaissance des arts, 1958, illus. p. 53.

Wilson, "Acquisitions 1977 to mid 1979," no. 1, p. 37, illus.

Gillian Wilson, "A Late Seventeenth-Century French Cabinet at the J. Paul Getty Museum," *The Art Institute of Chicago Centennial Lecture,* Museum Studies 10, 1983, pp. 119–131, illus.

Wilson, *Selections,* no. 3, pp. 6–67, illus.

COMMENTARY

The pair to this cabinet is in the collection of the Duke of Buccleuch at Drumlanrig Castle, Scotland. Four of the marquetry birds found on the drawer fronts of this cabinet are cut from the same templates as those on the top of the table in No. 56 of this handbook. This indicates that the marquetry birds, and therefore probably the pieces themselves, were made in the same workshop.

---

5 TWO COFFERS ON STANDS

Paris, circa 1680–1685
Attributed to André-Charles Boulle
Oak and walnut veneered with tortoiseshell, ebony, pewter, and brass; set with mirrored glass; gilt-bronze mounts
One stand stamped H.RASKIN at top of back for Henry Raskin, possibly a nineteenth-century restorer. Many mounts on each coffer and stand stamped with the crowned C for 1745–1749.
Height: 5′1⅝″ (156.6 cm); Width: 2′11⅜″ (89.9 cm); Depth: 1′10″ (55.9 cm)
Accession numbers 82.DA.109.1.a–b and 2.a–b

PROVENANCE

The coffers were reputedly made for Louis, Grand Dauphin of France.

Prince Anatole Demidov, San Donato Palace, Pratolino (near Florence). Sold, San Donato Palace, March 15, 1880, lots 1421 and 1422.

5a

5b

Marquis da Foz, Lisbon.

Mortimer L. Schiff, New York. Sold by his heir, John L. Schiff, Christie's, London, June 22, 1938, lot 68, to Gaston Bensimon, Paris.

Anna Gould (duchesse de Talleyrand), Palais Rose, Paris.

Violette de Talleyrand (Mme Gaston Palewski), Château de Marais, Seine-et-Oise. Offered for sale, Sotheby's, Monaco, May 26, 1980, lot 619, bought in.

Purchased by the J. Paul Getty Museum, 1982.

BIBLIOGRAPHY

Alfred de Champeaux, *Le Meuble,* 1885, vol. 2, p. 78, illus. p. 65.

A. Genevay, *Le Style Louis XIV,* 1886, p. 241, illus. fig. 31.

Henry Havard, *Les Boulles,* 1892, p. 40, illus. pp. 41, 45.

Molinier, *Le Mobilier,* p. 74, illus.

Pierre Verlet, "A propos de Boulle et du Grand Dauphin," *Nederland kunsthistorisch Jaarbuch* 3, 1980, pp. 285–288, illus.

Wilson, "Acquisitions 1982," no. 1, pp. 13–18, illus.

Wilson, *Selections,* no. 6, pp. 12–13, illus.

COMMENTARY

A coffer of this model appears in a 1689 inventory of the Grand Dauphin's possessions at Versailles. Coffer and stand number 82.DA.109.1.a–b can possibly be identified as having been sold from the collection of C. F. Julliot, Paris, November 20, 1777, lot 706.

6

6 CABINET

Paris, circa 1710–1715
Attributed to André-Charles Boulle
Oak veneered with tortoiseshell, brass and ebony; gilt-bronze mounts; *sarrancolin des Pyrénées* marble top
No marks
Height: 2′8½″ (82.5 cm); Width: 4′7¼″ (140.0 cm); Depth: 2′4½″ (72.5 cm)
Accession number 84.DA.58

PROVENANCE

Baron Gustave Salomon de Rothschild, Paris.

Baronne Cecilie de Rothschild, Paris.

Sir Philip Sassoon, Bt., London, by descent, 1912.

Sybil Sassoon (Marchioness of Cholmondeley, wife of the 5th Marquess, married 1913), Houghton Hall, Norfolk, by descent, after 1939. Sold, Christie's, London, April 12, 1984, lot 164.

Purchased at that sale by the J. Paul Getty Museum.

EXHIBITIONS

London. 25 Park Lane, *Three French Reigns,* February–April 1933, ex. cat., no. 71, illus.

BIBLIOGRAPHY

Pierre Verlet, *La Maison du XVIIIe siècle en France,* 1966, p. 38, illus. fig. 21.

Wilson, "Acquisitions 1984," no. 1, pp. 67–69, illus.

7

7 BOOKCASE

Paris, circa 1725
Maker unknown
Oak veneered with kingwood; gilt-bronze mounts
No marks
Height: 8′8¾″ (266.0 cm); Width: 5′10¾″ (179.7 cm); Depth: 1′11¼″ (59.0 cm)
Accession number 74.DA.14

PROVENANCE

(?) Prince Paul Demidov, Villa Demidov, Pratolino (near Florence), after 1872, or Marie Demidov (Princess Abamelek-Lazarev), daughter of Prince Paul Demidov, Villa Demidov, after 1885.

Prince Paul of Yugoslavia (nephew of Princess Abamelek-Lazarev), Villa Demidov. Offered for sale, Sotheby's, Villa Demidov, April 21–24, 1969, lot 266, bought in.

Purchased by J. Paul Getty, 1974.

COMMENTARY

A bookcase of this model is in the collection of the Duke of Northumberland at Alnwick Castle, Northumberland.

8

8 BOOKCASE
Paris, circa 1735–1740
Maker unknown
Oak and pine veneered with kingwood and mahogany; gilt-bronze mounts
No marks
Height: 9′2″ (279.4 cm); Width: 10′3″ (312.4 cm); Depth: 2′6″ (76.2 cm)
Accession number 83.DA.19

PROVENANCE

La Cour de Varenne, Paris, 1982.

Purchased by the J. Paul Getty Museum, 1983.

9 CABINET
Paris, circa 1735–1740
Attributed to Bernard van Risenburgh
Oak veneered with tulipwood, *bois satiné*, and cherry; gilt-bronze mounts; *brèche d'Alep* top
Inscribed DAVAL twice on back.
Height: 3′9 5/8″ (115.8 cm); Width: 15′4 1/2″ (468.6 cm); Depth: 1′9 1/2″ (54.5 cm)
Accession number 77.DA.91

PROVENANCE

Daval *(marchand-mercier)*, Paris, before 1822.

Henri, comte de Greffuhle, Paris. Sold by his widow, Sotheby's, London, July 23, 1937, lot 50, to Arnold Seligmann and Trevor and Co., for £1,400.

David Drey, London, 1950's.

Maurice Aveline, Paris, 1950's.

Antenor Patiño, Paris, circa 1957.

Aveline et Cie, Paris and Geneva.

Purchased by the J. Paul Getty Museum, 1977.

BIBLIOGRAPHY

Charles Guellette, "Les Cabinets d'art à Paris—La Collection de M. Henri de Greffuhle," *Gazette des beaux-arts* 15, 1877, p. 466.

Wilson, "Acquisitions 1977 to mid 1979," no. 3, p. 37, illus.

9

10

10 *CARTONNIER* WITH *SERRE-PAPIER* AND CLOCK
Paris, circa 1745–1749
By Bernard van Risenburgh; clock movement by Etienne Le Noir
Oak veneered with ebonized wood and painted with *vernis Martin;* enameled and painted metal; glass; gilt-bronze mounts
Cartonnier and *serre-papier* stamped B.V.R.B. on back; *cartonnier* also stamped with the name of E.J. CUVELLIER, who possibly restored it. Several mounts stamped with the crowned C for 1745–1749. Clock dial and movement signed *Etienne LeNoir AParis.* Metal plaque on rear of *cartonnier* engraved *Angela's 1835.*
Height: 6′3 5/8″ (192.0 cm); Width: 3′4 9/16″ (103.0 cm); Depth: 1′4 1/8″ (41.0 cm)
Accession number 83.DA.280

PROVENANCE

(?) Sir Francis Burdett, Bt., London.

Angela, Baroness Burdett-Coutts (daughter of Sir Francis Burdett, Bt.), London, probably given to her in 1835 on her twenty-first birthday.

Hon. William Bartlett Burdett-Coutts, M.P. (husband of Angela, Baroness Burdett-Coutts), by descent, 1906. Sold, Christie's, London, May 9, 1922, lot 144, to H. J. Simmons, for 4,200 guineas.

Rothschild collection, Paris. Confiscated after the German occupation of Paris in 1940.

José and Vera Espirito Santo, Lausanne, Switzerland, 1970's.

Purchased by the J. Paul Getty Museum, 1983.

BIBLIOGRAPHY

Sassoon, "Acquisitions 1983," no. 6, pp. 193–197, illus.

11

11 PAIR OF CABINETS

Paris, circa 1750–1755
By Bernard van Risenburgh
Oak veneered with *bois satiné,* kingwood, and cherry; gilt-bronze mounts
Each cabinet stamped B.V.R.B. on back, near center of upper rail.
Height: 4′10⅝″ (149.0 cm); Width: 3′3¾″ (101.0 cm); Depth: 1′7″ (48.3 cm)
Accession number 84.DA.24.1–2

PROVENANCE

Probably purchased by Sir John Hobart Caradoc, 2nd Lord Howden, Grimston Park, Yorkshire, circa 1840.

Albert Denison, Lord Londesborough, Grimston Park, 1850 (?).

(?) William Henry Forester, 2nd Lord Londesborough.

John Fielden, Grimston Park, 1850.

Captain John Fielden (great-nephew of John Fielden). Sold, Henry Spencer and Sons, Retford, Nottinghamshire, May 29–31, 1962, lot 372.

René Weiller, Paris.

Raymond Kraemer, Paris, 1960's.

Kraemer et Cie, Paris, 1970's.

Purchased by the J. Paul Getty Museum, 1984.

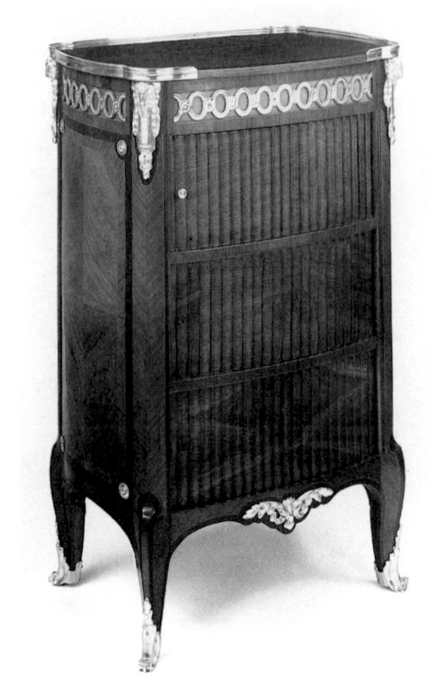

12

12 CABINET

Paris, circa 1765
By Roger Vandercruse called Lacroix
Oak veneered with *bois-de-rose,* amaranth, and green-stained wood; gilt-bronze mounts; white marble interior shelf
Stamped RVLC and JME inside the drawer at top right-hand side.
Height: 3′⅞″ (93.7 cm); Width: 1′11⅜″ (59.3 cm); Depth: 1′5¼″ (43.8 cm)
Accession number 70.DA.81

PROVENANCE

Henry Pelham Archibald Douglas, 7th Duke of Newcastle, Clumber, Nottinghamshire, by descent. Sold by his heir, Christie's, London, June 9, 1937, lot 253.

J. M. Botibol, London.

Purchased by J. Paul Getty, 1938.

13

14

13 CABINET
Paris, circa 1765
By Joseph Baumhauer or his son Gaspard-Joseph Baumhauer
Oak veneered with ebony, tulipwood, and amaranth; set with panels of seventeenth-century Japanese *kijimakie* lacquer; gilt-bronze mounts; yellow jasper top
Stamped JOSEPH between two fleur-de-lys under the apron.
Height: 2′11¼″ (89.6 cm); Width: 3′11⅜″ (120.2 cm); Depth: 1′11⅛″ (58.6 cm)
Accession number 79.DA.58

PROVENANCE

Kraemer et Cie, Paris, 1930–1939.

Private collection, Brussels.

Alexander and Berendt, Ltd., London, 1977.

Purchased by the J. Paul Getty Museum, 1979.

BIBLIOGRAPHY

Wilson, "Acquisitions 1979 to mid 1980," no. 4, pp. 6–7, illus.

Wilson, *Selections,* no. 34, pp. 68–69, illus.

14 CABINET
Paris, circa 1785–1790, with late seventeenth-century panels of marquetry and bronze mounts
Attributed to Philippe-Claude Montigny
Oak veneered with ebony; set with marquetry panels of brass, pewter, tortoiseshell, ebony, and amaranth; gilt-bronze mounts; nero antico marble top
No marks
Height: 3′5¼″ (104.8 cm); Width: 5′4⅝″ (164.2 cm); Depth: 1′10½″ (57.1 cm)
Accession number 72.DA.71

PROVENANCE

Arnold Seligmann, Paris. Sold, Galerie Jean Charpentier, Paris, June 4–5, 1935, lot 192.

François-Gérard Seligmann.

French and Company, New York, 1972.

Purchased by J. Paul Getty, 1972.

BIBLIOGRAPHY

Watson, *Louis XVI Furniture,* no. 236, illus.

Meuvret, *Les Ebénistes,* p. 37, illus.

Stürmer, *Möbelkunst,* illus. pp. 156, 288.

15

16

15 *BONHEUR DU JOUR*
Paris, circa 1785–1790
Attributed to Adam Weisweiler;
Wedgwood jasperware plaques designed by Elizabeth, Lady Templetown, and modeled by William Hackwood
Oak and mahogany veneered with amboyna, ebony, green-stained harewood, and sycamore; set with five Wedgwood green jasperware plaques; gilt-bronze mounts; white marble top and shelf
No marks
Height: 3′6⅜″ (107.6 cm); Width: 2′3¼″ (69.2 cm); Depth: 1′4¼″ (41.3 cm)
Accession number 72.DA.59

PROVENANCE

Private collection, Paris. Sold, Palais Galliera, Paris, March 2, 1972, lot 121.

Purchased at that sale by J. Paul Getty.

16 CABINET
Paris, 1788
By Guillaume Beneman; gilt-bronze mounts cast by Forestier (either Etienne-Jean or his brother Pierre-Auguste) from models by Gilles-François Martin, chased by Bardin and Pierre-Philippe Thomire, and gilded by André Galle
Oak veneered with ebony, mahogany, and lacquer; set with *pietre dure* plaques of seventeenth- and eighteenth-century date; gilt-bronze mounts; *bleu turquin* marble top
Stamped G. BENEMAN twice on top of carcass. Stenciled mark, possibly for the Château de Saint-Cloud, on back.
Height: 2′11$^{15}/_{16}$″ (91.3 cm); Width: 5′5⅛″ (165.4 cm); Depth: 2′1¼″ (64.1 cm)
Accession number 78.DA.361

PROVENANCE

Louis XVI, *chambre à coucher du Roi,* Château de Saint-Cloud, from October 4, 1788. One of a pair costing 5,954 *livres.* Listed in the same room in An II (1793/94).

Earls of Powis, Powis Castle, Wales, by 1848. Sold, Sotheby's, London, May 11, 1962, lot 262.

John Allnat. Sold, Sotheby's, London, June 21, 1974, lot 109, to Didier Aaron, Paris.

Aveline et Cie, Paris.

Purchased by the J. Paul Getty Museum, 1978.

EXHIBITIONS

London. Victoria and Albert Museum, on loan, 1969–1974.

BIBLIOGRAPHY

Meuvret, *Les Ebénistes,* pp. 306–307, illus.

Anthony Coleridge, "Clue to the Provenance of an Outstanding French Commode," *Connoisseur*, July 1966, illus.

Wilson, "Acquisitions 1977 to mid 1979," no. 11, pp. 46–49, illus.

COMMENTARY

This cabinet and its pair, now in the Palacio Real in Madrid, were returned to Beneman for alterations in 1790. They were originally decorated with panels of black oriental lacquer. They are possibly based on a design by Richard de Lalonde and were ordered by Thierry de Ville d'Avray and Jean Hauré.

17a

17b

17 PAIR OF CABINETS
Cabinets: Paris, (1) circa 1785 and (2) circa 1810
Pietre dure plaques: Italian and French, mid-seventeenth to late eighteenth century
Micromosaic roundels: Italian (Rome), early nineteenth century
Both cabinets attributed to Adam Weisweiler
Oak, pine, and beech veneered with ebony and mahogany; pewter stringing; set with *pietre dure* plaques and micromosaic roundels; gilt-bronze mounts; *portor d'Italie* marble tops
Cabinet 1 stamped JME.
Height: 3′4″ (101.6 cm); Width: 4′11⅛″ (150.5 cm); Depth: 1′8⅞″ (53.0 cm)
Accession number 76.DA.9.1–2

PROVENANCE

76.DA.9.1:
M. Marin, Paris. Sold, Paris, March 22, 1790, lot 712, for 3,100 *livres.*

Vincent Donjeux, Paris. Sold, Paris, April 29ff., 1793, lot 554, for 3,200 *livres.*

76.DA.9.1–2:
(?) William Beckford, Fonthill Abbey, Wiltshire.

(?) Susan Beckford (Duchess of Hamilton, wife of the 10th Duke, married 1810, died 1859), Hamilton Palace, Lanarkshire, Scotland.

William, 12th Duke of Hamilton, Hamilton Palace, by descent. Sold, Christie's, Hamilton Palace, June 19, 1882, lots 185 and 186.

Christopher Beckett-Denison, London. Sold, Christie's, London, June 6, 1885, lot 817, to Maclean, and lot 818, to Donaldson.

Moss Harris, London.

Maharanee of Baroda, Paris. Sold, Palais Galliera, Paris, November 29, 1973, lot 114 A and B.

Aveline et Cie, Paris.

Purchased by J. Paul Getty, 1976.

18

COMMODES

18 COMMODE
Paris, circa 1710–1715
Maker unknown
Pine and walnut veneered with tulipwood; gilt-bronze mounts
Stamped on the back with a crowned M, probably for the Château de Maisons, and an interlaced AT over G.M for the *garde-meuble* of the comte d'Artois.
Height: 2′9$\frac{1}{16}$″ (83.9 cm); Width: 4′7¼″ (140.3 cm); Depth: 1′11½″ (59.7 cm)
Accession number 78.DA.87

PROVENANCE

Comte d'Artois, Château de Maisons, after 1777.

(?) Léon Lacroix, Paris, 1938.

Purchased by J. Paul Getty, 1938.

COMMENTARY

The keyhole escutcheons are later replacements.

19

19 COMMODE
Paris, circa 1710–1715
Maker unknown
Oak and pine veneered with rosewood; gilt-bronze mounts; *rouge griotte de Félines* marble top
No marks
Height: 2′9½″ (85.1 cm); Width: 4′ (121.9 cm); Depth: 1′10⅜″ (56.8 cm)
Accession number 73.DA.66

PROVENANCE

Ducs d'Arenberg, Palais d'Arenberg, Brussels, until 1914.

Duchesse Mathildis d'Arenberg, Monte Carlo.

Gallet, Cannes.

French and Company, New York, 1973.

Purchased by J. Paul Getty, 1973.

20

20 COMMODE
Paris, circa 1710–1715
Attributed to the workshop of André-Charles Boulle
Oak and pine veneered with tulipwood and mahogany; gilt-bronze mounts; *brocatelle violette du Jura* marble top
Stamped C.M. COCHOIS on top of carcass.
Many mounts stamped with the crowned C for 1745–1749.
Height: 2′9¾″ (85.7 cm); Width: 4′3¾″ (131.4 cm); Depth: 1′11″ (58.4 cm)
Accession number 70.DA.80

PROVENANCE

(?) Henry Peter, 1st Lord Brougham, Cannes, 1840's or 1850's.

(?) William, 2nd Lord Brougham, England, after 1868.

(?) Hon. Wilfred Brougham, England, after 1886.

Maria Sophia Faunce (Hon. Mrs. Wilfred Brougham), England, after 1904.

J. M. Botibol, London, 1938.

Purchased by J. Paul Getty, 1938.

COMMENTARY

This commode was probably restored or sold in the 1740's by Charles-Michel Cochois.

21

21 COMMODE
Paris, circa 1725–1730
By Etienne Doirat
Oak and pine veneered with kingwood; gilt-bronze mounts; *brèche d'Alep* top
Stamped E. DOIRAT on top of carcass.
Height: 2′10″ (86.4 cm); Width: 5′6½″ (168.9 cm); Depth: 2′4¼″ (71.7 cm)
Accession number 72.DA.66

PROVENANCE

George Durlacher, London. Sold, Christie's, London, April 6–7, 1938, lot 176, to Sutch.

Sold, "Property of a Gentleman," Christie's, London, December 1, 1966, lot 70, to Perman.

Aveline et Cie, Paris, 1972.

Purchased by J. Paul Getty, 1972.

22

23

24

22 COMMODE
Paris, circa 1735
By Charles Cressent
Pine veneered with *bois satiné* and amaranth; gilt-bronze mounts; *brèche d'Alep* top
Corner mounts stamped with the crowned C for 1745–1749.
Height: 2′11½″ (90.2 cm); Width: 4′5¾″ (136.5 cm); Depth: 2′1½″ (64.8 cm)
Accession number 70.DA.82

PROVENANCE

Duveen Brothers, New York.

George J. Gould, Georgian Court, Lakewood, New Jersey. (?) Sold, Samuel Marx Inc., New York, April 28, 1924, lot 272.

Arnold Seligmann, Rey and Co., New York.

Purchased by J. Paul Getty, 1938.

BIBLIOGRAPHY

Ballot, *Cressent,* no. 132, p. 215.

Wilson, *Selections,* no. 19, pp. 38–39, illus.

COMMENTARY

This commode is described in some detail in the Cressent auction catalogue of February 15, 1757, lot 132.

23 COMMODE
Paris, circa 1740
By Bernard van Risenburgh
Oak set with panels of black Japanese lacquer and painted with *vernis Martin;* cherry and amaranth on interior of the doors; gilt-bronze mounts; *sarrancolin* marble top
Stamped B.V.R.B. on top of carcass.
Height: 2′10¾″ (88.3 cm); Width: 4′11¾″ (151.9 cm); Depth: 1′10¾″ (57.8 cm)
Accession number 65.DA.4

PROVENANCE

Colbert family, France, by repute from the eighteenth to the twentieth century.

Rosenberg and Stiebel, New York.

Purchased by J. Paul Getty, 1953.

BIBLIOGRAPHY

Wilson, *Selections,* no. 14, pp. 28–29, illus.

24 COMMODE
Paris, circa 1740
By Bernard van Risenburgh
Oak set with panels of red Japanese lacquer and painted with *vernis Martin;* gilt-bronze mounts; *brèche d'Alep* top
Stamped B.V.R.B. once and JME twice on top of carcass.
Height: 2′9″ (83.8 cm); Width: 3′9″ (114.3 cm); Depth: 1′9⅝″ (54.9 cm)
Accession number 72.DA.46

PROVENANCE

Private collection, Paris. Sold, Palais Galliera, Paris, March 2, 1972, lot 109.

Purchased at that sale by J. Paul Getty.

25

25 COMMODE

Paris, circa 1740
Attributed to Jean Desforges
Oak veneered with kingwood, walnut, amaranth, and padouk; gilt-bronze mounts; *brèche d'Alep* top
Stamped DF on top of carcass.
Height: 2′10¼″ (87.0 cm); Width: 5′1¼″ (155.5 cm); Depth: 2′1″ (63.5 cm)
Accession number 76.DA.15

PROVENANCE

Mrs. S. Shrigley-Feigel, Crag Hall, Lancashire.

Alexander and Berendt, Ltd., London, 1976.

Purchased by J. Paul Getty, 1976.

26

26 COMMODE

Paris, circa 1745–1750
By Jean-Pierre Latz
Oak veneered with *bois satiné*; gilt-bronze mounts; *fleur de pêcher* marble top
Stamped RESTAURE par P.SPOHN on top of carcass.
Height: 2′10½″ (87.7 cm); Width: 4′11⅝″ (151.5 cm); Depth: 2′2⅝″ (65.0 cm)
Accession number 83.DA.356

PROVENANCE

Sir Anthony de Rothschild, Bt., England.

Annie de Rothschild (Hon. Mrs. Eliot Yorke; daughter of Sir Anthony de Rothschild), England. Sold, Christie's, London, May 5, 1927, lot 138, to S. Founés, for 980 guineas.

Mme Duselschon, Château de Coudira, Prégny, Switzerland.

Mme Rouvière, Lausanne, Switzerland.

Maurice Segoura, Paris, 1983.

Purchased by the J. Paul Getty Museum, 1983.

BIBLIOGRAPHY

Wilson, "Acquisitions 1983," no. 7, pp. 197–198, illus.

COMMENTARY

A commode of the same form and decoration stamped I.P. LATZ is in the Palazzo Quirinale, Rome. It was taken by Madame Louise-Elisabeth, daughter of Louis XV, to Parma in 1753, by which time she had become the Duchess of Parma.

27

27 COMMODE

Paris, circa 1745–1749
Attributed to Jean Desforges
Oak veneered with rosewood, *bois satiné*, and other woods; gilt-bronze mounts; *brèche d'Alep* top
Stamped DF on top of carcass. Mounts stamped with the crowned C for 1745–1749.
Height: 2′8½″ (82.5 cm); Width: 3′5″ (104.1 cm); Depth: 1′7½″ (49.5 cm)
Accession number 79.DA.166

PROVENANCE

Mrs. Evelyn St. George, Cam House, London. Sold, Sotheby's, Cam House, July 24, 1939, lot 93.

Purchased at that sale by J. Paul Getty.

EXHIBITIONS

Woodside, California. Filoli, on loan, 1985–present.

28

28 PAIR OF COMMODES
Paris, circa 1750
By Bernard van Risenburgh
Oak veneered with tulipwood, kingwood, and amaranth; gilt-bronze mounts; one commode with a *brèche violette* top, one with a *brocatelle jaune* top
Each commode stamped B.V.R.B. twice on top of carcass.
Height: 2′10⅜″ (87.3 cm); Width: 3′4⅛″ (101.9 cm); Depth: 1′10″ (55.9 cm)
Accession number 71.DA.96.1–2

PROVENANCE

(?) Given by Louis, Dauphin of France (1729–1765), to his father-in-law, Frederick Augustus III, Elector of Saxony and King of Poland. Listed in inventories of the Residenz, Dresden, in 1794 and 1798.

Prince Ernst Heinrich von Wettin, Schloss Moritzburg (near Dresden), Saxony. Installed in the Tower Room circa 1924. Sold early 1930's.

C. Ball, Paris, 1934.

Anna Thomson Dodge, Rose Terrace, Grosse Pointe Farms, Michigan. Sold, Christie's, London, June 24, 1971, lot 102.

Purchased at that sale by J. Paul Getty.

BIBLIOGRAPHY

Adolf Feulner, *Kunstgeschichte des Möbels*, 1927, pp. 324–325.

Stürmer, *Möbelkunst*, illus. p. 67.

Wilson, *Selections*, no. 20, pp. 40–41, illus.

COMMENTARY

These commodes come from a set that contained three larger commodes—now at Schloss Pillnitz, near Dresden—and a pair of corner cupboards destroyed in Dresden during the Second World War.

29

29 COMMODE
Paris, circa 1750
Attributed to Joseph Baumhauer
Oak set with brown Japanese lacquer and painted with French *vernis Martin;* gilt-bronze mounts; *campan mélangé vert* marble top
One trade label of the *marchand-mercier* François-Charles Darnault pasted on top of carcass and one pasted underneath.
Height: 2′10¾″ (88.3 cm); Width: 4′9½″ (146.1 cm); Depth: 2′⅝″ (62.6 cm)
Accession number 55.DA.2

PROVENANCE

Sir Alfred Chester Beatty, London.

Purchased by J. Paul Getty, 1955, through Sir Robert Abdy.

BIBLIOGRAPHY

Wilson, *Selections*, no. 23, pp. 46–47, illus.

COMMENTARY

A commode of the same model, stamped by Joseph Baumhauer and decorated with lacquer panels, is in the Victoria and Albert Museum, London.

30

30 COMMODE
Paris, circa 1755
By Adrien-Faizelot Delorme
Oak veneered with tulipwood and kingwood; gilt-bronze mounts; *lumachella pavonazza* marble top
Stamped DELORME, JME, and N.PETIT on top of commode.
Height: 2′11½″ (90.1 cm); Width: 4′9″ (144.8 cm); Depth: 2′2¼″ (66.6 cm)
Accession number 70.DA.79

PROVENANCE

J. M. Botibol, London, 1938.

Purchased by J. Paul Getty, 1938.

BIBLIOGRAPHY

André Boutemy, "Joseph," *Connaissance des arts*, March 1965, illus. p. 84.

COMMENTARY

It is likely that this commode was made in the workshop of Adrien-Faizelot Delorme and later sold by Nicolas Petit, who, complying with guild regulations, stamped it with his name.

31

31 COMMODE

Paris, circa 1760
By Jean-François Oeben
Oak veneered with tulipwood, kingwood, sycamore, amaranth, and burl wood; gilt-bronze mounts; *campan mélangé vert* marble top
Stamped J.F.OEBEN and JME twice on top of carcass.
Height: 2′11⅞″ (91.1 cm); Width: 4′7⅜″ (140.6 cm); Depth: 1′6⅛″ (46.0 cm)
Accession number 72.DA.54

PROVENANCE

Private collection, Paris (possibly Goupil de Douilla).

Frank Partridge Ltd., London.

Guedes de Souza, Paris.

Etienne Lévy, Paris, and Frank Partridge Ltd., London, 1972.

Purchased by J. Paul Getty, 1972.

32

32 COMMODE

Paris, 1769
By Gilles Joubert
Oak veneered with kingwood, tulipwood, holly or boxwood, and ebony; gilt-bronze mounts; *sarrancolin* marble top
Painted in black ink on back with the inventory number *du N° 2556.2* of the Garde-Meuble de la Couronne.
Height: 3′⅝″ (93.0 cm); Width: 5′11¼″ (181.0 cm); Depth: 2′2½″ (67.3 cm)
Accession number 55.DA.5

PROVENANCE

Made for Madame Louise of France (youngest daughter of Louis XV), Château de Versailles, 1769.

Emmanuel-Felicité, duc de Duras, Maréchal de France, Château de Fontainebleau, 1785.

Lionel de Rothschild, Exbury, Hampshire.

Sir Alfred Chester Beatty, London.

Purchased by J. Paul Getty, 1955.

EXHIBITIONS

Paris. Hôtel de la Monnaie, *Louis XV: Un Moment de perfection de l'art français*, 1974, ex. cat., no. 422, pp. 320–321, illus.

BIBLIOGRAPHY

Watson, *Louis XVI Furniture*, no. 24, illus.

Douglas Cooper, *Great Private Collections*, 1963, p. 187, illus.

Pierre Verlet, *French Royal Furniture*, 1963, pp. 77, 111, illus.

Meuvret, *Les Ebénistes*, p. 68, illus.

Svend Eriksen, *Early Neo-Classicism in France*, 1974, illus. pl. 120.

Verlet, *Meubles français*, p. 27, illus. (detail).

COMMENTARY

This commode was one of a pair delivered by Gilles Joubert on August 28, 1769, for use in the bedroom of Madame Louise at Versailles. The present whereabouts of the companion piece is unknown.

33

33 COMMODE
Paris, circa 1870–1880
Maker unknown
Oak veneered with mahogany, satinwood, and various stained and natural woods; gilt-bronze mounts; gray-veined white marble top
Stamped with forged marks J.H.RIESENER, for Jean-Henri Riesener, and JME on top of carcass.
Height: 3′4⅛″ (101.9 cm); Width: 5′5¼″ (165.7 cm); Depth: 2′⅜″ (61.9 cm)
Accession number 67.DA.8

PROVENANCE

Arnold Seligmann, Rey and Co., New York, 1928.

Henry Walters, New York. Sold by his widow, Parke Bernet, New York, May 3, 1941, lot 1419.

Purchased at that sale by J. Paul Getty, through Duveen.

EXHIBITIONS

Woodside, California. Filoli, on loan, 1983–present.

COMMENTARY

In the 1941 Walters auction catalogue this commode was said to have been sold by the comte de Chastellux in 1858.

34a

34b

CORNER CUPBOARDS

34 PAIR OF CORNER CUPBOARDS
Paris, circa 1740
By Bernard van Risenburgh
Oak set with panels of black Japanese lacquer and painted with *vernis Martin;* gilt-bronze mounts; *sarrancolin* marble tops
Each cupboard stamped B.V.R.B. twice on top of carcass.
Height: 3′3⅛″ (99.4 cm); Width: 2′10¾″ (88.3 cm); Depth: 2′⅛″ (61.2 cm)
Accession number 72.DA.44.1–2

PROVENANCE

Kraemer et Cie, Paris, 1972.

Purchased by J. Paul Getty, 1972.

35

35 PAIR OF CORNER CABINETS
Paris, circa 1745
Attributed to Charles Cressent
Oak veneered with tulipwood, kingwood, and amaranth; gilt-bronze mounts
No marks
Height: 6′3½″ (191.8 cm); Width: 10′11″ (332.7 cm); Depth: 1′3½″ (39.4 cm)
Accession number 79.DA.2.1–2

PROVENANCE

(?) Baron Mayer Alphonse de Rothschild, Paris.

Baron Edouard de Rothschild, Paris.

Baron Guy de Rothschild, Paris.

Purchased by the J. Paul Getty Museum, 1979.

BIBLIOGRAPHY

Ballot, *Cressent,* pp. 128, 151–152.

Meuvret, *Les Ebénistes,* illus. p. 46.

Claude Frégnac and Wayne Andrews, *The Great Houses of Paris,* 1979, p. 257, illus.

Wilson, "Acquisitions 1977 to mid 1979," no. 15, p. 52, illus. (one).

36 PAIR OF CORNER CUPBOARDS

Paris, circa 1750–1755

Carcass and mounts attributed to Jean-Pierre Latz; marquetry panels attributed to the workshop of Jean-François Oeben

Oak veneered with amaranth, stained sycamore, boxwood, harewood, lignum vitae, and various stained fruitwoods; gilt-bronze mounts; *brèche d'Alep* tops

No marks

Height: 3′2¼″ (97.2 cm); Width: 2′9¾″ (85.7 cm); Depth: 1′11⅛″ (58.7 cm)

Accession number 72.DA.39.1–2

PROVENANCE

Leslie collection, England, 1911.

L. Currie, England, 1917.

Private collection, Berlin. Sold, Hugo Helbing Gallery, Berlin, June 23, 1936, lot 49.

Private collection, Germany. Sold, Lempertz Gallery, Cologne, March 11, 1938, lot 217.

Private collection, New York. Sold, Parke Bernet, New York, October 21–22, 1955, lot 358.

Philip R. Consolo, Palm Beach, Florida.

Frank Partridge Ltd., London, 1966.

Purchased by J. Paul Getty, 1972.

36a

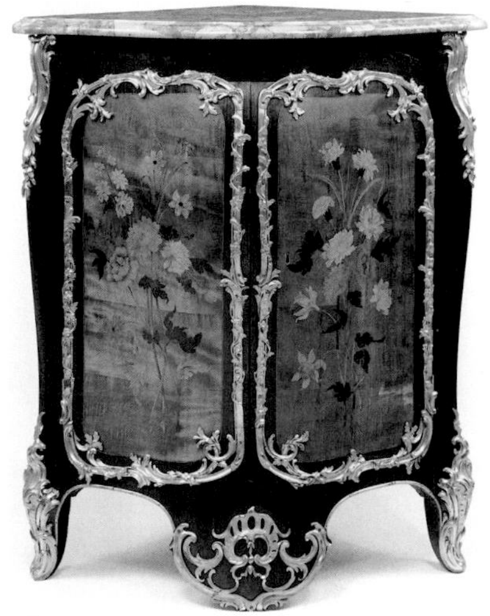

36b

EXHIBITIONS

London. Victoria and Albert Museum, on loan, 1913, from Mr. Leslie.

London. Victoria and Albert Museum, on loan, 1917, from L. Currie.

BIBLIOGRAPHY

Henry Hawley, "Jean-Pierre Latz, Cabinetmaker," *Bulletin of the Cleveland Museum of Art,* September/October 1970, no. 49, illus. (one).

Wilson, *Selections,* no. 24, pp. 48–49, illus.

COMMENTARY

The marquetry depiction of lilies is based on engravings of designs by Louis Tessier.

37 PAIR OF CORNER CUPBOARDS

Paris, circa 1750–1755

Carcass and mounts attributed to Jean-Pierre Latz; marquetry panels attributed to the workshop of Jean-François Oeben.

Oak veneered with amaranth, stained sycamore, rosewood, boxwood, and various stained fruitwoods; gilt-bronze mounts; *brèche d'Alep* tops

No marks

Height: 3′¼″ (92.1 cm); Width: 2′8¼″ (81.9 cm); Depth: 2′ (61.0 cm)

Accession number 72.DA.69.1–2

PROVENANCE

Sidney J. Block, London.

French and Company, New York, 1972.

Purchased by J. Paul Getty, 1972.

BIBLIOGRAPHY

Henry Hawley, "Jean-Pierre Latz, Cabinetmaker," *Bulletin of the Cleveland Museum of Art,* September/October 1970, no. 50, illus. (one).

37a

37b

38 CORNER CUPBOARD

Paris, circa 1755
By Jacques Dubois; clock movement by Etienne Le Noir
Oak veneered with *bois satiné*, tulipwood, and rosewood; enameled metal; gilt-bronze mounts
Stamped I.DUBOIS twice on back of carcass. Signed *Etienne Le Noir A Paris* on clock face and movement. Penciled with the Rothschild inventory number *AR 653* on back.
Height: 9′6″ (289.5 cm); Width: 4′3″ (129.5 cm); Depth: 2′4 3/8″ (72.0 cm)
Accession number 79.DA.66

PROVENANCE

Made for Count Jan Klemens Branicki, Warsaw. Ordered by General Mokronowski through the *marchand-mercier* Lullier of Warsaw in 1753.

Probably Christine Branicka (sister of Count Branicki), by descent.

Marianna Syzmanowska (née Potocka; granddaughter of Christine Branicka), by the 1820's.

Baron Nathaniel de Rothschild, Vienna, before 1896.

Baron Alphonse de Rothschild, Vienna.

Baroness Clarice de Rothschild, Vienna and New York, 1942.

Rosenberg and Stiebel, and Wildenstein, New York, 1940's.

Georges Wildenstein, New York, 1940's.

Daniel Wildenstein, New York.

Akram Ojjeh, 1978. Sold, Sotheby's, Monaco, June 25–26, 1979, lot 60.

Purchased at that sale by the J. Paul Getty Museum.

BIBLIOGRAPHY

Molinier, *Le Mobilier*, pp. 146–147, illus. pl. XIII.

Nathaniel de Rothschild, *Notizen über einige meiner Kunstgegenstände*, 1903, no. 80.

38

Robert Schmidt, *Möbel: Ein Handbuch für Sammler und Liebehaber*, 1920, illus. fig. 130.

Adolf Feulner, *Kunstgeschichte des Möbels*, 1926, p. 445, illus. p. 321.

Adolf Feulner, *Kunstgeschichte des Möbels seit dem Altertum*, 1927, pp. 330–331, Pineau design illus. p. 321.

Charles Packer, *Paris-Furniture*, 1956, p. 34, illus. fig. 40.

André Boutemy, "Des Meubles Louis XV à grands succès: Les Encoignures," *Connaissance des arts,* September 1959, p. 36, illus. p. 41.

Meuvret, *Les Ebénistes,* p. 101–102, illus. p. 100.

Comte François de Salverte, *Les Ebénistes du XVIIIe siècle,* rev. ed., 1963, p. 100, illus. pl. XVIII.

Alvar Gonzalez-Palacios, *Gli ebanisti del Luigi XV,* 1966, p. 67.

Claude Frégnac, *Les Styles français,* 1975, p. 100, illus. pl. 2.

Pierre Kjellberg, "Jacques Dubois," *Connaissance des arts,* December 1979, p. 115, illus.

Adolf Feulner, *Kunstgeschichte des Möbels,* 1980, illus. no. 292.

Wilson, "Acquisitions 1979 to mid 1980," no. 1, pp. 1–3, illus.

Wilson, *Selections,* no. 21, pp. 42–43, illus.

COMMENTARY

This cupboard is based on a drawing by Nicolas Pineau now in the Musée des Arts Décoratifs, Paris. The design was published in Paris in 1727 by Jean Mariette, and it was republished in Germany by Johann Georg Merz.

39a

39b

39 PAIR OF CORNER CUPBOARDS
Paris, circa 1755
By Jacques Dubois
Oak veneered with black Chinese (?) lacquer; gilt-bronze mounts; *brèche d'Alep* tops
Each cupboard stamped I. DUBOIS and JME on top of carcass.
Height: 3′2¼″ (97.1 cm); Width: 2′7½″ (80.0 cm); Depth: 1′11⅛″ (58.6 cm)
Accession number 78.DA.119.1–2

PROVENANCE

Baron Nathaniel de Rothschild, Vienna.

Baron Alphonse de Rothschild, Vienna.

Baroness Clarice de Rothschild, Vienna and New York, 1942.

Frank Partridge Ltd., London, 1950.

Purchased by J. Paul Getty, 1950.

40

40 PAIR OF CORNER CUPBOARDS
Paris, circa 1765
By Pierre Garnier
Oak veneered with ebony, tulipwood, and amaranth; gilt-bronze mounts; gray-veined white marble tops
Each cupboard stamped P.GARNIER on top of carcass. Incised 1 on top of one carcass, 4 on the other.
Height: 4′5¼″ (135.2 cm); Width: 2′ (61.0 cm); Depth: 1′4½″ (41.9 cm)
Accession number 81.DA.82.1–2

PROVENANCE

François-Ferdinand-Joseph Godefroy, Paris. Sold, Hôtel de Bullion, Paris, November 15, 1785, lot 238 *bis*, to Harcourt (?).

Espirito Santo family, Portugal, and Lausanne, Switzerland. Sold circa 1976.

Didier Aaron, New York, 1980.

Purchased by the J. Paul Getty Museum, 1981.

BIBLIOGRAPHY

Wilson, "Acquisitions 1981," no. 3, pp. 71–73, illus.

Wilson, *Selections*, no. 31, pp. 62–63, illus.

41

DESKS

41 DOUBLE DESK
Paris, circa 1750
By Bernard van Risenburgh
Oak veneered with tulipwood and kingwood; gilt-bronze mounts
Stamped B.V.R.B. underneath and on interior of carcass. Underside of carcass bears several red wax seals of the Duke of Argyll.
Height: 3′6½″ (107.8 cm); Width: 5′2½″ (158.7 cm); Depth: 2′9⅜″ (84.7 cm)
Accession number 70.DA.87

PROVENANCE

Purchased by Elizabeth Gunning (Duchess of Argyll, wife of the 5th Duke, married 1759, died 1790) in Paris in the 1760's.

Dukes of Argyll, Inverary Castle, Argyll, Scotland. Sold by Ian, 11th Duke of Argyll, 1951.

Sir Robert Abdy, London, 1951.

Rosenberg and Stiebel, New York, 1952.

Purchased by J. Paul Getty, 1952.

EXHIBITIONS

Paris. Hôtel de la Monnaie, *Louis XV: Un Moment de perfection de l'art français*, 1974, ex. cat., no. 430, pp. 327–328, illus.

BIBLIOGRAPHY

André Boutemy, "Les Vraies Formes du bureau dos d'âne," *Connaissance des arts*, July 1958, p. 43, illus.

Meuvret, *Les Ebénistes*, p. 78, illus.

Claude Frégnac, *Les Styles français*, 1975, illus. pl. 4.

Verlet, *Meubles français*, p. 27, illus. pl. 3. (detail).

Wilson, *Selections*, no. 22, pp. 44–45, illus.

42

42 ROLLTOP DESK
Paris, circa 1785–1790
By Bernard Molitor
Oak veneered with mahogany and lacquer; gilt-bronze mounts; *griotte de Flandre* marble top
Stamped B. MOLITOR on lip of one interior drawer.
Height: 4′5⅝″ (136.2 cm); Width: 5′9⅞″ (177.4 cm); Depth: 2′10¼″ (87.0 cm)
Accession number 67.DA.9

PROVENANCE

(?) Louis XVI, Château de Saint-Cloud.

Vandyck, London. Offered for sale Christie's, London, May 16, 1800, lot 101, and again February 12, 1801, lot 70, bought in.

(Octavius E. ?) Coope, London.

Mortimer L. Schiff, New York. Sold by his heir, John L. Schiff, Christie's, London, June 22, 1938, lot 59.

Purchased at that sale by J. Paul Getty.

43

SECRETAIRES

43 *SECRETAIRE*
Paris, circa 1755
By Jacques Dubois
Oak set with panels of red Chinese lacquer and painted with *vernis Martin*; gilt-bronze mounts; *brèche d'Alep* top
Stamped I.DUBOIS and JME at rear on right upright.
Height: 3′4½″ (102.8 cm); Width: 3′9″ (114.3 cm); Depth: 1′3⅛″ (38.4 cm)
Accession number 65.DA.3

PROVENANCE

Rosenberg and Stiebel, New York.

Purchased by J. Paul Getty, 1951.

44

44 *SECRETAIRE*
Paris, 1770
Attributed to Jean-François Leleu
Oak veneered with amaranth, ebony, kingwood, tulipwood, boxwood, and amboyna; gilt-bronze mounts; *brèche d'Alep* top
Inked *1770* inside carcass. Label printed *Earl of Rosebery* pasted on back.
Height: 3′5⅞″ (106.3 cm); Width: 3′11¼″ (120.0 cm); Depth: 1′5¼″ (43.8 cm)
Accession number 82.DA.81

PROVENANCE

Baron Mayer Amschel de Rothschild, Mentmore Towers, Buckinghamshire, late nineteenth century.

Hannah de Rothschild (Countess of Rosebery, wife of the 5th Earl, married 1878, died 1890), Mentmore Towers.

Harold, 6th Earl of Rosebery, Mentmore Towers.

Neil, 7th Earl of Rosebery, Mentmore Towers. Sold, Sotheby's, Mentmore Towers, May 18, 1977, lot 24.

Private collection, London, 1977.

Purchased by the J. Paul Getty Museum, 1982.

BIBLIOGRAPHY

Wilson, "Acquisitions 1982," no. 12, pp. 56–60, illus.

Wilson, *Selections*, no. 37, pp. 56–57, illus.

45 *SECRETAIRE*
Paris, circa 1775
By René Dubois
Oak veneered with kingwood, tulipwood, and lemonwood; incised with colored mastics; set with mother-of-pearl; gilt-bronze mounts; white marble top
Stamped I.DUBOIS and JME on back.
Height: 5′3″ (160.0 cm); Width: 2′3⅝″ (70.2 cm); Depth: 1′1¼″ (33.7 cm)
Accession number 72.DA.60

PROVENANCE

Sir Richard Wallace, Paris.

Sir John Murray Scott, London. Sold, Christie's, London, June 24, 1913, lot 54, to E. M. Hodgkins.

Jacques Seligmann, Paris.

Henry Walters, New York. Sold by his widow, Parke Bernet, New York, April 26, 1941, lot 712.

Baron and Baroness Cassel van Doorn, Paris. Sold, Galerie Jean Charpentier, Paris, March 9, 1954, lot 90.

Guedes de Souza, Paris.

Frank Partridge Ltd., London, 1972.

Purchased by J. Paul Getty, 1972.

BIBLIOGRAPHY

Jean Nicolay, *L'Art et la manière des maîtres ébénistes français au XVIIIème siècle*, 1956, p. 153, illus.

Watson, *Louis XVI Furniture*, no. 89, illus.

Meuvret, *Les Ebénistes*, p. 221, illus.

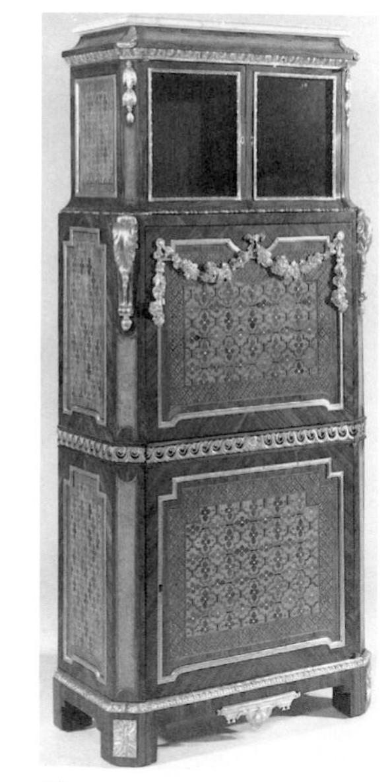

45

46

46 *SECRETAIRE*
Paris, circa 1775
By Martin Carlin; circular Sèvres porcelain plaque painted by Jean-Jacques Pierre *le jeune*
Oak veneered with kingwood, boxwood, and ebony; incised with colored mastics; set with eight soft paste Sèvres porcelain plaques; gilt-bronze mounts; white marble top
Stamped M.CARLIN and JME twice on lower back. Circular porcelain plaque painted with blue crossed L's of the Sèvres Manufactory, enclosing the date letter X for 1775, and with the *P'* mark of Pierre *le jeune* and a black number *216*. Four other plaques painted with blue crossed L's, enclosing the date letter X, and with an unidentified painter's mark. Central plaque in the frieze painted with the crossed L's in gold and a rubbed gilder's mark. Rothschild inventory number KKU 859 chalked on back of carcass.
Height: 3′11¼″ (120.0 cm); Width: 3′1½″ (95.2 cm); Depth: 1′1³⁄₁₆″ (33.5 cm)
Accession number 65.DA.2

PROVENANCE

Baron Nathaniel de Rothschild, Vienna.

Baron Alphonse de Rothschild, Vienna.

Baroness Clarice de Rothschild, Vienna and New York, 1942.

Rosenberg and Stiebel, New York, 1950.

Purchased by J. Paul Getty, 1950.

BIBLIOGRAPHY

Nathaniel de Rothschild, *Notizen über einige meiner Kunstgegenstände*, 1903, no. 319.

Stürmer, *Möbelkunst*, p. 47, illus.

47

47 *SECRETAIRE*
Paris, circa 1776, with early twentieth-century stand
By Claude-Charles Saunier; replaced stand by F. Durand *fils*; the Sèvres porcelain plaques painted by Jean-Baptiste Tandart and gilded by Baudouin *père*
Oak veneered with tulipwood and amaranth; set with four soft paste Sèvres porcelain plaques; gilt-bronze mounts; white marble top
Stamped C.C.SAUNIER on upper back; stamped F. DURAND Fils on side rail of stand. Plaques painted on their reverses with the blue crossed L's of the Sèvres Manufactory—two enclosing the date letter Y for 1776, two flanked by two date letter Y's. Two plaques painted with Tandart's three-dot mark and four with Baudouin's mark *BD*. Each plaque bears paper price label (only one intact) printed with crossed L's and inked *132* [*livres*]. Inscribed in pencil *Saunier le Jeune 1776* on carcass.
Height: 4′1⅞″ (126.8 cm); Width: 2′4⅝″ (72.8 cm); Depth: 1′4⅝″ (42.2 cm)
Accession number 67.DA.7

PROVENANCE

Prince Narishkine, New York (?).

Henry Walters, New York. Sold by his widow, Parke Bernet, New York, May 3, 1941, lot 1399.

Purchased at that sale by J. Paul Getty, through Duveen.

48

48 *SECRETAIRE*
Paris, circa 1776–1777
By Martin Carlin; the two smaller Sèvres porcelain plaques in the fall front painted by Jean-Charles Sioux *l'aîné*
Oak veneered with tulipwood, satinwood, amaranth, and ebony; set with five soft paste Sèvres porcelain plaques; enameled metal; gilt-bronze mounts; white marble top
Stamped M.CARLIN and JME twice under drawer front. All porcelain plaques painted on their reverses with the blue crossed L's of the Sèvres Manufactory. The two larger plaques bear the blue date letter Y for 1776. The left drawer-front plaque painted with Sioux's mark of dots in black; the central plaque bears an unidentified painter's mark in blue and the date letter Z for 1777 with a paper price label printed with crossed L's and inked 36 [*livres*]; the right plaque painted with Sioux's mark of dots in black, the marks X and 10 in gold, and the blue date letter Z.
Height: 3′6¼″ (107.9 cm); Width: 3′3¾″ (101.0 cm); Depth: 1′2″ (35.5 cm)
Accession number 81.DA.80

PROVENANCE

(?) Don Francesco de Borja Alvarez de Toledo, 16th Duke of Medina-Sidonia and 12th Marquess of Villafranca.

Don Pedro de Alcantara Alvarez de Toledo, 17th Duke of Medina-Sidonia. Sold by his heir, the Marquess of Villafranca, Hôtel Drouot, Paris, April 21, 1870, lot 23.

Purchased at that sale by Richard, 4th Marquess of Hertford, Paris, through Nieuwenhuys.

Sir Richard Wallace, Paris, by descent, 1870.

Lady Wallace, Paris, by descent, 1890.

Sir John Murray Scott, Paris, by descent, 1897.

Victoria, Lady Sackville, Paris, by descent, 1912.

Jacques Seligmann, Paris.

Baron and Baronne Edouard de Rothschild, Paris.

Mr. and Mrs. Habib Sabet, Paris, early 1970's.

Purchased by the J. Paul Getty Museum, 1981.

BIBLIOGRAPHY

Wilson, "Acquisitions 1981," no. 1, pp. 63–66, illus.

Dorothée Guilleme-Brulon, "Les Plaques en porcelaine de Sèvres dans le mobilier," *L'Estampille*, November 1983, pp. 42–43, illus.

Wilson, *Selections*, no. 39, pp. 78–79.

49 *SECRETAIRE*

Paris, circa 1780
Attributed to Adam Weisweiler; two of the Sèvres porcelain plaques gilded by Henry-François Vincent *le jeune*
Oak veneered with amboyna and ebonized wood; set with five soft paste Sèvres porcelain plaques; gilt-bronze mounts; white marble top
One of the porcelain plaques painted in gold on its reverse with the crossed L's of the Sèvres Manufactory and the gilder Vincent's mark *2000*; it also bears a torn, printed Sèvres price label inked *72*.
Height: 4′7/8″ (124.2 cm); Width: 2′8¼″ (81.9 cm); Depth: 1′2⅝″ (37.2 cm)
Accession number 70.DA.83

PROVENANCE

Jules Lowengard, Paris.

Baron Nathaniel de Rothschild, Vienna.

Baron Alphonse de Rothschild, Vienna.

Baroness Clarice de Rothschild, Vienna and New York, 1942.

Rosenberg and Stiebel, New York.

Purchased by J. Paul Getty, 1950.

BIBLIOGRAPHY

Seymour de Ricci, *Louis XVI Furniture*, 1913, p. 127, illus.

Watson, *Louis XVI Furniture*, no. 86, illus.

Meuvret, *Les Ebénistes*, p. 286, illus. (erroneously described as being in the Metropolitan Museum of Art, New York).

49

50

50 *SECRETAIRE*

Paris, circa 1785
Attributed to Jean-Henri Riesener; gilt-bronze plaque of the *Sacrifice to Cupid* after a model attributed to Clodion
Oak veneered with panels of black Japanese lacquer and ebony; gilt-bronze mounts; black marble top
Two paper labels inked *Hamilton Palace* on back.
Height: 5′1″ (154.9 cm); Width: 3′8½″ (113.0 cm); Depth: 1′6⅜″ (46.6 cm)
Accession number 71.DA.104

PROVENANCE

George Watson Taylor, Erlestoke Mansion, Wiltshire. Sold, Erlestoke, July 9ff., 1832, lot 26.

Alexander, 10th Duke of Hamilton, Hamilton Palace, Lanarkshire, Scotland. Listed in the duke's dressing room in an inventory of 1835–1840.

William, 12th Duke of Hamilton, Hamilton Palace. Sold, Christie's, Hamilton Palace, July 10, 1882, lot 1296, to Samuel Wertheimer.

Cornelius Vanderbilt.

William K. Vanderbilt.

Gladys Vanderbilt (Countess Laszlo Szechenyi). Sold by her heirs, Sotheby's, London, November 26, 1971, lot 71.

Purchased at that sale by J. Paul Getty.

BIBLIOGRAPHY

Seymour de Ricci, *Louis XVI Furniture*, 1913, p. 147, illus.

Ronald Freyberger, "Eighteenth-Century French Furniture from Hamilton Palace," *Apollo*, December 1981, p. 405, illus.

51

52

51 *SECRETAIRE*
Paris, circa 1824
Attributed to Alexandre-Louis Bellangé
Oak veneered with amaranth, thuya, ebony, and pewter; set with twelve hard paste porcelain plaques, mirror, and painted glass; gilt-bronze mounts; *rouge griotte* marble top
No marks
Height: 5′3⁄8″ (153.4 cm); Width: 2′10 5⁄16″ (87.2 cm); Depth: 1′4 3⁄4″ (42.6 cm)
Accession number 66.DA.1

PROVENANCE

Sold, probably by Alexandre-Louis Bellangé, Paris, April 19, 1825, lot 97.

Purchased at that sale by Marie-Pierre-Hubert, duc de Cambacérès, Paris.

Purchased from his eventual heirs by Charles Michel, Paris, 1938.

W. Ball, New York, 1938.

Purchased by J. Paul Getty, 1938.

52 *SECRETAIRE*
Paris (?), mid- to late nineteenth century; circular Sèvres porcelain plaque, circa 1775
Maker unknown
Oak veneered with mahogany, satinwood, and tulipwood; set with one soft paste and seven hard paste porcelain plaques; gilt-bronze mounts; white marble top
Stamped LELEU—a forged stamp for Jean-François Leleu—and JME at top left and top right corners of back. Painted with MA under a crown, a false mark for Marie-Antoinette, on back. Circular Sèvres plaque painted in blue with the crossed L's of the Sèvres Manufactory on the reverse. Metal label stamped Hamilton Place underneath carcass.
Height: 4′2 11⁄16″ (128.8 cm); Width: 2′10 1⁄4″ (87.0 cm); Depth: 1′2″ (35.6 cm)
Accession number 63.DA.1

PROVENANCE

Alfred de Rothschild, London.

Edmund de Rothschild, London.

Sold, Messrs. Frank Green, Ashwick House, Dulverton, Somerset, September 19, 1947.

Frank Partridge Ltd., London.

Purchased by J. Paul Getty, 1950.

53

TABLES

53 READING AND WRITING TABLE

Paris, circa 1670–1675
Maker unknown
Oak veneered with ivory, blue-painted horn, and ebony; gilt-bronze moldings
No marks
Height: 2′1″ (63.5 cm); Width: 1′7⅛″ (48.5 cm); Depth: 1′2″ (35.5 cm)
Accession number 83.DA.21

PROVENANCE

Made for Louis XIV.

Damour and Baudoint families, Château de Cornillion, Loire.

Bernard Barouch Steinitz, Paris, 1982.

Purchased by the J. Paul Getty Museum, 1983.

COMMENTARY

A detailed, measured description of this table is recorded as number 651 in the posthumous inventory of Louis XIV's possessions dated 1729.

---

54 TABLE

Paris, circa 1680
Attributed to Pierre Golle
Oak veneered with ebony, tortoiseshell, pewter, olive wood, and brass; carved and gilded wood; gilt-bronze mounts
No marks
Height: 2′6½″ (76.7 cm); Width: 1′4½″ (42.0 cm); Depth: 1′2¼″ (36.1 cm)
Accession number 82.DA.34

PROVENANCE

(?) Louis, Grand Dauphin of France.

Henry James Laird, Ardmore House, Blackheath Park, Middlesex. Sold, Christie's, London, March 19, 1936, lot 147.

Private collection, Scotland. Sold, Phillips, Glasgow, April 16, 1981, lot 305.

Alexander and Berendt, Ltd., London, 1981.

Purchased by the J. Paul Getty Museum, 1982.

BIBLIOGRAPHY

Wilson, "Acquisitions 1982," no. 2, pp. 18–23, illus.

Wilson, *Selections*, no. 5, pp. 10–11, illus.

COMMENTARY

The presence of tortoiseshell fleur-de-lys and dolphins in the marquetry of this table suggests that it was made for the Grand Dauphin. The central circular scene of marquetry inside the top is based on a design that was later engraved by Daniel Marot. A table in the British Royal Collection, on loan to the Victoria and Albert Museum, London, forms a pair to this table.

54a

54b

55

55 TABLE

Paris, circa 1680
Attributed to the Gobelins Manufactory
Oak veneered with ebony, tortoiseshell, horn, pewter, brass, ivory, and various woods; gilt-bronze mounts
No marks
Height: 2′8¼″ (82.0 cm); Width: 3′9⅞″ (116.5 cm); Depth: 2′2″ (66.0 cm)
Accession number 83.DA.22

PROVENANCE

Bernheimer, Munich, 1920's.

Private collection, Saxony. Taken to Munich, 1945.

Purchased by the J. Paul Getty Museum, 1983.

BIBLIOGRAPHY

Herman, Graf von Armin and Willi Boelcke, *Muskau: Standesherrschaft zwischen Spree und Neiße*, 1978, illus. p. 27.

COMMENTARY

The top panel of this table is removable. It is possible that the table formed a stand for a medal cabinet that is decorated with similar marquetry and is now in the Staatliche Münzsammlung, Munich.

56a

56b

56 TABLE

Paris, circa 1680
Attributed to the Gobelins Manufactory
Oak veneered with tortoiseshell, pewter, brass, ebony, horn, ivory, boxwood, cherry, sycamore, and amaranth; gilt-bronze mounts
No marks
Height: 2′4⅜″ (72.0 cm); Width: 3′7½″ (110.5 cm); Depth: 2′5″ (73.6 cm)
Accession number 71.DA.100

PROVENANCE

Le Despencer family, Mereworth Castle, Kent. Sold, circa 1831, to Levy, Maidstone, Kent, for £35.

London art market, 1831.

Richard, 2nd Duke of Buckingham and Chandos, Stowe House, Buckinghamshire. Sold, Christie's, Stowe House, August 15ff., 1848, lot 256, to Redfern, for £59.

William Humble, 11th Baron Ward (created 1st Earl of Dudley, 1860), 1848.

William Humble, 2nd Earl of Dudley, Dudley House, London.

Sir Joseph C. Robinson, Bt., purchased with the contents of Dudley House.

Dr. Joseph Labia (son-in-law of Sir Joseph C. Robinson), London. Sold, Sotheby's, London, May 17, 1963, lot 137.

Ronald Lee, London, 1970.

Alexander and Berendt Ltd., London, 1971.

Purchased by J. Paul Getty, 1971.

BIBLIOGRAPHY

Henry R. Forster, *The Stowe Catalogue, Priced and Annotated*, 1848, no. 256, p. 16.

Stürmer, *Möbelkunst*, pp. 35, 215, illus.

Gillian Wilson, "A Late Seventeenth-Century French Cabinet at the J. Paul Getty Museum," *The Art Institute of Chicago Centennial Lecture*, Museum Studies 10, 1983, pp. 119–131, illus.

Wilson, *Selections*, no. 4, pp. 8–9 illus.

COMMENTARY

The four marquetry birds on the top of this table are cut from the same templates as those found on drawer fronts of the cabinet in No. 4 of this handbook. This indicates that the marquetry birds, and therefore probably the pieces themselves, were made in the same workshop.

57

58

57 CARD TABLE
Paris, circa 1725
Maker unknown
Oak and pine veneered with *satiné rouge* and kingwood; walnut drawers; gilt-bronze mounts
No marks
Closed: Height: 2′6¼″ (76.8 cm); Width: 3′3⅞″ (101.3 cm); Depth: 1′8¼″ (51.4 cm)
Opened: Height: 2′5⅛″ (74.0 cm); Width: 3′3⅞″ (101.3 cm); Depth: 3′4″ (101.6 cm)
Accession number 75.DA.2

PROVENANCE

Jane, Countess of Westmorland (wife of the 10th Earl, married 1800, died March 1857), Cotterstock Hall, Northamptonshire, from the late eighteenth century.

Lieutenant Colonel Hon. Henry Fane (son of Jane, Countess of Westmorland; died May 1857), Cotterstock Hall.

Henry Dundas, 5th Viscount Melville (cousin of Hon. Henry Fane), Cotterstock Hall.

Dundas family, Melville Castle, Scotland, until 1967.

Alexander and Berendt, Ltd., London.

French and Company, New York.

Purchased by J. Paul Getty, 1975.

58 TABLE
Paris, circa 1725
Attributed to the workshops of Boulle *fils*
Oak and pine veneered with *satiné rouge* and amaranth; modern leather top; gilt-bronze mounts
Black and white chalk drawing, possibly for a corner mount, on an interior panel.
Height: 2′6⅛″ (76.5 cm); Width: 6′7⅝″ (202.2 cm); Depth: 2′11¼″ (89.5 cm)
Accession number 67.DA.10

PROVENANCE

H. H. A. Josse, Paris. Sold, Galerie Georges Petit, Paris, May 29, 1894, lot 151.

Purchased at that sale by Edouard Chappey, Paris. Sold privately, after 1900.

E. Cronier, Paris. Sold, Galerie Georges Petit, Paris, December 4–5, 1905, lot 135, to Jacques Seligmann, Paris.

François Coty, Paris. Sold, Galerie Jean Charpentier, Paris, November 30–December 1, 1936, lot 84, to B. Fabre et Fils, Paris.

Confiscated by the Third Reich, 1940–1945.

Cameron, London, 1949.

Purchased by J. Paul Getty, 1949.

EXHIBITIONS

Paris. *Exposition universelle de 1900*, no. 2904.

BIBLIOGRAPHY

Alfred de Champeaux, *Portefeuille des arts décoratifs*, 1888–1889, p. 578, illus.

Molinier, *Le Mobilier*, p. 99.

Ballot, *Cressent*, pp. 113–114, 136–137, 145.

Adolf Feulner, *Kunstgeschichte des Möbels seit dem Altertum*, 1927, p. 314.

Pierre Verlet, *La Maison du XVIIIe siècle en France*, 1966, no. 133, pp. 168–169, illus.

Wilson, *Selections*, no. 10, pp. 20–21, illus.

COMMENTARY

A table of this model appears in a portrait by Jacques-André-Joseph Aved of Said Pasha, the ambassador from the Sublime Porte (Constantinople). The painting was exhibited in the Salon of 1742 and now hangs in the Château de Versailles.

59

60

59 TABLE
Paris, circa 1735
Attributed to the workshops of Boulle *fils*
Oak veneered with tulipwood; modern leather top; gilt-bronze mounts
No marks
Height: 2′7⅞″ (81.0 cm); Width: 6′4¼″ (193.7 cm); Depth: 3′1½″ (95.2 cm)
Accession number 55.DA.3

PROVENANCE

F. F. Uthemann, Saint Petersburg, late nineteenth century. In Helsinki by 1921.

Sir Alfred Chester Beatty, London.

Purchased by J. Paul Getty, 1955.

EXHIBITIONS

Oslo, Norway. Nasjonalgalleriet, on loan, 1921–1923.

60 TABLE
Paris, circa 1745
Attributed to Joseph Baumhauer
Oak veneered with *satiné rouge*; modern leather top; gilt-bronze mounts
All mounts stamped with the crowned C for 1745–1749.
Height: 2′7¹⁄₁₆″ (78.9 cm); Width: 5′11⅜″ (181.3 cm); Depth: 3′3⅝″ (100.7 cm)
Accession number 71.DA.95

PROVENANCE

(?) Either Empress Elizabeth of Russia, given by Louis XV, 1745, or Count Vorontsov, Saint Petersburg, purchased in Paris, 1745.

Empress Catherine II of Russia by descent, 1762, or purchased with the Vorontsov Palace.

Helen, Duchess of Mecklenburg-Strelitz (Princess of Saxe-Altenburg), Chinese Palace, Oranienbaum (near Saint Petersburg), by 1904.

Duveen Brothers, New York.

Anna Thomson Dodge, Rose Terrace, Grosse Pointe Farms, Michigan, by 1935. Sold, Christie's, London, June 24, 1971, lot 98.

Purchased at that sale by J. Paul Getty.

EXHIBITIONS

Saint Petersburg. *Exposition rétrospective d'objets d'art*, 1904, ex. cat., illus. p. 232.

BIBLIOGRAPHY

Denis Roche, *Le Mobilier français en Russie*, 1912, vol. 1, illus. pl. XVIII.

André Boutemy, "B.V.R.B. et la morphologie de son style," *Gazette des beaux-arts*, 1957, p. 174.

André Boutemy, "Joseph," *Connaissance des arts*, March 1965, illus. p. 88.

COMMENTARY

A table of this description was given by Louis XV to Empress Elizabeth of Russia in 1745. It was ordered in April of that year from the *marchand-mercier* Hébert and was sent with a clock and a *cartonnier* with a *serre-papier*. The *cartonnier* and *serre-papier*, which are similar in form to No. 10 in this handbook, are now in the State Hermitage, Leningrad. They may have been made en suite with this table. Another table of this model with a Russian provenance exists; it is stamped JOSEPH for Joseph Baumhauer.

61

62

61 TABLE
Paris, circa 1745–1749
By Bernard van Risenburgh
Oak veneered with tulipwood and ebony; modern leather top; gilt-bronze mounts
Stamped B.V.R.B. underneath. Some mounts stamped with the crowned C for 1745–1749.
Height: 2′7″ (78.7 cm); Width: 5′4½″ (163.8 cm); Depth: 2′7⅜″ (79.6 cm)
Accession number 78.DA.84

PROVENANCE

Henry Hirsch, London. Sold, Christie's, London, June 11, 1931, lot 171.

J. M. Botibol, London, 1931.

Purchased by J. Paul Getty, circa 1940.

BIBLIOGRAPHY

Barry Shifman, "A Newly-Found Table by Edward Holmes Baldock," *Apollo*, January 1984, pp. 38–42, illus.

COMMENTARY

This table was probably once set with panels of black lacquer in the frieze. It was copied in the 1830's or 1840's by the London dealer Edward Holmes Baldock.

62 MECHANICAL WRITING AND TOILET TABLE
Paris, circa 1750
By Jean-François Oeben
Oak veneered with tulipwood, amaranth, *satiné rouge*, kingwood, and various stained woods; iron mechanism; gilt-bronze mounts
Stamped J.F.OEBEN and JME underneath.
Height: 2′4¾″ (73.0 cm); Width: 2′5⅛″ (73.9 cm); Depth: 1′2⅞″ (37.8 cm)
Accession number 70.DA.84

PROVENANCE

B. Fabre et Fils, Paris.

Cameron, London.

Purchased by J. Paul Getty, 1949.

63a

63b

63 WRITING AND TOILET TABLE

Paris, circa 1750–1755
By Jean-François Oeben
Oak veneered with burl ash, holly, tulipwood, and other stained and exotic woods; leather; gilt-bronze mounts
Stamped J.F.OEBEN and JME underneath table. Label underneath table printed *Mrs John D. Rockefeller, Jr.*; label inside drawer inked *C.13478 J.D.R.* and *JM.*
Height: 2′4″ (71.1 cm); Width: 2′7$\frac{1}{2}$″ (80.0 cm); Depth: 1′4$\frac{7}{8}$″ (42.8 cm)
Accession number 71.DA.103

PROVENANCE

John George Murray, 8th Duke of Atholl, Marquess of Tullibardine, Scotland.

Mary Gavin (Hon. Mrs. Robert Baillie-Hamilton).

Lady Harvey, London.

Lewis and Simmons, Paris.

Judge Elbert H. Gary, New York. Sold, American Art Association, April 21, 1928, lot 272, when the above provenance was given.

Duveen Brothers, New York.

Martha Baird (Mrs. John D. Rockefeller, Jr.). Sold, Parke Bernet, New York, October 23, 1971, lot 712.

The Antique Porcelain Company, New York, 1971.

Purchased by J. Paul Getty, 1971

BIBLIOGRAPHY

Wilson, *Selections*, no. 27, pp. 54–55, illus.

COMMENTARY

A similar table is shown in a portrait by François Guérin of the marquise de Pompadour and her daughter Alexandrine, painted before 1754. That table is now in the Musée du Louvre, Paris.

64

64 WRITING TABLE

Paris, circa 1755
By Bernard van Risenburgh
Oak and pine veneered with tulipwood, kingwood, amaranth, and laburnum; modern leather panel; gilt-bronze mounts
Stamped B.V.R.B. and JME twice under front rail. A label pasted underneath printed *Londesborough* under a coronet. Another label printed *J.J.Allen, Furniture Depositories, London,* and inked *Countess of Londesborough.*
Height: 2′5$\frac{1}{2}$″ (74.9 cm); Width: 3′1$\frac{7}{8}$″ (96.2 cm); Depth: 1′10$\frac{11}{16}$″ (57.6 cm)
Accession number 65.DA.1

PROVENANCE

Lady Grace Adelaide Fane (Countess of Londesborough, wife of the 2nd Earl, married 1887, died 1933), London. Sold, Hampton Sons, London, July 24, 1933, lot 123.

J. M. Botibol, London, by 1937.

Purchased by J. Paul Getty, 1938.

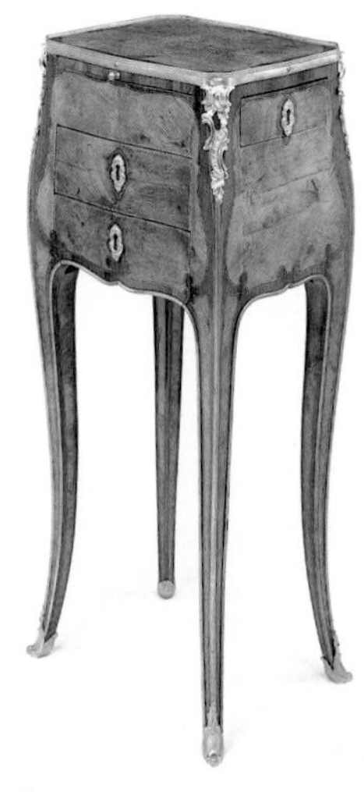

65

65 TABLE
Paris, circa 1760
By Adrien Faizelot Delorme
Oak veneered with amaranth and green-stained burl yew; leather panel; modern silvered fittings for ink, sand, and sponge; gilt-bronze mounts
Stamped DELORME twice and JME once on drawer panel.
Height: 2′3⅛″ (68.9 cm); Width: 11⅝″ (29.4 cm); Depth: 9⅝″ (24.4 cm)
Accession number 72.DA.64

PROVENANCE

Paris art market, early 1970's.

Rosenberg and Stiebel, New York, 1972.

Purchased by J. Paul Getty, 1972.

66

66 CARD TABLE
Paris, circa 1760
By Jean-François Oeben
Oak veneered with tulipwood, kingwood, and green-stained burl wood; modern baize top; gilt-bronze mounts
Stamped J.F.OEBEN underneath.
Height: 2′3¾″ (70.5 cm); Width: 2′9⅜″ (84.7 cm); Depth: 1′1⅝″ (34.6 cm)
Accession number 71.DA.105

PROVENANCE

Probably purchased by Sir Charles Mills or his son Charles Henry, created Lord Hillingdon in 1886.

Charles, 4th Lord Hillingdon, Essex, by descent. Sold, Christie's, London, May 14, 1970, lot 102.

Frank Partridge Ltd., London, 1970.

Purchased by J. Paul Getty, 1971.

67

67 TOILET TABLE
Paris, circa 1760–1765
Attributed to Jean-François Leleu
Oak veneered with kingwood, amaranth, sycamore, maple, holly, boxwood, ebony, and *bois satiné*; gilt-bronze mounts
The number 499 cast into the reverse of each mount. Paper label inked *B.f.a.a. 1913 Meyer Sassoon Esq.* inside drawer. Paper label printed *BURLINGTON FINE ARTS CLUB EXHIBITION OF THE FRENCH SCHOOL OF THE XVIIIth CENT. 1913* and another label inked *Mr. A. Barker présenté par M. Chenue, 24 rue . . . . des petits Charr . . . . .* underneath table.
Height: 2′3⅝″ (70.2 cm); Width: 1′10⅜″ (56.9 cm); Depth: 1′3⅞″ (40.3 cm)
Accession number 72.DA.49

PROVENANCE

Alexander Barker, probably acquired in Paris. Sold, Christie's, London, June 11, 1874, lot 693.

(?) Edmund, 1st Lord Grimthorpe.

Leopold George Frederick, 5th Viscount Clifden. Sold, Robinson and Fisher, May 21ff., 1895, lot 606, to Seligmann, Paris, for 750 guineas.

Mr. and Mrs. Meyer Sassoon, Pope's Manor, Berkshire.

Violet Sassoon (Mrs. Derek C. Fitzgerald), Heathfield Park, Sussex. Offered for sale, Sotheby's, London, November 22, 1963, lot 132, bought in. Sold, Christie's, London, March 23, 1972, lot 88.

Purchased at that sale by J. Paul Getty.

EXHIBITIONS

London. The Burlington Fine Arts Club, 1913.

London. Morton Lee and Mallett and Sons, *The Royal Cabinetmakers of France*, July 1951, ex. cat., no. 8, illus.

68

68 TABLE

Paris, circa 1770
Attributed to Martin Carlin
Oak veneered with tulipwood, ebony, and holly; set with four soft paste Sèvres porcelain plaques; gilt-bronze mounts; white marble lower shelf
Circular porcelain plaque painted on reverse with the blue crossed L's of the Sèvres Manufactory enclosing the date letter L for 1764.
Height: 2′3¾″ (70.5 cm); Diameter: 1′3⅜″ (39.1 cm)
Accession number 70.DA.74

PROVENANCE

Alfred de Rothschild, Halton, Buckinghamshire.

Almina Wombwell (daughter of Alfred de Rothschild; Countess of Carnarvon, wife of the 5th Earl, married 1895, died 1969), 1918.

Henry Symons and Co., London, 1919.

French and Company, New York, 1919.

Mortimer L. Schiff, New York, 1919. Sold by his heir, John L. Schiff, Christie's, London, June 22, 1938, lot 52.

Purchased at that sale by J. Paul Getty.

---

69 TABLE

Paris, circa 1773
Table by Martin Carlin; circular porcelain plaque painted by Marie-Claude-Sophie Xhrouet
Oak veneered with tulipwood, holly, and ebony; set with four soft paste Sèvres porcelain plaques; gilt-bronze mounts
Stamped M.CARLIN and JME underneath top section. Circular plaque painted with the blue crossed L's of the Sèvres Manufactory, the date *1773*, and the painter Xhrouet's mark *X*.
Height: 2′4⅞″ (73.3 cm); Diameter: 1′3¾″ (40.0 cm)
Accession number 70.DA.75

PROVENANCE

Alfred de Rothschild, Halton, Buckinghamshire.

Almina Wombwell (daughter of Alfred de Rothschild; Countess of Carnarvon, wife of the 5th Earl, married 1895, died 1969), 1918.

Henry Symons and Co., London, 1920.

French and Company, New York, 1920.

Mortimer L. Schiff, New York, 1920. Sold by his heir, John L. Schiff, Christie's, London, June 22, 1938, lot 51.

Purchased at that sale by J. Paul Getty.

69

70

70 MUSIC STAND

Paris, circa 1770–1775
Attributed to Martin Carlin
Oak veneered with tulipwood and pearwood; incised with colored mastics; gilt-bronze mounts
Stamped JME under oval shelf.
Height: (max.) 4′10½″ (148.6 cm), (min.) 3′1 1/16″ (94.2 cm); Width: 1′7¾″ (50.2 cm); Depth: 1′2⅜″ (36.5 cm)
Accession number 55.DA.4

PROVENANCE

Sir Alfred Chester Beatty, London.

Purchased by J. Paul Getty, 1955.

BIBLIOGRAPHY

Watson, *Louis XVI Furniture*, no. 125, illus.

---

71 TABLE

Paris, 1777
By Jean-Henri Riesener
Oak veneered with satinwood and amaranth; modern leather top; gilt-bronze mounts
Underside of table painted in black with the partly effaced French royal inventory mark *No. 2905*. Stamped under same panel, in the form of a circle that is half cut away, [GARDE-MEUB]LE DE LA REINE, enclosing the monogram MA. Also painted underneath table is a crown that originally appeared over the letters CT, which are now cut away.
Height: 2′5½″ (74.9 cm); Width: 4′5½″ (135.9 cm); Depth: 2′3⅞″ (70.8 cm)
Accession number 71.DA.102

PROVENANCE

Ordered by Marie-Antoinette for the *cabinet* of Louis XVI in the Petit Trianon, Versailles. Delivered August 6, 1777.

John Partridge, London, 1967–1971.

Purchased by J. Paul Getty, 1971.

BIBLIOGRAPHY

Geoffrey de Bellaigue, *Furniture, Clocks, and Gilt Bronzes*, the James A. de Rothschild Collection at Waddesdon Manor, 1974, vol. 1, no. 69; vol. 2, no. 103.

COMMENTARY

This table was delivered by Jean-Henri Riesener in 1777 with a *secrétaire* and a small table, now at Waddesdon Manor, Buckinghamshire, and a commode now returned to the Petit Trianon, Versailles.

71

72 TOILET TABLE

Paris, circa 1777–1780
Maker unknown
Oak and pine veneered with tulipwood and stained holly; marquetry panels of amaranth, satinwood, pearwood, tulipwood, applewood, ebony, and other stained fruitwoods; gilt-bronze mounts
No marks
Height: 2′4⅛″ (71.3 cm); Width: 2′7¾″ (80.6 cm); Depth: 1′4¾″ (42.5 cm)
Accession number 72.DA.67

PROVENANCE

Sold anonymously, Christie's, London, December 2, 1971, lot 112.

French and Company, New York, 1971.

Purchased by J. Paul Getty, 1972.

COMMENTARY

The marquetry trophies on the top of the table are copied from engravings by P.-F. Tardieu (after designs by Jean-Charles Delafosse) published after 1776.

72a

72b

73 WRITING TABLE
Paris, circa 1778
Table by Martin Carlin; some Sèvres porcelain plaques gilded by Jean-Baptiste-Emmanuel Vandé
Oak veneered with tulipwood; set with fourteen soft paste Sèvres porcelain plaques; modern leather top; gilt-bronze mounts
Stamped M.CARLIN (partly effaced) and JME under front-right rail. Printed paper trade label of Dominique Daguerre underneath left-rear rail; three Russian inventory numbers painted on carcass; central drawer contains a paper label inked with the twentieth-century inventory number 29615. Porcelain plaques painted variously (not all are marked) with the crossed L's of the Sèvres Manufactory in red, the date letters AA for 1778, Vandé's mark *VD*, and paper labels printed with the crossed L's and inked with the prices 30 and 96 [*livres*].
Height: 2′6½″ (77.5 cm); Width: 4′3⅝″ (131.2 cm); Depth: 2′⅜″ (62.0 cm)
Accession number 83.DA.385

PROVENANCE

Grand Duchess Maria Feodorovna of Russia (later czarina of Paul I), purchased in 1784 from the *marchand-mercier* Dominique Daguerre in Paris, installed in her state bedroom at Pavlovsk (near Saint Petersburg), Russia.

Russian Imperial Collections, Palace of Pavlovsk.

Duveen and Co., New York, purchased in 1931 from the Soviet government.

Anna Thomson Dodge, Rose Terrace, Grosse Pointe Farms, Michigan, 1931. Sold Christie's, London, June 24, 1971, lot 135.

Habib Sabet, Geneva, 1971. Sold, Christie's, London, December 1, 1983, lot 54.

Purchased at that sale by the J. Paul Getty Museum.

73

BIBLIOGRAPHY

Alexandre Benois, *Les Trésors d'art en Russie*, 1907, vol. 3, p. 373; vol. 7, p. 186, illus. pl. 20.

Denis Roche, *Le Mobilier français en Russie*, 1913, vol. 2, illus. pl. LV.

Duveen and Co., *A Catalogue of Works of Art in the Collection of Anna Thomson Dodge*, 1939, vol. 1, illus.

Anthony Coleridge, "Works of Art with a Royal Provenance from the Collection of the Late Mrs. Anna Thomson Dodge," *Connoisseur*, May 1971, pp. 34–36, illus.

Sassoon, "Acquisitions 1983," no. 10, p. 201, 204–207, illus.

74

74 TABLE

Paris (?), circa 1880
Maker unknown
Oak veneered with ebony, tortoiseshell, and brass; modern leather top; gilt-bronze mounts
No marks
Height: 2′8″ (81.3 cm); Width: 5′11″ (180.5 cm); Depth: 3′5/8″ (93.0 cm)
Accession number 81.DA.30

PROVENANCE

Richard G. Roberts, Los Angeles. Bequeathed to the J. Paul Getty Museum, 1981.

COMMENTARY

This table is a copy of an early eighteenth-century *bureau plat* now in the Musée des Arts Décoratifs, Paris. Another version of this model is in the Wallace Collection, London.

75

75 TABLE

Paris, 1761 and early twentieth century
Carcass perhaps by an imitator of Bernard van Risenburgh; Sèvres porcelain top painted by Charles-Nicolas Dodin after a design by François Boucher
Painted oak; set with a soft paste Sèvres porcelain plaque; gilt-bronze mounts
Stamped B.V.R.B. and JME underneath drawer. Underside of porcelain plaque painted with the blue crossed L's of the Sèvres Manufactory, enclosing the date letter I for 1761, and with Dodin's mark *k*.
Height: 2′2 3/8″ (66.9 cm); Width: 1′1 5/8″ (34.6 cm); Depth: 11 1/8″ (28.3 cm)
Accession number 70.DA.85

PROVENANCE

Rosenberg and Stiebel, New York, 1949.

Purchased by J. Paul Getty, 1949.

BIBLIOGRAPHY

Adrian Sassoon, "New Research on a Table Stamped by Bernard van Risenburgh," *The J. Paul Getty Museum Journal* 9, 1981, pp. 167–174, illus.

COMMENTARY

It is possible that the panel of wood bearing the genuine B.V.R.B. stamp comes from another piece of furniture. The green pigment used in the paint on the carcass was not in commercial use until 1862. The porcelain top is painted with a scene entitled *Le Pasteur galant*, taken from an engraving by André Laurent of a painting by François Boucher of about 1738. The top has been broken and is believed to have come from a similar table now in the Musée du Louvre, Paris, that has a replacement top of white marble. The Louvre table has *vernis Martin* trellis decoration that matches that on the Sèvres top of this table.

76

77

78

CLOCKS

76 MODEL FOR A MANTEL CLOCK

Paris, circa 1700
Maker unknown
Terracotta; enameled metal plaques
No marks
Height: 2′7″ (78.7 cm); Width: 1′8½″ (52.1 cm); Depth: 9½″ (24.2 cm)
Accession number 72.DB.52

PROVENANCE

Dalva Brothers, New York, 1972. Acquired in Europe in the 1930's.

Purchased by J. Paul Getty, 1972.

EXHIBITIONS

New York. The Metropolitan Museum of Art, *Magnificent Time-Keepers*, January 1971–March 1972, no. 67.

BIBLIOGRAPHY

Wilson, *Clocks*, no. 1, pp. 8–11, illus.

Wilson, *Selections*, no. 7, pp. 14–15, illus.

77 WALL CLOCK

Paris, circa 1710
Case attributed to André-Charles Boulle
Gilt bronze; blue-painted horn; enameled metal
Label on the back inked *Vernon House, Staircase.*
Height: 2′4″ (71.1 cm); Width: 11¼″ (28.6 cm); Depth: 4½″ (11.4 cm)
Accession number 73.DB.74

PROVENANCE

Charles William, 2nd Lord Hillingdon, Vernon House, London.

Charles, 4th Lord Hillingdon. Sold, Christie's, London, June 29, 1972, lot 56.

French and Company, New York, 1972.

Purchased by J. Paul Getty, 1973.

BIBLIOGRAPHY

Wilson, *Clocks*, no. 3, pp. 18–21, illus.

COMMENTARY

The movement is a later English replacement.

78 MANTEL CLOCK

Paris, circa 1715–1725
Case attributed to André-Charles Boulle; movement by Jacques Gudin
Oak veneered with tortoiseshell, blue-painted horn, brass, and ebony; enameled metal; gilt-bronze mounts
Engraved *Gudin lejeune A PARIS* on back-plate of movement. Painted *GUDIN LE JEUNE APARIS* on clock face.
Height: 3′3¾″ (100.9 cm); Width: 1′6⅛″ (46.0 cm); Depth: 11¼″ (28.6 cm)
Accession number 72.DB.55

PROVENANCE

Count János Pálffy. Sold, Bad Pistyan, Czechoslovakia, June 30, 1924, lot 285.

Etienne Lévy, Paris, 1971.

French and Company, New York.

Purchased by J. Paul Getty, 1972.

EXHIBITIONS

Paris. Hôtel George V, *Haute Joaillerie de France*, June 1971.

New York. The Frick Collection, *French Clocks in North American Collections*, November 1982–January 1983, ex. cat., no. 38, illus. p. 46.

BIBLIOGRAPHY

Wilson, *Clocks*, no. 4, pp. 22–25, illus.

---

79 PEDESTAL CLOCK
Paris, circa 1715–1720
Case attributed to André-Charles Boulle; movement by Julien Le Roy
Oak veneered with tortoiseshell, ebony, and brass; enameled metal plaques; gilt-bronze mounts
Engraved *Julien Le Roy* on backplate of movement and painted with same name on enamel plaque on the front. Engraved *Karel Solle 1846* and *4869* on movement.
Height: 9′4″ (284.5 cm); Width: 2′3⅜″ (69.5 cm); Depth: 1′1″ (33.0 cm)
Accession number 74.DB.1

PROVENANCE

English collection, nineteenth century.

The Duke of Medinaceli, Spain.

Manuel Gonzales, Madrid, circa 1965.

French and Company, New York, 1972.

Purchased by J. Paul Getty, 1974.

EXHIBITIONS

Madrid. Sociedad Española de Amigos del Arte, *El reloj en arte*, May–June 1965, ex. cat., no. 10, illus.

BIBLIOGRAPHY

Luis Montañes, "Un péndulo desconocido de Julien Le Roy," *Dersa*, no. 34, July 1967, pp. 8–16, illus.

Wilson, *Clocks*, no. 2, pp. 12–17, illus.

Wilson, *Selections*, no. 9, pp. 18–19, illus.

---

80 LONG-CASE MUSICAL CLOCK
Paris, circa 1725
Movement by J.-F. Dominicé; movement repaired and face and hands replaced by Pierre-Henry Lepaute; stand attributed to André-Charles Boulle
Oak veneered with brass and red-painted tortoiseshell; enameled metal; gilt-bronze mounts
Engraved *J.F.Dominicé A Paris* on movement and *LEPAUTE* on dial. Signed by various repairers on movement.
Height: 8′7″ (261.6 cm); Width: 3′½″ (92.7 cm); Depth: 1′3″ (38.1 cm)
Accession number 72.DB.40

PROVENANCE

Sir Peter Burrell, 1st Lord Gwydir. Sold, Christie's, London, March 11–12, 1829, lot 103, to Samuel Fogg, London.

Henry George Brownlow, 4th Marquess of Exeter. Sold, Christie's, London, June 7–8, 1888, lot 261, to Charles Davies, London.

Cornelius Vanderbilt.

William K. Vanderbilt.

Gladys Vanderbilt (Countess Laszlo Szechenyi).

Purchased from Countess Szechenyi's heirs by Rosenberg and Stiebel, New York, 1971.

French and Company, New York, 1971.

Purchased by J. Paul Getty, 1971.

BIBLIOGRAPHY

Wilson, *Clocks*, no. 5, pp. 26–33, illus.

79

80

81 BAROMETER ON BRACKET

Paris, circa 1735–1755
Mechanism by Digue; case attributed to Charles Cressent; bracket attributed to Jean-Joseph de Saint Germain
Gilt bronze; enameled metal
Engraved *DIGUE A PARIS* on dial.
Height: 4′2″ (127.0 cm); Width: 1′5½″ (44.3 cm); Depth: 7¼″ (18.4 cm)
Accession number 71.DB.116

PROVENANCE

George Jay Gould, Georgian Court, Lakewood, New Jersey.

Duveen Brothers, New York.

Anna Thomson Dodge, Rose Terrace, Grosse Pointe Farms, Michigan. Sold, Christie's, London, June 24, 1971, lot 40 (with No. 82 in this handbook).

Purchased at that sale by J. Paul Getty.

BIBLIOGRAPHY

Theodore Dell, "The Gilt-Bronze Cartel Clocks of Charles Cressent," *Burlington Magazine*, April 1967, pp. 210–217.

Wilson, *Clocks*, nos. 8–9 (with No. 82 in this handbook), pp. 44–51, illus.

COMMENTARY

The case originally housed a clock movement. The bracket is not contemporary with the case and was probably made about twenty years later.

81

82

82 CLOCK ON BRACKET

Paris, circa 1750–1755
Movement by Jean Romilly; clock case attributed to Charles Cressent; bracket by Jean-Joseph de Saint Germain
Gilt bronze; enameled metal
Stamped *ST. GERMAIN* on bracket.
Painted *Romilly A Paris* on dial and movement. Stamped E on reverse of all gilt-bronze elements.
Height: 4′2″ (127.0 cm); Width: 1′5¾″ (45.1 cm); Depth: 7¼″ (18.4 cm)
Accession number 71.DB.115

PROVENANCE

George Jay Gould, Georgian Court, Lakewood, New Jersey.

Duveen Brothers, New York.

Anna Thomson Dodge, Rose Terrace, Grosse Pointe Farms, Michigan. Sold, Christie's, London, June 24, 1971, lot 40 (with No. 81 in this handbook).

Purchased at that sale by J. Paul Getty.

BIBLIOGRAPHY

Theodore Dell, "The Gilt-Bronze Cartel Clocks of Charles Cressent," *Burlington Magazine*, April 1967, pp. 210–217.

Wilson, *Clocks*, nos. 8–9 (with No. 81 in this handbook), pp. 45–51, illus.

COMMENTARY

The mainspring of the movement is dated 1758. It is likely that Cressent had the clock case in stock for a few years before it was fitted with a movement.

83 WALL CLOCK

Paris, circa 1735–1740
Case attributed to Charles Cressent; movement by Jean-Jacques Fieffé *père*
Gilt bronze; enameled metal
Painted *FIEFFE DELOBSERVATOIR* on dial.
Engraved *Fieffé A Paris* on backplate of

83

84

85

movement. Engraved with restorer's name *J. E. Villamarina* on movement.
Height: 4′4½″ (133.3 cm); Width: 2′2½″ (67.3 cm); Depth: 5⅝″ (14.4 cm)
Accession number 72.DB.89

PROVENANCE

Baron Mayer Alphonse de Rothschild, Château de Ferrières, Tarn.

Baron Edouard de Rothschild, Château de Ferrières.

Baron Guy de Rothschild, Château de Ferrières. Sold, Sotheby's, London, November 24, 1972, lot 7.

Purchased at that sale by J. Paul Getty.

BIBLIOGRAPHY

Eveline Schlumberger, "Caffiéri, le bronzier de Louis XV," *Connaissance des arts,* May 1965, illus. p. 83.

Wilson, *Clocks*, no. 6, pp. 34–37, illus.

Gérard Mabille, *Le Style Louis XV*, 1978, p. 175, illus.

84 WALL CLOCK

Paris and Chantilly Manufactory, circa 1740
Movement by Charles Voisin
Soft paste Chantilly porcelain; gilt bronze; enameled metal
Painted *CHARLES VOISIN APARIS* on dial and engraved with same on movement.
Height: 2′5½″ (74.9 cm); Width: 1′2″ (35.6 cm); Depth: 4⅜″ (11.1 cm)
Accession number 81.DB.81

PROVENANCE

Jacques Kugel, Paris, 1980.

Purchased by the J. Paul Getty Museum, 1981.

BIBLIOGRAPHY

Wilson, "Acquisitions 1981," no. 2, pp. 66–71, illus.

Wilson, *Selections*, no. 13, pp. 26–27, illus.

85 MANTEL CLOCK

Paris, circa 1742
Movement by Julien Le Roy; maker of case unknown; enamel dial by Antoine-Nicolas Martinière
Gilt bronze; enameled metal
Painted *.JULIEN.LE ROY. .DELA. SOCIETE DES ARTS* on dial. Engraved *Julien Le Roy AParis* on backplate of movement. Inscribed in ink *a.n. martiniere 1742* on reverse of dial.
Height: 1′6⅛″ (46.0 cm); Width: 1′¾″ (32.4 cm); Depth: 8⅛″ (20.6 cm)
Accession number 79.DB.4

PROVENANCE

Jacques Kugel, Paris, 1978.

Purchased by the J. Paul Getty Museum, 1979.

EXHIBITIONS

New York. The Frick Collection, *French Clocks in North American Collections*, November 1982–January 1983, ex. cat., no. 52, illus p. 13.

BIBLIOGRAPHY

Wilson, "Acquisitions 1977 to mid 1979," no. 14, pp. 50–52, illus.

86

86 PLANISPHERE CLOCK

Paris, circa 1745–1749
Case attributed to Jean-Pierre Latz; movement (now missing) by Alexandre Fortier
Oak veneered with kingwood; bronze mounts
Engraved *Inventé par A. Fortier* on upper middle dial. All mounts on base section stamped with the crowned C for 1745–1749.
Height: 9′3″ (282.0 cm); Width: 3′½″ (92.7 cm); Depth: 1′3½″ (39.5 cm)
Accession number 74.DB.2

PROVENANCE

Henri Ephrussi, Paris. Sold, Galerie Georges Petit, May 22, 1911, lot 63.

Sold, "Property of a Lady of Title," Sotheby's, London, November 24, 1972, lot 34.

Rosenberg and Stiebel, New York, 1974.

Purchased by J. Paul Getty, 1974.

EXHIBITIONS

New York. The Metropolitan Museum of Art, *The Grand Gallery*, CINOA, October 1974–January 1975, no. 44.

BIBLIOGRAPHY

Wilson, *Clocks*, no. 7, pp. 38–43, illus.

Wilson, *Selections*, no. 18, pp. 36–37, illus.

87 WALL CLOCK

Paris, circa 1747
Case by Jacques Caffiéri; movement by Julien Le Roy; enamel dial by Antoine-Nicolas Martinière
Gilt bronze; enameled metal
Case engraved *Fait par Caffieri* and stamped twice with the crowned C for 1745–1749. Painted *.JULIEN. ·LE·ROY·* on face. Engraved *Julien le Roy AParis* on movement. Inscribed in ink *a.n. Martiniere*

87

Privilégié [?] *Du Roi 1747* on reverse of dial.
Height: 2′6½″ (77.5 cm); Width: 1′4″ (40.6 cm); Depth: 4½″ (11.4 cm)
Accession number 72.DB.45

PROVENANCE

Sold anonymously, Christie's, London, July 15, 1971, lot 21.

French and Company, New York, 1972.

Purchased by J. Paul Getty, 1972.

BIBLIOGRAPHY

Wilson, *Clocks*, no. 10, pp. 52–55, illus.

88

88 MANTEL CLOCK

Paris, circa 1750
Case attributed to Robert Osmond; movement by Etienne Le Noir
Patinated and gilt bronze; enameled metal
Painted *Etienne le Noir AParis* on dial.
Engraved *Etienne le Noir AParis No. 396* on movement.
Height: 1′9⅜″ (54.3 cm); Width: 1′5¾″ (45.1 cm); Depth: 9⅛″ (23.2 cm)
Accession number 73.DB.85

PROVENANCE

Sold, "Property of a Nobleman," Christie's, London, July 5, 1973, lot 31.

Purchased at that sale by J. Paul Getty.

BIBLIOGRAPHY

Wilson, *Clocks*, no. 11, pp. 56–59, illus.

89

89 WALL CLOCK ON BRACKET

Paris, circa 1765
Case by Antoine Foullet; movement by Lapina
Oak veneered with panels of green, red, and cream-painted horn; brass; enameled metal; gilt-bronze mounts
Stamped *ANT FOVLLET JME* on case and bracket. Engraved *Lapina A Paris* on movement.
Height: 3′10¾″ (118.7 cm); Width: 1′7½″ (49.5 cm); Depth: 11¼″ (28.6 cm)
Accession number 75.DB.7

PROVENANCE

Private collection, Cornwall.

Alexander and Berendt, Ltd., London, 1974.

Purchased by J. Paul Getty, 1974.

BIBLIOGRAPHY

Wilson, *Clocks*, no. 12, pp. 60–63, illus.

90

90 MANTEL CLOCK

Paris, circa 1765
Case attributed to Etienne Martincourt; movement by Charles Le Roy
Gilt bronze; enameled metal
Painted *CHARLES LE ROY A PARIS* on dial.
Engraved *Ch*^{les} *LeRoy A Paris #2417* on backplate of movement.
Height: 2′4″ (71.1 cm); Width: 1′11⅜″ (59.3 cm); Depth: 1′1⅛″ (33.3 cm)
Accession number 73.DB.78

PROVENANCE

Made for Louis XVI. Listed in his *chambre à coucher* at the Palais de Tuileries, Paris, 1793.

Possibly marquis de Saint-Cloud. Sold, Hôtel Drouot, Paris, February 25–26, 1861, lot 1.

Private collection, Paris.

Kraemer et Cie, Paris, 1972.

Purchased by J. Paul Getty, 1973.

EXHIBITIONS

New York. The Frick Collection, *French Clocks in North American Collections*,

November 1982–January 1983, ex. cat., no. 63, illus. p. 68.

BIBLIOGRAPHY

Wilson, *Clocks*, no. 13, pp. 64–67, illus.

Wilson, *Selections*, no. 32, pp. 64–65, illus.

COMMENTARY

A drawing for this model of clock case survives, signed by Etienne Martincourt.

---

91 MANTEL CLOCK

Paris, circa 1785
Attributed to Pierre-Philippe Thomire
Gilt and patinated bronze; enameled metal; *vert Maurin des Alpes* marble; white marble
No marks
Height: 1′9″ (53.3 cm); Width: 2′1⅛″ (63.8 cm); Depth: 9¼″ (23.5 cm)
Accession number 82.DB.2

PROVENANCE

Private collection, Sweden. In Sweden by the 1880's, and possibly from the 1820's. Sold, Sotheby's, London, December 11, 1981, lot 99.

Purchased at that sale by the J. Paul Getty Museum.

BIBLIOGRAPHY

Wilson, "Acquisitions 1981," no. 5, pp. 79–84, illus.

Alvar Gonzalez-Palacios, *The Adjectives of History*, ex. cat., P. & D. Colnaghi and Co., London, 1983, pp. 44–45.

Wilson, *Selections*, no. 42, pp. 84–85, illus.

COMMENTARY

A clock of this model is illustrated in a drawing for a fireplace arrangement, attributed to Jean-Démosthène Dugourc, in the Musée des Arts Décoratifs, Paris. The standing bronze figure on this clock closely compares with a drawing by Jacques-Louis David now in the Musée du Louvre, Paris.

91

92 MANTEL CLOCK

Paris, circa 1790–1800
Movement by Nicolas-Alexandre Folin; enamel plaques by G. Merlet
Gilt bronze; enameled metal; white marble base; glass and gilded metal case
Painted *Folin l'ainé A PARIS* on dial. Painted *G. Merlet* on one enamel ring.
Height: 1′6″ (45.7 cm); Width: 10⅞″ (27.6 cm); Depth: 5½″ (14.0 cm)
Accession number 72.DB.57

PROVENANCE

Louis Guiraud, Paris. Sold, Palais Galliera, Paris, December 10, 1971, lot 35.

French and Company, New York, 1971.

Purchased by J. Paul Getty, 1972.

BIBLIOGRAPHY

Wilson, *Clocks*, no. 14, pp. 68–71, illus.

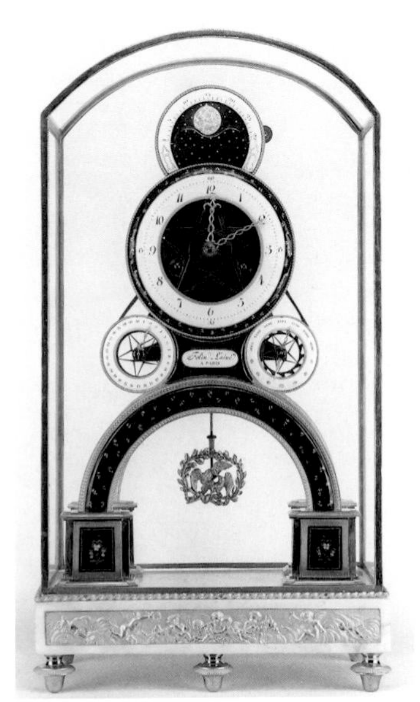

92

93

94

95

SEAT FURNITURE

93 SIDE CHAIR
Paris, late seventeenth century
Maker unknown
Gilded walnut
No marks
Height: 3′10″ (116.8 cm); Width: 1′10½″ (57.1 cm); Depth: 2′1″ (63.5 cm)
Accession number 75.DA.62

PROVENANCE

Frederick Victoria Inc., New York.

Nicolas Landau, Paris.

Purchased by J. Paul Getty, 1975.

---

94 DESK CHAIR
Paris, circa 1735
Attributed to Etienne Meunier
Carved walnut; leather upholstery; velvet pocket linings; brass studs
No marks
Height: 2′11¾″ (90.8 cm); Width: 2′4″ (71.1 cm); Depth: 2′1¼″ (64.1 cm)
Accession number 71.DA.91

PROVENANCE

Duveen Brothers, New York.

Anna Thomson Dodge, Rose Terrace, Grosse Pointe Farms, Michigan. Sold, Christie's, London, June 24, 1971, lot 48.

Purchased at that sale by J. Paul Getty.

COMMENTARY

A desk chair of the same model stamped by Meunier was on the Paris art market in 1984.

---

95 FOUR ARMCHAIRS
Paris, circa 1735
Maker unknown
Carved and gilded walnut; modern velvet upholstery
No marks
Height: 3′5¼″ (104.8 cm); Width: 2′1¼″ (64.1 cm); Depth: 1′10¾″ (57.8 cm)
Accession number 75.DA.8.1–4

PROVENANCE

Jacques Kugel, Paris, 1975.

Purchased by J. Paul Getty, 1975.

96a

96 TWO ARMCHAIRS AND TWO SIDE CHAIRS

Paris, circa 1735–1740
Maker unknown
Carved and gilded beech; modern silk upholstery
No marks
Armchairs: Height: 3′7½″ (110.5 cm); Width: 2′6⅛″ (76.6 cm); Depth: 2′8⅞″ (83.7 cm)
Side chairs: Height: 3′1″ (94.1 cm); Width: 2′⅜″ (62.0 cm); Depth: 2′3⅜″ (69.4 cm)
Accession number 82.DA.95.1–4

PROVENANCE

Private collection, England, from the eighteenth century until 1979.

William Redford, London, 1979.

Alexander and Berendt, Ltd., London, 1979.

Purchased by the J. Paul Getty Museum, 1982.

BIBLIOGRAPHY

Sassoon, "Acquisitions 1982," no. 4, pp. 28–33, illus.

96b

97 PAIR OF ARMCHAIRS AND A SETTEE

Paris, circa 1750–1755
By Jean Avisse
Gilded oak; modern upholstery
Each chair stamped IAVISSE once beneath rear rail. Settee stamped IAVISSE twice beneath rear rail.
Chairs: Height: 3′5¼″ (104.7 cm); Width: 2′6″ (76.2 cm); Depth: 1′11 7/16″ (59.6 cm)
Settee: Height: 3′6″ (106.7 cm); Width: 7′½″ (214.5 cm); Depth: 3′ (91.4 cm)
Accession numbers: chairs 83.DA.230.1–2; settee 84.DA.70

PROVENANCE

Chairs:

Mrs. Rose Freda, New York.

Matthew Schutz Ltd., New York, 1982.

Purchased by the J. Paul Getty Museum, 1983.

Settee:

Mrs. Rose Freda, New York. Sold Sotheby's, New York, May 4, 1984, lot 41.

Purchased at that sale by the J. Paul Getty Museum.

BIBLIOGRAPHY

Bremer-David, "Acquisitions 1983," no. 8, pp. 98–199, illus.

COMMENTARY

Another pair of armchairs from this set was sold at Sotheby's, New York, in 1981 and again on November 17, 1984, as lot 290.

97a

97b

98

98 ARMCHAIR

Paris, circa 1755
By Nicolas Heurtaut
Carved and gilded wood; modern silk upholstery
Stamped N.HEURTAUT under rear rail.
Height: 3′3¾″ (101.0 cm); Width: 2′7¾″ (80.6 cm); Depth: 2′5¾″ (75.5 cm)
Accession number 84.DA.69

PROVENANCE

Private collection, New York.

Matthew Schutz Ltd., New York, circa 1960. Sold, Sotheby's, New York, May 4, 1984, lot 59.

Purchased at that sale by the J. Paul Getty Museum.

99

99 PAIR OF ARMCHAIRS

Paris, 1762, with nineteenth-century tapestry upholstery
Frames by Nicolas-Quinibert Foliot
Gilded wood; wool tapestry
Each armchair stamped N Q FOLIOT inside rear rail and stenciled in same place with a crowned *F* and the number *832* for the Château de Fontainebleau.
Height: 3′¾″ (93.3 cm); Width: 2′2⅝″ (67.6 cm); Depth: 1′9⅞″ (55.5 cm)
Accession number 70.DA.70.1–2

PROVENANCE

Château de Versailles, 1762.

Château de Fontainebleau. Listed as in the lodgings of Charles-Claude de Taillepied, seigneur de la Garenne, on November 1, 1786, and again in 1787.

Mme Annette Lefortier, Paris. Sold, American Art Association, New York, November 20, 1937, lot 151.

Purchased at that sale by J. Paul Getty.

COMMENTARY

These chairs were part of one of two deliveries received at Versailles in May and September of 1762. A total of fourteen armchairs, twenty-eight side chairs, nine beds, and seven screens were delivered. In 1762 these armchairs were upholstered with crimson damask, supplied by Capin and held with gilded nails. By 1786 when M. de la Garenne owned these two armchairs, as well as four side chairs from the set, their frames were described as being painted. In 1790 when these six chairs were re-covered with crimson velvet, the frames were painted white.

100

100 PAIR OF SIDE CHAIRS

Paris, circa 1765–1770
By Jean Boucault
Carved and gilded beech; modern silk velvet upholstery
Each chair stamped J.BOUCAULT and

branded with a crowned double V, the mark of the Château de Versailles, under seat rail. Each also stenciled with various later royal inventory numbers.
Height: 2′11⅝″ (90.4 cm); Width: 1′10⅝″ (57.4 cm); Depth: 1′9″ (53.3 cm)
Accession number 71.DA.92.1–2

PROVENANCE

Château de Versailles.

Jacques, comte de Béraudière. Sold, Paris, May 18–30, 1885, lot 902 (part).

Duveen Brothers, New York.

Anna Thomson Dodge, Rose Terrace, Grosse Pointe Farms, Michigan. Sold, Christie's, London, June 24, 1971, lot 65.

Purchased at that sale by J. Paul Getty.

COMMENTARY

Two more side chairs from this set are in the Nelson-Atkins Museum of Art, Kansas City, Missouri. Two *marquises* from this set are at the Château de Versailles; one *bergère* is in a French private collection; and a pair of *fauteuils*, also from this set, was on the Paris art market in 1985. A large *canapé* was also with the set when it was sold at auction in 1885.

101 FOUR ARMCHAIRS AND ONE SETTEE

Paris, circa 1770–1775
By Jean-Baptiste Tilliard *fils*
Carved and gilded beech; modern silk velvet upholstery
Each piece stamped TILLIARD under rear seat rail.
Chairs: Height: 3′4″ (101.6 cm); Width: 2′5″ (73.6 cm); Depth: 2′5½″ (74.9 cm)
Settee: Height: 3′11⅜″ (120.3 cm); Width: 7′6½″ (229.7 cm); Depth: 3′½″ (92.7 cm)
Accession number 78.DA.99.1–5

PROVENANCE

Mortimer L. Schiff, New York. Sold by his heir, John L. Schiff, Christie's, London, June 22, 1938, lot 55.

Purchased at that sale by J. Paul Getty.

BIBLIOGRAPHY

Wilson, *Selections*, no. 46, pp. 92–93, illus.

COMMENTARY

A pair of armchairs from this set is in the Cleveland Museum of Art.

101a

101b

102 FOUR SIDE CHAIRS

Paris, circa 1780
By Georges Jacob
Carved and gilded beech; modern silk upholstery
One chair stenciled GARDE MEUBLE DE LA REINE under seat rail. Another bears a label *Ex museo L.Double.*
Height: 2′11⅛″ (89.2 cm); Width: 1′9¾″ (55.3 cm); Depth: 1′7¾″ (50.1 cm)
Accession number 71.DA.93.1–4

PROVENANCE

Marie-Antoinette, Petit Trianon, Versailles.

Léopold Double, Paris. Sold, Paris, May 30–June 1, 1881, lot 427.

Henri, comte de Greffuhle, Paris.

Duveen Brothers, New York.

Anna Thomson Dodge, Rose Terrace, Grosse Pointe Farms, Michigan. Sold, Christie's, London, June 24, 1971, lot 66.

Purchased at that sale by J. Paul Getty.

COMMMENTARY

The carving of the seat rails has been altered. Two other pieces from this set—a *bergère* with the Petit Trianon mark, CT under a crown, and a side chair stamped by Georges Jacob—are in separate French private collections.

102

103

103 PAIR OF FOLDING STOOLS

Paris, circa 1786
By Jean-Baptiste-Claude Sené; carved by Nicolas Vallois
Carved, painted, and gilded beech; modern upholstery
Each stool branded with three fleur-de-lys beneath a crown, and with TH, the mark of the Tuileries.
Height: (without cushion) 1′4¾″ (42.6 cm); Width: 2′4⅜″ (72.1 cm); Depth: 1′7⅛″ (48.5 cm)
Accession number 71.DA.94.1–2

PROVENANCE

Marie-Antoinette. From a set of sixty-four folding stools supplied, at the cost of 720 *livres* each, for her gaming rooms in the Château de Fontainebleau and the Château de Compiègne. Ordered in two batches by Jean Hauré in 1786.

Palais du Luxembourg or Palais des Tuileries, Paris, 1797–circa 1806.

Michel, Paris, 1933.

Anna Thomson Dodge, Rose Terrace, Grosse Pointe Farms, Michigan. Sold, Christie's, London, June 24, 1971, lot 69.

Purchased at that sale by J. Paul Getty.

BIBLIOGRAPHY

Pierre Verlet, "Les Meubles sculptés du XVIIIe siècle, quelques identifications," *Bulletin de la Société de l'histoire française*, 1937, pp. 259–263.

Pierre Verlet, *French Royal Furniture*, 1963, pp. 35–36.

Verlet, *Meubles français*, p. 227.

COMMENTARY

These stools, possibly after a design by Gilles-Pierre Cauvet, were partly painted white and partly gilded by Chatard. The bosses were gilded by Chaudron, and the stools were upholstered by Capin.

104

104 SWIVEL CHAIR

Paris, circa 1787
By Georges Jacob; carved by Triquet and Rode
Carved beech; caning; modern silk velvet upholstery
Painted 8758 under the rail.
Height: 2′9½″ (85.1 cm); Width: 1′10¾″ (57.8 cm); Depth: 1′9½″ (54.6 cm)
Accession number 72.DA.51

PROVENANCE

Made for Marie-Antoinette's *chambre à coucher du treillage* in the Petit Trianon, Versailles, 1787. Ordered by Bonnefoy-Duplan.

Edith M. K. Wetmore and Maude A. K. Wetmore, Château-sur-Mer, Newport, Rhode Island. Offered for sale, Parke Bernet, Château-sur-Mer, September 16–18, 1969, lot 1037, bought in. Sold, Parke Bernet, New York, February 20, 1971, lot 122.

Dalva Brothers, New York, 1971.

Purchased by J. Paul Getty, 1972.

COMMENTARY

This chair was originally painted by Chaillot and covered with silk made by Desfarges of Lyons. The set from which the chair comes has now returned to the Petit Trianon, except for the bed, which is not known to have survived.

105 SETTEE, TWO *BERGERES*, AND EIGHT *FAUTEUILS*

Paris, circa 1810
Frames attributed to Jacob-Désmalter et Cie
Mahogany; gilt-bronze mounts; silk and wool tapestry upholstery
No marks
Settee: Height: 3′4½″ (102.9 cm); Width: 6′2⅞″ (190.2 cm); Depth: 2′⅛″ (61.3 cm)
Chairs: Height: 3′3⅝″ (100.6 cm); Width: 2′1″ (63.5 cm); Depth: 1′7″ (48.2 cm)
Accession number 67.DA.6.1–11

PROVENANCE

Traditionally Eugène Beauharnais, Duke of Leuchtenberg, Munich.

If so, then inherited by Maximilian, 3rd Duke of Leuchtenberg, and his wife Grand Duchess Maria Nikolaevna.

Museums and Palaces Collections, Leningrad. Sold, Lepke, Berlin, November 7, 1928, lot 73.

Ives, comte de Cambacérès, Paris.

Edouard Mortier, 5ᵉ duc de Trévise, Paris. Sold, Galerie Jean Charpentier, Paris, May 19, 1938, lot 47.

Purchased at that sale by J. Paul Getty.

105a

105b

CARVED TABLES

106 CONSOLE TABLE
Paris, circa 1725
Maker unknown
Carved and gilded oak; *lumachella pavonazza* marble top
Remains of Christie Robert's printed label underneath.
Height: 2′10⅜″ (87.3 cm); Width: 4′11⅞″ (152.1 cm); Depth: 1′11¼″ (59.1 cm)
Accession number 72.DA.68

PROVENANCE

Christie Robert, London, circa 1885–1916.

Baroness van Zuylen, Paris, by 1964. Palais Galliera, Paris, June 8, 1971, lot 77.

Rosenberg and Stiebel, New York, 1972.

Purchased by J. Paul Getty, 1972.

COMMENTARY

This table is carved with a coat of arms, possibly for a cadet branch of the Besard family of Lorraine.

107

106

107 SIDE TABLE
Paris, circa 1730
Maker unknown
Carved and gilded oak; *brèche violette* top
No marks
Height: 2′11⅛″ (89.3 cm); Width: 5′7″ (170.2 cm); Depth: 2′8″ (81.3 cm)
Accession number 79.DA.68

PROVENANCE

Vicomtesse de B . . . , Paris. Sold, Hôtel Drouot, Paris, April 26, 1923, lot 21.

François-Gérard Seligmann, Paris.

Purchased by the J. Paul Getty Museum, 1979.

BIBLIOGRAPHY

Wilson, "Acquisitions 1979 to mid 1980," no. 3, p. 5, illus.

108a

108b

108 CENTER TABLE

Top: Italian (Rome), circa 1600
Support: Paris, circa 1745
Makers unknown
Carved and gilded wood; marble top inlaid with semiprecious stones
No marks
Height: 2′10½″ (87.6 cm); Width: 6′5⅝″ (197.1 cm); Depth: 3′9⅝″ (115.8 cm)
Accession number 72.DA.58

PROVENANCE

Alfred de Rothschild, Halton, Buckinghamshire.

Lionel de Rothschild, Exbury, Hampshire, by descent, 1918.

Edmund de Rothschild, Exbury, Hampshire, by descent, 1942.

Frank Partridge Ltd., London, 1972.

Purchased by J. Paul Getty, 1972.

SUPPORTS

109 WALL BRACKET

Paris, circa 1715–1720
Maker unknown
Carved and gilded oak
No marks
Height: 1′6″ (45.7 cm); Width: 1′9½″ (54.6 cm); Depth: 8½″ (21.6 cm)
Accession number 84.DH.86

PROVENANCE

Private collection, New York.

Matthew Schutz Ltd., New York, 1984.

Purchased by the J. Paul Getty Museum, 1984.

109

110 PAIR OF *TORCHERES*

Paris, circa 1725
Maker unknown
Carved and gilded wood
No marks
Height: 5′8¼″ (173.3 cm); Diameter (at top): 1′3¾″ (40.0 cm); (at base): 1′10½″ (57.1 cm)
Accession number 71.DA.98.1–2

PROVENANCE

Duveen Brothers, New York.

Anna Thomson Dodge, Rose Terrace, Grosse Pointe Farms, Michigan. Sold, Christie's, London, June 24, 1971, lot 75.

Purchased at that sale by J. Paul Getty.

110

PANELING

111 PANELING

Paris, 1725–1726, with twentieth-century additions
By Jacques Gaultier after the designs of Armand-Claude Mollet
Painted and gilded wood; *brèche d'Alep* mantelpiece; modern mirrored glass
No marks
Height: 13′ (396.2 cm); Width: 26′9″ (815.0 cm); Depth: 22′ (670.6 cm)
Accession number 71.DH.118

111

PROVENANCE

Guillaume Cressart, Hôtel Cressart, 18, place Vendôme. Paris, Installed in 1725 and 1726 in the *chambre à coucher.*

Louis-Auguste Duché, Hôtel Cressart, 1733.

Jean-Baptiste Duché (brother of Louis-Auguste Duché), Hôtel Cressart, by 1743.

Elisabeth-Louise Duché (wife of Jacques Bertrand, marquis de Scépeaux et de Beaupreau), Hôtel Cressart, after 1743.

Elisabeth-Louise-Adélaïde de Scépeaux de Beaupreau (wife of the comte de La Tour d'Auvergne), Hôtel Cressart, 1769.

Jean-Louis Milon d'Inval, Hôtel Cressart, 1774, ownership passed to his wife Antoinette Bureau Seraudey (Mme d'Inval), in An III (1794/95). Sold by her heirs in 1836.

Sophie Dawes (baronne de Feuchères), Hôtel Cressart, 1836. The *chambre à coucher* became the *salon* at this time. Sold by her heirs after her death in 1841.

Marquise de Las Marismas del Guadalquivir (Mme Alexandre Aguado), Hôtel Cressart, 1842.

Union Artistique, Hôtel Cressart, 1865.

André Carlhian, Paris. *Boiseries* removed in 1936.

Duveen Brothers, 1939. Stored in Paris until removed to New York in 1959.

Norton Simon, New York, 1965.

Purchased by J. Paul Getty, 1971.

BIBLIOGRAPHY

René Colas, *Paris qui reste*, 1914, vol. 1, p. 105, illus.

Bruno Pons, "Les Boiseries de l'Hôtel Cressart au J. Paul Getty Museum," *The J. Paul Getty Museum Journal* 11, 1983, pp. 67–88, illus.

COMMENTARY

The Hôtel Cressart was leased many times in the eighteenth century, the tenants included Elie Randon, Pierre-Louis-Paul Randon de Boisset, the comte de Stainville, the comte de La Marck, the Russian ambassador Count Saltykov, and Sainte-Amarande.

112

112 FOUR PANELS

Paris, circa 1730–1735
Maker unknown
Oak
No marks
Panels 1 and 2: Height: 9′2¼″ (280.0 cm); Width: 4′½″ (123.0 cm)
Panels 3 and 4: Height: 9′2¼″ (280.0 cm); Width: 4′6½″ (139.0 cm)
Accession number 84.DH.52.1–4

PROVENANCE

Château de Marly-Le-Roi, Yvelines, by repute.

Mallet family, Louveciennes, early nineteenth century.

Mme Claude Melin, Louveciennes, 1984, by descent.

Purchased by the J. Paul Getty Museum, 1984.

113

113 FRAME FOR AN ALCOVE OR MIRROR

Paris, circa 1740
Maker unknown
Carved, painted, and gilded oak
No marks
Height: 9′7″ (292.1 cm); Width: 7′4″ (223.5 cm)
Accession number 72.DH.70

PROVENANCE

Gift of Deane and Anne Johnson, Los Angeles, 1972.

114a

114b

114 PAIR OF PAINTED PANELS

Paris, circa 1745
Maker unknown
Painted canvas and raised leather
No marks
Height: 8′ (243.8 cm); Width: 8′ (243.8 cm)
Accession number 76.DH.38.1–2

PROVENANCE

Gift of Neil Sellin, New York, 1976.

COMMENTARY

These panels are from a series, other examples of which are in the Cooper-Hewitt Museum, New York.

115

115 PANELING

Paris, circa 1755
Maker unknown
Painted and gilded oak; four oil-on-canvas overdoor paintings; *brèche d'Alep* mantelpiece; modern mirrored glass; gilt-bronze hardware
No marks
Height: 14′4″ (436.9 cm); Width: 23′6½″ (718.0 cm); Depth: 25′6″ (777.0 cm)
Accession number 73.DH.107

PROVENANCE

A hôtel on the quai Malaquais, Paris, until 1900.

Mme Doucet, Paris, 1900–1907.

Duc de Gramont, avenue Georges Mandel, Paris, 1907. Offered for sale (still in situ), Ader Picard, Paris, October 9, 1969, bought in.

R. and M. Carlhian, Paris.

Purchased by J. Paul Getty, 1973.

BIBLIOGRAPHY

Gérard Mabille, "Un Demi-Siècle à l'Hôtel Gramont," *Connaissance des arts*, November 1963, p. 92, illus.

116

116 PANELED ROOM

Paris, circa 1770–1775
Maker unknown
Painted and gilded oak; plaster overdoors; modern mirrored glass; *brèche d'Alep* mantelpiece; gilt-bronze hardware
No marks
Height: (without cornice) 15′5/16″ (458.0 cm); Width: 30′4 3/16″ (925.0 cm); Depth: 20′6 7/8″ (627.0 cm)
Accession number 84.DH.34

PROVENANCE

Jacques Seligmann, Paris, 1920's.

François-Gérard Seligmann, Paris.

Purchased by the J. Paul Getty Museum, 1984.

117

118

117 PANELING
Paris, circa 1780
Maker unknown
Painted oak; modern mirrored glass; gilt-bronze hardware; contemporary gray-veined white marble mantelpiece from a separate source
No marks
Height: 11′8″ (355.6 cm); Width: 21′5″ (652.8 cm); Depth: 30′6″ (929.6 cm)
Accession numbers: paneling 61.DH.1; mantelpiece 72.DH.88

PROVENANCE

Paneling:

Installed in Mr. Getty's Malibu home, 1950's.

Mantelpiece:

R. and M. Carlhian, Paris.

Purchased by J. Paul Getty, 1972.

118 NEWEL POST
Paris, circa 1735
Maker unknown
Gilded iron
No marks
Height: 2′11⅝″ (90.5 cm); Width: 11½″ (29.2 cm); Depth: 1′3¾″ (40.0 cm)
Accession number 79.DH.164

PROVENANCE

A. Gignoux, Paris.

Installed in Mr. Getty's Malibu home, 1950's.

119

LIGHTING: CANDELABRA

119 PAIR OF GIRANDOLES
Paris, circa 1730
Maker unknown
Rock crystal; gilt bronze
No marks
Height: 2′10″ (86.3 cm); Width: 2′$\frac{1}{2}$″ (62.3 cm); Depth: 1′2$\frac{3}{4}$″ (37.5 cm)
Accession number 75.DF.53.1–2

PROVENANCE

Kraemer et Cie, Paris.

Purchased by J. Paul Getty, 1975.

120

120 PAIR OF CANDELABRA
Elephants: German (Meissen Manufactory), circa 1741–1745
Flowers: Vincennes Manufactory (?), circa 1745–1750
Mounts: Paris, circa 1750
Elephants modeled by Peter Reinicke in 1741
Hard paste porcelain elephants; soft paste porcelain flowers; gilt-bronze mounts
No marks
Height: 9$\frac{1}{8}$″ (23.2 cm); Width: 9$\frac{3}{4}$″ (24.7 cm); Depth: 4$\frac{1}{8}$″ (10.5 cm)
Accession number 75.DI.68.1–2

PROVENANCE

Baron Maximilian von Goldschmidt-Rothschild, Frankfurt.

Rosenberg and Stiebel, New York, 1975.

Purchased by J. Paul Getty, 1975.

121

121 PAIR OF CANDELABRA
Paris, circa 1775
Attributed to Pierre Gouthière
Gilt bronze
No marks
Height: 1′2$\frac{13}{16}$″ (37.6 cm); Width: 8$\frac{1}{2}$″ (21.6 cm); Depth: 7$\frac{7}{8}$″ (19.9 cm)
Accession number 72.DF.43.1–2

PROVENANCE

(?) Baron Henri de Rothschild, Paris.

Jacques Seligmann, Paris, 1948.

Carreras Savedra, Buenos Aires.

Jacques Helft, Argentina and Paris.

French and Company, New York, 1972.

Purchased by J. Paul Getty, 1972.

122

122 PAIR OF CANDELABRA
Paris, circa 1784
Attributed to L.-F. Feuchère
Blued metal; gilt bronze
No marks
Height: 3′8¾″ (113.7 cm); Width: 1′5¾″ (45.1 cm); Depth: 10½″ (26.7 cm)
Accession number 71.DF.99.1–2

PROVENANCE

Baron Mayer Amschel de Rothschild, Mentmore Towers, Buckinghamshire.

Hannah de Rothschild (Countess of Rosebery, wife of the 5th Earl, married 1878, died 1890), Mentmore Towers.

Harold, 6th Earl of Rosebery, Mentmore Towers, by inheritance. Sold, Sotheby's, London, April 17, 1964, lot 25.

Claude Sère, Paris, 1964.

Private collection, Paris, late 1960's.

Frank Partridge Ltd., London, 1971.

Purchased by J. Paul Getty, 1971.

EXHIBITIONS

London. 25 Park Lane, *Three French Reigns*, February–April 1933, ex. cat., no. 485, illus.

123

LIGHTING: CANDLESTICKS

123 PAIR OF CANDLESTICKS
Paris, circa 1680–1690
Maker unknown
Gilt bronze
No marks
Height: 10″ (25.4 cm); Diameter: 5¾″ (14.6 cm)
Accession number 72.DF.56.1–2

PROVENANCE

Baron Nathaniel de Rothschild, Vienna.

Baron Alphonse de Rothschild, Vienna.

Baroness Clarice de Rothschild, Vienna and New York, 1942.

Rosenberg and Stiebel, New York, 1971.

Purchased by J. Paul Getty, 1972.

124

124 PAIR OF CANDLESTICKS
Paris, circa 1780
By Etienne Martincourt
Gilt bronze
Each candlestick stamped MARTINCOURT under base. One inscribed *Louis Antoine Blois* and *LA* inside base.
Height: 11¾″ (29.9 cm); Diameter: 5⅜″ (13.7 cm)
Accession number 72.DF.48.1–2

PROVENANCE

Mr. and Mrs. Meyer Sassoon, Pope's Manor, Berkshire, by 1914.

Violet Sassoon (Mrs. Derek C. Fitzgerald), Heathfield Park, Sussex. Sold, Christie's, London, March 23, 1972, lot 59.

Purchased at that sale by J. Paul Getty, 1972.

EXHIBITIONS

London. The Burlington Fine Arts Club, 1914, no. 117.

COMMENTARY

These candlesticks are possibly based on a design by Jean-Charles Delafosse.

125

LIGHTING: CHANDELIERS

125 CHANDELIER
Paris, circa 1710
Attributed to André-Charles Boulle
Gilt bronze
Each element stamped with the crowned C for 1745–1749.
Height: 2′6½″ (77.5 cm); Diameter: 2′8″ (81.3 cm)
Accession number 76.DF.13

PROVENANCE

Antenor Patiño, Paris.

Kraemer et Cie, Paris, 1976.

Purchased by J. Paul Getty, 1976.

126

126 CHANDELIER
Paris, circa 1710–1715
Maker unknown
Colored and plain glass; colored foils; rock crystal; gilt and silvered bronze
No marks
Height: 2′5½″ (75.0 cm); Diameter: 2′8″ (81.3 cm)
Accession number 74.DH.29

PROVENANCE

Private collection, Turin.

Jacques Kugel, Paris.

Kraemer et Cie, Paris, 1974.

Purchased by J. Paul Getty, 1974.

127

127 CHANDELIER
Paris, circa 1818–1819
By André Galle
Glass; enameled metal; gilt bronze
No marks
Height: 4′3″ (129.5 cm); Diameter: 3′2″ (96.5 cm)
Accession number 73.DH.76

PROVENANCE

Sold, Hôtel Drouot, Paris, early 1960's.

Sold, Hôtel Drouot, Paris, February 7, 1972, lot 83.

Kraemer et Cie, Paris, 1972.

Purchased by J. Paul Getty, 1973.

BIBLIOGRAPHY

Michael Shapiro, "Monsieur Galle, *Bronzier et Doreur*," *The J. Paul Getty Museum Journal* 6–7, 1978–1979, pp. 61–66, illus.

COMMENTARY

This model of chandelier is described by Galle as a "lustre à poissons" in a list of objects that he offered for sale to the Garde-Meuble de la Couronne of Louis XVIII in 1820. It had been made by him for the 1819 *Exposition des produits de l'industrie française* in Paris.

128

129

130

LIGHTING: WALL LIGHTS

128 PAIR OF WALL LIGHTS

Paris, circa 1715–1720
Maker unknown; partly based on an engraved design by André-Charles Boulle, later published in Paris by Jean Mariette, circa 1725
Gilt bronze
No marks
Height: 1′8$\frac{1}{16}$″ (51.0 cm); Width: 1′2″ (35.5 cm); Depth: 9$\frac{13}{16}$″ (25.0 cm)
Accession number 83.DF.195.1–2

PROVENANCE

Samuel Kahn, Paris.

Bernard Barouch Steinitz, Paris, 1982.

Purchased by the J. Paul Getty Museum, 1983.

BIBLIOGRAPHY

Bremer-David, "Acquisitions 1983," no. 4, p. 187, illus.

129 PAIR OF WALL LIGHTS

Paris (possibly German), circa 1735
Maker unknown
Gilt bronze
No marks
Height: 1′11″ (58.5 cm); Width: 11$\frac{1}{8}$″ (28.3 cm); Depth: 8″ (20.3 cm)
Accession number 78.DF.89.1–2

PROVENANCE

Cameron, London, 1950.

Purchased by J. Paul Getty, 1950.

130 FOUR WALL LIGHTS

Paris, circa 1750
Attributed to Jacques Caffiéri
Gilt bronze
Two lights stamped with a crown flanked by *CR* for *Casa Reale* and the inventory numbers *C.562.1* and *C.562.2* on front near base. Two other lights stamped similarly *C.1068.1* and *C.1068.2*.
Height: 3′1″ (94.0 cm); Width: 1′10$\frac{3}{4}$″ (57.8 cm); Depth: 1′1$\frac{3}{8}$″ (34.0 cm)
Accession number 84.DF.41.1–4

PROVENANCE

Madame Louise-Elisabeth of France (Duchess of Parma), Palazzo di Colorno (near Parma), circa 1753.

Ducal collection of Parma.

Private collection, France. Sold, Ader, Picard et Tajan, Paris, December 12, 1978, lot 48.

Partridge (Fine Arts) Ltd., London, 1978.

Private collection, London.

Partridge (Fine Arts) Ltd., London, 1983.

Purchased by the J. Paul Getty Museum, 1984.

BIBLIOGRAPHY

Bremer-David, "Acquisitions 1984," no. 3, pp. 76–79, illus.

131

131 FOUR WALL LIGHTS

Paris, circa 1750
Maker unknown
Soft paste porcelain flowers; gilt bronze
No marks
Height: 1′6″ (45.7 cm); Width: 1′1½″ (34.3 cm); Depth: 7¾″ (19.7 cm)
Accession number 75.DF.4.1–4

PROVENANCE

Henry Seymour, London (together with another pair).

French and Company, New York (six). Two lights sold to Arnold Seligmann, Rey and Co., 1941 (later in the Georges Lurcy collection, New York).

Rita Lydig, New York (?), 1927.

Sidney J. Lamon, New York. Sold, Christie's, London, November 29, 1973, lot 69.

Frank Partridge Ltd., London, 1973.

Purchased by J. Paul Getty, 1975.

132 FOUR WALL LIGHTS

Paris, 1756
By François-Thomas Germain
Gilt bronze
Two wall lights engraved FAIT PAR F.T. GERMAIN.SCULP.ORF.DU ROI AUX GALLERIES DU LOUVRE.1756 at lower right and left. Two stamped on lower front with Palais du Luxembourg inventory number 1051 LUX 1, and two with 1051 LUX 2. All stamped with Château de Compiègne inventory marks *CP* under a crown and *N° 28*, at lower rear. Various numbers stamped on bobèches and drip pans.
1.a: Height: 3′3¼″ (99.6 cm); Width: 2′⅞″ (63.2 cm); Depth: 1′4⅛″ (41.0 cm)
1.b: Height: 3′1¼″ (94.6 cm); Width: 1′10⅝″ (57.5 cm); Depth: 1′1⅝″ (34.6 cm)
2.a: Height: 3′4½″ (102.9 cm); Width: 2′1″ (63.5 cm); Depth: 1′1½″ (34.3 cm)
2.b: Height: 2′11⅛″ (89.2 cm); Width: 1′10⅜″ (56.8 cm); Depth: 1′3⅞″ (40.3 cm)
Accession numbers 81.DF.96.1.a–b and 2.a–b

PROVENANCE

Made for Louis-Philippe, duc d'Orléans. Four pairs installed in the Chambre d'Apparat and the Salon des Jeux of the Palais Royal, Paris, circa 1756. Sold privately in 1786 by Louis-Philippe-Joseph, duc d'Orléans, and purchased by the *bronzier* Feuchère (probably Pierre-François Feuchère) for Louis XVI.

Mobilier Royal, Paris, purchased August 30, 1786, four pairs, for 700 *livres* a pair; described as having damaged gilding.

Château de Compiègne. Two pairs regilded at the order of Jean Hauré in the first six months of 1787 for 500 *livres* a pair, and installed in the Salon des Nobles de la Reine. Listed at Compiègne in 1791.

Government of France, Palais du Luxembourg, Paris, after 1792.

132a

132b

Baron Mayer Amschel de Rothschild, Mentmore Towers, Buckinghamshire, late nineteenth century (in the Great Dining Room).

Hannah de Rothschild (Countess of Rosebery, wife of the 5th Earl, married 1878, died 1890), Mentmore Towers.

Harold, 6th Earl of Rosebery, Mentmore Towers. Sold, Sotheby's, London, April 17, 1964, lot 18, to François-Gérard Seligmann, Paris.

Private collector, Argentina and Switzerland. Offered for sale by his heirs, Sotheby's, Monaco, June 14–15, 1981, lot 148a and b, bought in.

Purchased by the J. Paul Getty Museum, 1981.

BIBLIOGRAPHY

Denis Diderot and Jean Le Rond d'Alembert, *Encyclopédie ou dictionnaire raisonné des sciences, planches*, 1762, vol. I, s. v. "*architecture*," illus. pls. XXXII, XXXIII.

Axelle de Broglie de Gaigneron, "Le 3ème Témoin de l'art de F-Th. Germain, bronzier," *Connaissance des arts*, September 1968, pp. 76–77, illus.

Max Terrier, "L'Applique: Sa Provenance," *Connaissance des arts*, November 1968, pp. 32–33.

Svend Eriksen, *Early Neo-Classicism in France*, 1974, p. 349, illus. pl. 202.

Pierre Verlet, "Bronzes d'ameublement français du XVIIIe siècle: Notes et documents," *Bulletin de la Société de l'histoire de l'art français*, 1980, pp. 200–201, illus. p. 203.

Michel Beurdeley, *La France à l'encan 1789–1799*, 1981, p. 167, illus. pls. 177–178.

Wilson, "Acquisitions 1981," no. 4, pp. 73–78 (with a note on conservation by Barbara Roberts).

Wilson, *Selections*, no. 25, pp. 50–51, illus.

COMMENTARY

The whereabouts of the remaining two pairs of wall lights is not known. After 1787 they were sent to the Ecole Militaire and hung in the Salle du Conseil or the Salon des Maréchaux.

133

133 SIX WALL LIGHTS

Paris, circa 1765–1770
By Philippe Caffiéri
Gilt bronze
Lights number 78.DF.263.1 and 82.DF.35.1 stenciled *No 151* on back. Light number 82.DF.35.1 engraved *fait par Caffiery* on one drip pan and stamped with the numbers 2 and 3 on back. Number 82.DF.35.2 stamped with the number 4 on back.
Height: 2′1½″ (64.8 cm); Width: 1′4½″ (41.9 cm); Depth: 1′¼″ (31.1 cm)
Accession numbers 78.DF.263.1–4 and 82.DF.35.1–2

PROVENANCE

78.DF.263.1–4:

(?) Sold, Hôtel Drouot, Paris, May 26–27, 1921, lot 99, to de Friedel.

M. and Mme Robert Daublay, Paris. Sold, Etude Couturier Nicolay, Paris, April 6, 1978, lot 52.

Alexander and Berendt, Ltd., London, 1978.

Purchased by the J. Paul Getty Museum, 1978.

82.DF.35.1–2:

Private collection, Los Angeles. Probably purchased in Paris.

Lee Greenway, Los Angeles. Sold, Sotheby's, Los Angeles, October 21, 1980, lot 787A.

Alexander and Berendt, Ltd., London, 1980.

Purchased by the J. Paul Getty Museum, 1982.

BIBLIOGRAPHY

Wilson, "Acquisitions 1977 to mid 1979," no. 7, pp. 42–43, illus. (one).

Sassoon, "Acquisitions 1982," no. 10, pp. 52–53, illus.

Wilson, *Selections*, no. 35, pp. 70–71, illus. (one).

COMMENTARY

A drawing for this model of wall light is in the University Library, Warsaw. It is inscribed *Inventé & Executé par P. Caffieri Sculpteur Et Sizeleur Du Roy A paris 1765*.

Another pair of wall lights of this model was formerly in a private collection in Los Angeles and was probably en suite in the twentieth century with the Museum's pair 82.DF.35.1–2. It is now in a private collection in New Jersey.

134 SIX WALL LIGHTS

Paris, circa 1775
Maker unknown
Gilt bronze
No marks
Height: 2′3″ (68.6 cm); Width: 1′1¼″ (33.7 cm); Depth: 10½″ (26.7 cm)
Accession numbers 74.DF.3.1–2 and 77.DF.29.1–4

PROVENANCE

74.DF.3.1–2:

Alexander and Berendt, Ltd., London, 1974.

Purchased by J. Paul Getty, 1974.

134

77.DF.29.1–4:

Sold, Christie's, London, December 2, 1976, lot 3.

Alexander and Berendt, Ltd., London, 1976.

Purchased by the J. Paul Getty Museum, 1977.

COMMENTARY

A watercolor of a *salon* in the prince de Condé's Château de Chantilly shows lights similar to this model. The watercolor is in an album that was presented by the prince to the future Czar Paul I of Russia in 1782 and has since been returned to the Musée Condé at Chantilly. A drawing showing a two-armed light similar to this model is in the J. Paul Getty Museum's collection, illustrated as No. 232 in this handbook.

135

135 PAIR OF WALL LIGHTS

Paris, circa 1780
Attributed to Pierre Gouthière, after a design by François-Joseph Bellanger
Gilt bronze
No marks
Height: 1′8½″ (52.1 cm); Width: 10 15/16″ (27.8 cm); Depth: 7″ (17.8 cm)
Accession number 74.DF.5.1–2

PROVENANCE

Kraemer et Cie, Paris, 1974.

Purchased by J. Paul Getty, 1974.

COMMENTARY

A pair of wall lights of this description formed lot 292 in the 1781 auction of the possessions of the late duchesse de Mazarin in Paris. They were described as being "par Gouttier."

136

136 PAIR OF WALL LIGHTS

Paris, circa 1787
Attributed to Pierre-Philippe Thomire
Gilt bronze
No marks
Height: 3′6½″ (107.9 cm); Width: 1′10 7/16″ (57.0 cm); Depth: 11 7/8″ (30.1 cm)
Accession number 83.DF.23.1–2

PROVENANCE

Ducs de Mortemart Rochechouart, Château de Saint-Vrain, Seine-et-Oise, from the eighteenth century, by descent until 1982.

Maurice Segoura, Paris, 1982.

Purchased by the J. Paul Getty Museum, 1983.

BIBLIOGRAPHY

Sassoon, "Acquisitions 1983," no. 11, pp. 207–208, 211, illus.

137

138

137 PAIR OF WALL LIGHTS

Paris, circa 1788
Attributed to L.-F. Feuchère
Gilt bronze
No marks
Height: 2′¼″ (61.6 cm); Width: 1′9⁹⁄₁₆″ (32.0 cm); Depth: 7¼″ (18.5 cm)
Accession number 78.DF.90.1–2

PROVENANCE

Jacques Bardac, Paris.

Paul Dutasta, Paris. Sold, Galerie Georges Petit, Paris, June 4, 1926, lot 105.

(?) Rothschild collection, Paris.

Rosenberg and Stiebel, New York.

Purchased by J. Paul Getty, 1953.

COMMENTARY

A similar pair of wall lights, but with an additional arm, was supplied by L.-F. Feuchère for Marie-Antoinette's *cabinet de toilette* at the Château de Saint-Cloud in 1788. They are now in the Musée du Louvre, Paris.

138 SIX WALL LIGHTS

Paris, circa 1880
Maker unknown
Gilt bronze
One inscribed SIII on back; another, VIII.
Height: 3′5″ (104.1 cm); Width: 1′11¾″ (60.3 cm); Depth: 9⅜″ (23.8 cm)
Accession numbers 78.DF.88.1–4 and 78.DF.242.1–2

PROVENANCE

78.DF.88.1–4:

Duc de Choiseul-Praslin, Château de Chanteloup, by repute.

Comte Philippe de La Rochefoucauld, Château de Beaumont, Côte d'Or. Sold, Parke Bernet, New York, May 17, 1952, lots 347 and 348.

Purchased at that sale (?) by J. Paul Getty.

78.DF.242.1–2

French and Company, New York, 1950.

Purchased by J. Paul Getty, 1950.

EXHIBITIONS

Woodside, California. Filoli, on loan, 1979–present.

139a

139b

FIREDOGS

139 PAIR OF FIREDOGS

Paris, circa 1735
Maker unknown
Gilt bronze
No marks
Left: Height: 1′2⅛″ (35.9 cm); Width: 1′3″ (38.1 cm); Depth: 9⅝″ (24.4 cm)
Right: Height: 1′¾″ (32.3 cm); Width: 1′3¼″ (38.7 cm); Depth: 8⅞″ (22.6 cm)
Accession number 71.DF.114.1–2

PROVENANCE

Duveen Brothers, New York.

Anna Thomson Dodge, Rose Terrace, Grosse Pointe Farms, Michigan. Sold, Christie's, London, June 24, 1971, lot 18.

Purchased at that sale by J. Paul Getty.

140

140 PAIR OF FIREDOGS

Paris, circa 1735
By Charles Cressent
Gilt bronze
No marks
Height: 1′3¼″ (38.7 cm); Width: 1′2⅜″ (36.4 cm); Depth: 8⅛″ (20.6 cm)
Accession number 73.DF.63.1–2

PROVENANCE

Didier Aaron, Paris, by 1971.

French and Company, New York, 1972.

Purchased by J. Paul Getty, 1973.

EXHIBITIONS

Amsterdam. Amsterdams Historisch Museum, *Fourth International Exhibition Presented by CINOA*, March–May 1970, ex. cat., no. 237.

BIBLIOGRAPHY

Ballot, *Cressent*, p. 218.

Wilson, *Selections*, no. 17, p. 34, illus.

COMMENTARY

A pair of firedogs of this model formed lot 163 in the Cressent auction catalogue of February 15, 1757.

141

141 PAIR OF FIREDOGS

Paris, circa 1780
Attributed to Pierre Gouthière
Gilt bronze; dark blue enameled panels
Some elements stamped with the letter A.
Height: 1′3⅝″ (39.7 cm); Width: 1′2$^{15}/_{16}$″ (37.9 cm); Depth: 5½″ (13.9 cm)
Accession number 62.DF.1.1–2

PROVENANCE

(?) Duchesse de Mazarin, Paris. Sold, Paris, December 10–15, 1781, lot 285.

(?) Comtesse de Clermont-Tonnerre, Paris. Sold, Hôtel Drouot, Paris, October 10–13, 1900, lot 290.

(?) Private collection, Paris. Sold, Hôtel Drouot, Paris, February 4, 1909, lot 96.

Mortimer L. Schiff, New York. Sold by his heir, John L. Schiff, Christie's, London, June 22, 1938, lot 45.

Purchased at that sale by J. Paul Getty.

COMMENTARY

In the 1781 auction catalogue of the duchesse de Mazarin's possessions, a pair of firedogs of this model is described as being "par Gouttier."

142

143

144

INKSTANDS

142 INKSTAND AND PAPERWEIGHTS
Paris, circa 1715
Maker unknown
Gilt bronze
No marks
Inkstand: Height: 4¼″ (10.8 cm); Width: 1′2 11/16″ (37.2 cm); Depth: 11⅛″ (28.2 cm)
Paperweights: Height: 2⅝″ (6.7 cm); Width: 6⅜″ (16.2 cm); Depth: 4½″ (11.4 cm)
Accession number 75.DF.6.1–3

PROVENANCE

Kraemer et Cie, Paris, 1975.

Purchased by J. Paul Getty, 1975.

COMMENTARY

Inkstands of a similar model but of larger size are shown in two portraits, one by Jacques-André-Joseph Aved of Jean-Gabriel de la Porte du Theil, dated 1740, in the Cleveland Museum of Art, and the other by Marie-Louise-Elisabeth Vigée-Lebrun of Charles-Alexandre Calonne, dated 1784, in the British Royal Collection.

143 INKSTAND
Porcelain: Chinese, early eighteenth century—two outer cups (Jingdezhen), figure group and central cup (Dehua)
Lacquer: French, circa 1750
Mounts: Paris, circa 1750
Makers unknown
Hard paste porcelain; *vernis Martin*; gilt-bronze mounts
No marks
Height: 8″ (20.3 cm); Width: 1′2″ (35.6 cm); Depth: 10½″ (26.7 cm)
Accession number 76.DI.12

PROVENANCE

B. Fabre et Fils, Paris, 1976.

Purchased by J. Paul Getty, 1976.

BIBLIOGRAPHY

Wilson et al., *Mounted Oriental Porcelain*, no. 14, pp. 68–69, illus.

144 INKSTAND
Paris, circa 1810
Maker unknown
White marble; gilt bronze; velvet
No marks
Height: 3½″ (8.9 cm); Width: 1′6½″ (47.0 cm); Depth: 9½″ (24.1 cm)
Accession number 73.DJ.67

PROVENANCE

Adolphe Lion, Paris, 1929.

Mrs. Benjamin Stern, New York. Sold, American Art Association, New York, April 4–7, 1934, lot 848.

Frederick Victoria Inc., New York.

Mallett and Son, Ltd., London, 1973.

Purchased by J. Paul Getty, 1973.

145

145 INKSTAND

Paris (?), late nineteenth century
Maker unknown
Oak veneered with rosewood; set with hard paste porcelain plaques; gilt-bronze mounts
One plaque bears an unidentified mark in script. Base pasted with paper label printed *Palace of Pavlovsk* in Russian, inked with the inventory number 1004, and overstamped with a French customs stamp. Another paper label inked with the inventory number 29652 and another stenciled with a French customs stamp. Base painted 1044 in white and Uh.6522 in blue.
Height: 3⅞″ (9.8 cm); Width: 11¼″ (28.6 cm); Depth: 7¼″ (18.4 cm)
Accession number 71.DH.97

PROVENANCE

Russian Imperial Collections, Palace of Pavlovsk (near Saint Petersburg), until the early twentieth century.

Duveen Brothers, New York.

Anna Thomson Dodge, Rose Terrace, Grosse Pointe Farms, Michigan. Sold, Christie's, London, June 24, 1971, lot 33.

Purchased at that sale by J. Paul Getty.

EXHIBITIONS

Detroit. The Detroit Institute of Arts, *French Taste in the Eighteenth Century*, April–June 1956, ex. cat., no. 174, illus. p. 50.

SILVER

146 FOUNTAIN

Paris, 1661–1663, with English alterations of 1695, 1758, and circa 1762
Maker unknown; probably altered in London in 1695 by Ralph Leeke, in 1758 by Phillips Garden, and again later in the eighteenth century
Silver
Marked on body with an unknown Parisian maker's mark of HR flanking a scepter, and with a crowned R (the Paris date letter for 1661). Scratched with the weights *348 14* (partially obliterated) and *363 13* under base. Engraved with the arms of Curzon and Colyear on central cartouche.
Height: 2′1⅝″ (65.2 cm); Width: 1′2⅛″ (35.9 cm); Depth: 1′2¼″ (36.2 cm)
Accession number 82.DG.17

PROVENANCE

In England by 1694, when probably adapted from a lidded one-handled vase with a spout mounted higher, and when a matching fountain and two basins were made by Ralph Leeke.

Sir Nathaniel Curzon, 1st Baron Scarsdale (born 1726; married Caroline Colyear 1750; died 1804), Kedleston Hall, Derbyshire, by 1750.

Barons of Scarsdale, Kedleston Hall, by descent. Offered for sale, Christie's, London, July 16, 1930, lot 42, bought in. Offered for sale, Christie's, London, November 7, 1945, bought in. Sold to Jacques Helft, Paris, 1940's.

Arturo Lopez-Willshaw, Paris, late 1940's.

Patricia Lopez-Willshaw (widow of Arturo Lopez-Willshaw), Paris. Offered for sale, Sotheby's, Monaco, June 23, 1976, lot 48, bought in.

Purchased by the J. Paul Getty Museum, 1982.

EXHIBITIONS

Paris. Musée des Arts Décoratifs, *Louis XIV: Faste et décors*, May–October 1960, ex. cat., no. 378, illus. pl. LVII.

146

BIBLIOGRAPHY

C. Jackson, *An Illustrated History of English Plate*, 1911, figs. 265–266 (illustrates the original form of this fountain at Welbeck Abbey).

Jacques Helft, *French Master Goldsmiths and Silversmiths*, 1966, pp. 60–61, illus.

Wilson, *Selections*, no. 2, pp. 4–5, illus.

Gillian Wilson, "The Kedleston Fountain: Its Development from a Seventeenth-Century Vase," *The J. Paul Getty Museum Journal* 11, 1983, pp. 1–12, illus.

COMMENTARY

A pair of unaltered silver fountains of this model bearing the arms of Harley, Earl of Oxford, are in the collection of the Duke of Portland at Welbeck Abbey. The Museum's fountain and the Ralph Leeke copy are shown in four drawings by Robert Adam.

147

147 MODEL FOR A SILVER VESSEL (?)

Paris, circa 1720–1728
Maker unknown
Terracotta
No marks; modeled with the arms, monogram, and coronet (now partly missing) of Louis-Henri, duc de Bourbon, prince de Condé.
Height: 1′¾″ (32.4 cm); Width: 11¾″ (29.8 cm); Depth: 11¾″ (29.8 cm)
Accession number 83.DE.36

PROVENANCE

Louis-Henri, duc de Bourbon, prince de Condé, Château de Chantilly.

D. David-Weill, Paris.

Didier Aaron, Paris, 1981.

Purchased by the J. Paul Getty Museum, 1983.

BIBLIOGRAPHY

Wilson, "Acquisitions 1983," no. 5, pp. 187, 189–192, 194, illus.

COMMENTARY

This model is similar to designs for various pieces of silver by Juste-Aurèle Meissonier engraved in 1723 by Jacques-Gabriel Huquier and inscribed . . . *executé pour M.r le Duc* . . . [de Bourbon].

148

148 PAIR OF TUREENS, LINERS, AND STANDS

Paris, 1726–1728
By Thomas Germain, with arms added in 1764 by his son François-Thomas Germain
Silver
Marked variously on tureens, liners, and stands with a crowned K (the Paris date letter for 1726); a crowned A overlaid with crowned L's (the Paris *charge* mark for May 1722–September 1727 under Charles Cordier); a crowned M (the Paris date letter for 1728); a crowned A (the Paris *charge* mark for September 1727–December 1732 under the *sous-fermier* Jacques Cottin); a crowned bell (the Paris *contremarque* for 1727–1732); an artichoke mark (for modified works in silver, applied in the 1760's); and three obliterated marks, probably of Thomas Germain ([?] removed by his son). One tureen, stand, and liner engraved *N°.1*, the others *N°.2*; tureens engraved with the weights $48^{m}.1^{on}.2^{d}$ and $48^{m}3^{on}.2^{d}$, stands engraved with the weights $48^{m}2^{d}$ and $48^{m}5^{d}$. Both stands, one with the added date 1764, engraved FAIT.PAR.F.T. GERMAIN.ORF. SCULP. DU.ROY.AUX GALLERIES.DU LOUVRE. APARIS. The coat of arms of the Mello e Castro family engraved on stands and applied on tureens.
Tureens: Height: 6⅞″ (17.4 cm); Width: 1′6½″ (47.0 cm); Depth: 10″ (25.4 cm)
Stands: Height: 1 7/16″ (3.7 cm); Width: 1′10 7/16″ (57.0 cm); Depth: 1′4″ (40.6 cm)
Accession number 82.DG.12.1–2

PROVENANCE

Probably sold circa 1764 to Martinho de Mello e Castro, the Portuguese ambassador in Paris from 1763. Listed in the 1796 inventory of his possessions (taken after his death) with their lids decorated with artichokes, cauliflowers, birds, and fish. These lids were lost in the beginning of the nineteenth century.

Mello e Castro de Vilhena family, Portugal, by descent.

Galveias family, Portugal and Paris, by descent.

Sold, Christie's, Geneva, November 11, 1975, lot 230.

Jean Rossignol, Geneva, 1975.

Purchased by the J. Paul Getty Museum, 1982.

EXHIBITIONS

Lisbon. Museu Nacional de Arte Antiga, *Exposição de arte francesa*, May–June 1934, nos. 230–231.

Paris. Musée des Arts Décoratifs, *Les Trésors de l'orfèvrerie du Portugal*, November 1954–January 1955, ex. cat., no. 453.

BIBLIOGRAPHY

Daniel Alcouffe, *Louis XV: Un Moment de perfection de l'art français*, Hôtel de la Monnaie, Paris, 1974, ex. cat., p. 358.

Thomas Milnes-Gaskell, "Thomas Germain," *Christie's Review of the Season*, 1976, pp. 219–221, illus.

Wilson, "Acquisitions 1982," no. 3, pp. 24–28, illus.

Wilson, *Selections*, no. 11, pp. 22–23, illus.

COMMENTARY

Single tureens of this model without lids are shown in two paintings by Alexandre-François Desportes. The paintings are in the National-museum, Stockholm, and in a French private collection.

149

149 LIDDED *ECUELLE*

Paris, 1727
By Claude-Gabriel Dardet
Silver gilt
Marked on bowl and lid with a crowned L (the Paris *charge* mark for 1727) and the maker's mark of a fleur-de-lys under a crown, CGD, a dart, and two dots.
Engraved on bowl with the coat of arms of the Moulinet family, probably in the nineteenth century.
Height: 4¼" (10.8 cm); Width: 11¾" (29.9 cm); Depth: 7⅜" (18.7 cm)
Accession number 71.DG.77

PROVENANCE

Moulinet family, Ile-de-France.

Marquis collection, Paris. Sold, Hôtel Drouot, Paris, February 10–18, 1890, lot 110 (?).

D. David-Weill, Paris. Sold, Palais Galliera, Paris, November 24, 1971, lot 17.

Purchased at that sale by J. Paul Getty.

BIBLIOGRAPHY

Emile Dacier, *L'Art au XVIIIème siècle*, 1951, no. 192, p. 110, illus.

150 PAIR OF LIDDED TUREENS, LINERS, AND STANDS

Paris, 1744–1750
By Thomas Germain
Silver
Marked variously on tureens, liners, lids, and stands with a crowned I (the Paris date letter for 1749); a crowned K (the Paris date letter for 1750–1751); a laurel leaf (the Paris *contremarque* for October 1756–November 1762 under the *sous-fermier* Eloy Brichard); a hen's head (the Paris *décharge* mark for October 1750–October 1756 under the *sous-fermier* Julien Berthe); a boar's head (the Paris *décharge* mark for large pieces of silver used October 1750–October 1756); and several obliterated marks. One tureen, liner, lid, and stand engraved with *DU N° 3*; the other with *DU N° 4*. Stands scratched with various dealers' marks of twentieth-century date. Originally engraved with a cardinal's coat of arms, now partly erased and replaced with the arms of Robert, 1st Lord Carrington.
Tureens: Height: 11$^{13}/_{16}$" (30.0 cm); Width: 1′1¾" (34.9 cm); Depth: 11⅛" (28.2 cm)
Stands: Height: 1⅝" (4.2 cm); Width: 1′6$^{3}/_{16}$" (46.2 cm); Depth: 1′6$^{9}/_{16}$" (47.2 cm)
Accession number 82.DG.13.1–2

PROVENANCE

Possibly made for a Portuguese cardinal.

Robert, 1st Lord Carrington (created Baron in 1796), England.

S. J. Phillips, London, 1920's or 1930's.

150

Mr. and Mrs. Meyer Sassoon, Pope's Manor, Berkshire, by the 1930's.

S. J. Phillips, London.

Jacques Helft, Paris.

José and Vera Espirito Santo, Paris, by 1954. Sold, Christie's, Geneva, April 27, 1976, lot 446.

Private collection, Geneva, 1976.

Purchased by the J. Paul Getty Museum, 1982.

EXHIBITIONS

Paris. Musée des Arts Décoratifs, *Les Trésors de l'orfèvrerie du Portugal*, November 1954–January 1955, ex. cat., no. 455, illus.

BIBLIOGRAPHY

Thomas Milnes-Gaskell, "Thomas Germain," *Christie's Review of the Season*, 1976, pp. 219–221, illus.

Wilson, "Acquisitions 1982," no. 7, pp. 39–45, illus.

151

151 TRAY
Paris, 1750
By François-Thomas Germain
Silver
Marked underneath with the maker's mark of a fleur-de-lys under a crown; two dots, FTG, and a *toison*; a crowned K (the warden's mark for 1750–1751); a crowned A with palm and laurel branches (the Paris *charge* mark for 1750–1756); and the cow symbol (the Paris *décharge* mark for 1733 [?]–1755 used on work intended for export). Engraved in the center with the arms of the marquis de Menars.
Height: 1 3/8" (3.8 cm); Width: 8 5/8" (21.9 cm); Depth: 7 7/8" (20.0 cm)
Accession number 71.DG.78

PROVENANCE

Marquis de Menars.

(?) Junius Morgan, New York.

Puiforcat, Paris, by 1926, and through 1938.

D. David-Weill, Paris. Sold, Palais Galliera, Paris, November 24, 1971, lot 24.

Purchased at that sale by J. Paul Getty.

EXHIBITIONS

Paris. Musée des Arts Décoratifs, *Exposition d'orfèvrerie française civile du XVIe siècle au début du XIXe*, April–May 1926, ex. cat., no. 91.

London. 25 Park Lane, *Three French Reigns*, February–April 1933, ex. cat., no. 388.

New York. The Metropolitan Museum of Art, *French Domestic Silver*, May–September 1938, ex. cat., no. 149, illus. pl. 85.

BIBLIOGRAPHY

S. Brault and Y. Bottineau, *L'Orfèvrerie française du XVIIIe siècle*, 1959, p. 186, illus. pl. XVII.

Faith Dennis, *Three Centuries of French Domestic Silver: Its Makers and Its Marks*, 1960, vol. 1, p. 116, illus. fig. 149.

Henry Nocq, *Le Poinçon de Paris*, 1968, vol. 2, p. 243, illus. opposite p. 244.

COMMENTARY

A contemporary design for a similar tray, bearing two lidded beakers and displaying the French royal coat of arms, is in a private collection in Paris.

152

152 LIDDED BOWL AND COVER
Lacquer: Japanese, early eighteenth century
Mounts: Paris, circa 1727–1738
Makers unknown
Wood lacquered with red pigment and gold powder; silver-gilt mounts
Each handle marked with the unidentified maker's mark PLR with a crescent, two grains, and a fleur-de-lys, and with a crowned bell (the Paris *contremarque* for 1727–1732 under the *sous-fermier* Jacques Cottin). The mount on the base of the bowl is marked with PLR and another unidentified mark. The rim of the tray is marked with a crowned S (the Paris date letter for 1734–1735). There is an unidentified mark on the inside lip of the lid.
Bowl: Height: 5 3/16" (13.2 cm); Width: 7 3/8" (18.7 cm); Depth: 5 3/8" (13.6 cm)
Stand: Height: 7/8" (2.3 cm); Diameter: 7 3/16" (18.2 cm)
Overall height: 5 9/16" (14.1 cm)
Accession number 84.DH.74.1, .2A, .2B

PROVENANCE

Hans Backer, London.

Martin Norton, London.

Purchased by the J. Paul Getty Museum, 1984.

BIBLIOGRAPHY

Nieda, "Acquisitions 1984," no. 2, pp. 72–76, illus.

153

153 SAUCEBOAT ON STAND

Paris, 1762
By Jean-Baptiste-François Cheret
Silver; parcel-gilt
Sauceboat and stand marked with maker's mark of a fleur-de-lys under a crown, JBC, a key, and two dots; a crowned Y (the Paris *charge* mark for 1762); a crowned A with a laurel branch; and a pointer's head (the Paris *décharge* mark for 1762–1768). A coat of arms has probably been burnished off the cartouche on the sauceboat.
Height: 4¾" (12.1 cm); Width: 5⅝" (14.3 cm); Depth: 7¾" (19.8 cm)
Accession number 71.DG.76

PROVENANCE

Dukes of Buckingham and Chandos, London. Sold 1903.

J. H. Fitzhenry, London. Sold, Christie's, London, November 20, 1913, lot 214.

Gaston Bensimon, Paris.

A. M. David-Weill, Paris.

D. David-Weill, Paris. Sold, Palais Galliera, Paris, November 24, 1971, lot 14.

Purchased at that sale by J. Paul Getty.

EXHIBITIONS

Paris, Musée des Arts Décoratifs, *Exposition d'orfèvrerie française civile du XVIe siècle au début du XIXe*, April–May 1926, ex. cat., no. 108, on loan from A. M. David-Weill.

BIBLIOGRAPHY

Henry Nocq, *Le Poinçon de Paris*, 1968, vol. 1, p. 259, illus.

154

154 PAIR OF CANDELABRA

Paris, 1779–1782
By Robert-Joseph Auguste
Silver
Marked variously with maker's mark RJA under a crown; a monogram of the five letters of the word PARIS (the Paris *charge* mark for 1775–1781); a bull's head (the Paris *décharge* mark for 1775–1781); a crowned P (the Paris date letter for July 18, 1778–July 21, 1779); crossed L's (the Paris *charge* mark for 1781–1783); a crowned S (the Paris date letter for August 1, 1781–July 13, 1782). Each base engraved with the monogram GR III under a crown.
Height: 1'10⅛" (56.1 cm); Width: 1'3⅛" (38.5 cm); Depth: 1'2⅜" (36.5 cm)
Accession number 84.DG.42.1–2

PROVENANCE

From a service made for George III of England.

(?) Ernst Augustus, Duke of Cumberland and of Brunswick-Lüneburg, King of Hanover, 1837.

(?) Ernst Augustus, Duke of Cumberland and of Brunswick-Lüneburg, 1851. Sold after his death, circa 1924.

A. Cartier Ltd., London, by 1926.

Louis Cartier, Paris, by the 1960's.

Claude Cartier, Paris, 1970's. Sold, Sotheby's, Monaco, November 25–27, 1979, lot 824, with another pair of matching candelabra.

Veronique Cartier, Paris.

Purchased by the J. Paul Getty Museum, 1984.

EXHIBITIONS

Paris, Musée des Arts Décoratifs, *Exposition d'orfèvrerie française civile du XVIe siècle au début du XIXe*, April–May 1926, ex. cat., no. 144, on loan from A. Cartier, Ltd., London.

Paris. Galerie Mellerio, *L'Orfèvrerie et le bijou d'autrefois*, 1935, no. 70.

BIBLIOGRAPHY

Faith Dennis, *Three Centuries of French Domestic Silver: Its Makers and Its Marks*, 1960, vol. 1, no. 20, p. 45, illus.; vol. 2, p. 31.

Claude Frégnac et al., *Les Grands Orfèvres de Louis XVIII à Charles X*, Collection connaissance des arts, 1965, pp. 240–241, illus. fig 2.

Jacques Helft, *French Master Goldsmiths and Silversmiths*, 1966, p. 240, illus. fig. 2.

Serge Grandjean et al., *Cinq Années d'enrichissement du patrimoine national 1975–1980*, Grand Palais, Paris, November 1980–March 1981, ex. cat., pp. 128–129.

EXHIBITIONS

New York. Cooper-Hewitt Museum, *Design in the Service of Tea*, August–October 1984.

BIBLIOGRAPHY

Sassoon, "Acquisitions 1982," no. 5, pp. 33–36, illus.

155

CERAMICS: CHANTILLY MANUFACTORY

155 TEA SERVICE

Chantilly Manufactory, circa 1730–1735
Maker unknown
Soft paste porcelain
No marks
Tray: Height: $\frac{13}{16}$" (2.1 cm); Width: $8\frac{13}{16}$" (22.4 cm); Depth: $8\frac{15}{16}$" (22.7 cm)
Cups: Height: $1\frac{9}{16}$" (4.0 cm); Width: $3\frac{1}{4}$" (8.2 cm); Depth: $2\frac{5}{8}$" (6.7 cm)
Saucers: Height: $\frac{15}{16}$" (2.3 cm); Width: $4\frac{9}{16}$" (11.6 cm); Depth: $4\frac{17}{32}$" (11.5 cm)
Sugar Bowl: Height: $3\frac{1}{8}$" (7.7 cm); Width: $4\frac{3}{8}$" (11.1 cm); Depth: $4\frac{1}{16}$" (10.3 cm)
Teapot: Height: $3\frac{1}{2}$" (8.9 cm); Width: $5\frac{1}{8}$" (13.1 cm); Depth: $3\frac{5}{16}$" (8.4 cm)
Accession number 82.DE.167.1–5

PROVENANCE

Mme Polès, Paris, 1979.

Klaber and Klaber, London, 1980.

Winifred Williams Ltd., London, 1982.

Purchased by the J. Paul Getty Museum, 1982.

156

156 CHAMBER POT *(bourdaloue)*

Chantilly Manufactory, circa 1740
Maker unknown
Soft paste porcelain
Painted on the base with the iron-red hunting horn mark of the Chantilly Manufactory.
Height: $3\frac{13}{16}$" (9.8 cm); Width: $7\frac{11}{16}$" (19.6 cm); Depth: $4\frac{5}{8}$" (11.8 cm)
Accession number 82.DE.9

PROVENANCE

Regainy, Paris, 1957.

Wilfred J. Sainsbury, England.

Kate Foster, Rye, England.

Rosenberg and Stiebel, New York, 1977.

Purchased by the J. Paul Getty Museum, 1982.

BIBLIOGRAPHY

Sassoon, "Acquisitions 1982," no. 6, pp. 36–38, illus.

157

CERAMICS: MENNECY MANUFACTORY

157 BUST OF LOUIS XV
Mennecy Manufactory, circa 1750–1755
Maker unknown
Soft paste porcelain
No marks
Height: 1′5″ (43.2 cm); Width: 9 9/16″ (24.5 cm); Depth: 5 11/16″ (14.5 cm)
Accession number 84.DE.46

PROVENANCE

Saget collection, Tours. Sold, Hôtel Drouot, Paris, March 14, 1910, lot 44.

Vandermeersch, Paris, late 1940's.

Mr. and Mrs. William Brown Meloney, Riverdale, New York, late 1940's.

The Antique Porcelain Company, London, from late 1950's.

Purchased by the J. Paul Getty Museum, 1984.

BIBLIOGRAPHY

Babette Craven, "French Soft Paste Porcelain in the Collection of Mr. and Mrs. William Brown Meloney," *Connoisseur*, May 1959, pp. 135–142, illus. fig. 10.

158a

158b

CERAMICS: VINCENNES MANUFACTORY

158 PAIR OF FIGURE GROUPS: *THE FLUTE LESSON* AND *THE GRAPE EATERS*
Vincennes Manufactory, circa 1752
Maker unknown
Soft paste biscuit porcelain
The Flute Lesson incised F on back.

The Flute Lesson: Height: 8¾″ (22.3 cm); Width: 10″ (25.4 cm); Depth: 6″ (15.2 cm)
The Grape Eaters: Height: 9″ (22.9 cm); Width: 9¾″ (24.8 cm); Depth: 7″ (17.8 cm)
Accession number 70.DE.98.1–2

PROVENANCE

Goury de Rosland. Sold, Galerie Georges Petit, Paris, May 29–30, 1905, lot 108.

Mortimer L. Schiff, New York. Sold by his heir, John L. Schiff, Christie's, London, June 22, 1938, lot 27.

Purchased at that sale by J. Paul Getty.

COMMENTARY

The Flute Lesson is based on an engraving by R. Gaillard of a painting by François Boucher exhibited in the Salon of 1748. *The Grape Eaters* is based on a painting by François Boucher of 1749. By about 1900, A. Aucoq mounted these figure groups on silver-gilt bases, which have since been removed.

159 VASE *(caisse à fleurs en tombeau, première grandeur)*
Vincennes Manufactory, 1753
Possibly painted by Jean-Pierre Ledoux
Soft paste porcelain; *bleu céleste* ground color; colored enamel decoration; gilding
Painted underneath with the blue crossed L's of the Vincennes Manufactory enclosing the date letter A for 1753, and with the painter's mark of a crescent.

Height: 9¼" (23.4 cm); Width: 11⅞" (30.0 cm); Depth: 8½" (21.6 cm)
Accession number 73.DE.64

PROVENANCE

Possibly sold by the Sèvres Manufactory between January 1 and August 20, 1756, to the *marchand-mercier* Lazare Duvaux, Paris, for 840 *livres* less the *marchand's* discount.

Possibly sold by Lazare Duvaux on March 1, 1756, to Count Moltke of Denmark, as part of a *garniture* of five vases.

(?) Gilbert Lévy, Paris, early twentieth century.

Private collection, Paris.

Rosenberg and Stiebel, New York, early 1970's.

Purchased by J. Paul Getty, 1973.

BIBLIOGRAPHY

Louis Courajod, ed., *Le Livre-Journal de Lazare Duvaux, marchand-bijoutier, 1748–1758*, 1873, vol. 2, no. 2420, p. 274.

COMMENTARY

The painter's mark of a crescent, generally attributed to Jean-Pierre Ledoux, is found on several pieces of Vincennes and Sèvres porcelain dated before 1758, the first year in which Ledoux is recorded as working at Sèvres.

159

160

160 WATERING CAN *(arrosoir d'appartement, deuxième grandeur)*
Vincennes Manufactory, 1754
Painted by Bardet
Soft paste porcelain; colored enamel decoration; gilding
Painted underneath with the blue crossed L's of the Vincennes Manufactory (with a dot at their apex) enclosing the date letter B for 1754, and with Bardet's mark of two short parallel lines. Incised 4.

Height: 7¾" (19.7 cm); Width: 9⁹⁄₁₆" (24.5 cm); Depth: 5⅛" (13.0 cm)
Accession number 84.DE.89

PROVENANCE

Florence, Countess of Northbrook (wife of the 2nd Earl, married 1899, died 1946). Sold, Christie's, London, November 28, 1940, lot 78 (part).

Hugh Burton-Jones, England, 1940.

Kathleen Burton-Jones (Mrs. Gifford-Scott). Sold, Sotheby's, London, June 12, 1984, lot 172.

Winifred Williams Ltd., London, 1984.

Purchased by the J. Paul Getty Museum, 1984.

BIBLIOGRAPHY

Adrian Sassoon, "Vincennes and Sèvres Porcelain Acquired by the J. Paul Getty Museum in 1984," *The J. Paul Getty Museum Journal* 13, 1985, pp. 89–91, illus.

161 PAIR OF POTPOURRI VASES *(pot-pourri Pompadour, troisième grandeur)*
Vincennes Manufactory, 1755
Model attributed to Jean-Claude Duplessis; painted by Jean-Louis Morin after engraved designs by François Boucher
Soft paste porcelain; *bleu lapis* ground color; carmine red decoration; gilding
Each vase painted underneath with the blue crossed L's of the Vincennes Manufactory enclosing the date letter C for 1755, and with Morin's mark M in blue and two blue dots. Each vase incised 2 under the base.

Height: 10″ (25.5 cm); Diameter: 6″ (15.2 cm)
Accession number 84.DE.3.1–2

PROVENANCE

Sold anonymously, Sotheby's, London, March 5, 1957, lot 96.

The Antique Porcelain Company, London, 1957.

Private collection, England (?).

The Antique Porcelain Company, London, 1983.

Purchased by the J. Paul Getty Museum, 1984.

BIBLIOGRAPHY

Adrian Sassoon, "Vincennes and Sèvres Porcelain Acquired by the J. Paul Getty Museum in 1984," *The J. Paul Getty Museum Journal* 13, 1985, pp. 91–94, illus.

161

162

CERAMICS: SEVRES MANUFACTORY

162 BASKET *(panier, deuxième grandeur)*
Sèvres Manufactory, 1756
Maker unknown
Soft paste porcelain; green ground color; gilding
Painted underneath with the blue crossed L's of the Sèvres Manufactory enclosing the date letter D for 1756, and with three dots. Incised with *répareur's* mark *PZ* under the base.

Height: 8 5/8″ (22.0 cm); Width: 7 7/8″ (20.1 cm); Depth: 7 1/8″ (18.0 cm)
Accession number 82.DE.92

PROVENANCE

French private collection. Sold, Christie's, London, June 28, 1982, lot 19.

Armin B. Allen, New York, 1982.

Purchased by the J. Paul Getty Museum, 1982.

BIBLIOGRAPHY

Sassoon, "Acquisitions 1982," no. 8, pp. 45–47, illus.

Wilson, *Selections*, no. 26, pp. 52–53, illus.

COMMENTARY

A basket of this size and color (valued at 240 *livres*) was given to the painter François Boucher by the Sèvres Manufactory in December 1757. One other basket of this type is known; it was sold from the Hillingdon collection in 1983.

163 EWER AND BASIN *(broc et jatte feuille d'eau, première grandeur)*
Sèvres Manufactory, 1757
Possibly modeled after a design by Jean-Claude Duplessis
Soft paste porcelain; pink ground color; colored enamel decoration; gilding
Basin painted underneath with the blue crossed L's of the Sèvres Manufactory enclosing the date letter E for 1757, and with an unidentified painter's mark. Ewer incised *. T.m*; basin incised *C.N.*

Ewer: Height: 7 9/16" (19.2 cm); Width: 5 5/8" (14.4 cm); Depth: 3 3/16" (8.1 cm)
Basin: Height: 2 3/4" (7.1 cm); Width: 11 1/2" (29.1 cm); Depth: 8 7/16" (22.1 cm)
Accession number 84.DE.88.a-b

PROVENANCE

Duke and Duchess of Portland. Sold, Henry Spencer and Sons, Retford, Nottinghamshire, July 23, 1970, lot 288.

Winifred Williams Ltd., London, 1970.

Eric Robinson, Mereworth Castle, Kent, 1970. Sold, Sotheby's, London, June 12, 1984, lot 213.

Winifred Williams Ltd., London, 1984.

Purchased by the J. Paul Getty Museum, 1984.

BIBLIOGRAPHY

Adrian Sassoon, "Vincennes and Sèvres Porcelain Acquired by the J. Paul Getty Museum in 1984," *The J. Paul Getty Museum Journal* 13, 1985, pp. 95–98, illus.

163

164

164 TRAY *(plateau carré)*
Sèvres Manufactory, 1758
Maker unknown
Soft paste porcelain; pink ground color; colored enamel decoration; gilding
Painted underneath with the blue crossed L's of the Sèvres Manufactory enclosing the date letter F for 1758, and with a blue painter's mark of an *E*. Incised *60* underneath.

Height: 15/16" (2.3 cm); Width: 5" (12.7 cm); Depth: 5 1/16" (12.8 cm)
Accession number 72.DE.75

PROVENANCE

Deane and Anne Johnson, Los Angeles. Sold, Sotheby's, New York, December 9, 1972, lot 27.

Purchased at that sale by J. Paul Getty.

165a

165b

165c

165d

165 PAIR OF CUPS AND SAUCERS
(gobelets Calabre et soucoupes)
Sèvres Manufactory, 1759
Painted by Charles Buteux *l'aîné*
Soft paste porcelain; pink and green ground colors; colored enamel decoration; gilding
Saucers painted underneath with the blue crossed L's of the Sèvres Manufactory enclosing the date letter *g* for 1759, and with Buteux's mark of a blue anchor. One cup incised under the base with an *h*; the other cup incised with an indecipherable mark in script.

Cups: Height: 3¼″ (8.3 cm); Width: 4″ (10.2 cm); Depth: 3⅛″ (7.9 cm)
Saucers: Height: 1⅝″ (4.1 cm); Diameter: 6$^{3}/_{16}$″ (15.7 cm)
Accession number 72.DE.74.1–2

PROVENANCE

Otto and Magdalena Blohm, Hamburg. Sold, Sotheby's, London, July 5, 1960, lots 126 and 127.

Deane and Anne Johnson, Los Angeles. Sold, Sotheby's, New York, December 9, 1972, lot 21.

Purchased at that sale by J. Paul Getty.

BIBLIOGRAPHY

Robert Schmidt, *Early European Porcelain as Collected by Otto Blohm*, 1953, p. 101, illus.

166a

166b

166c

166d

166 PAIR OF VASES *(vases pot-pourri à bobèches)*

Sèvres Manufactory, 1759

Painted by Charles-Nicolas Dodin

Soft paste porcelain; pink and green ground colors; colored enamel decoration; gilding

One vase painted underneath with the blue crossed L's of the Sèvres Manufactory enclosing the date letter G for 1759, and with Dodin's mark *k*. Various paper collectors' labels pasted under the base. One vase unmarked.

Height: 9 13/16" (24.9 cm); Width: 5 11/16" (14.4 cm); Depth: 3 11/16" (9.4 cm)

Accession number 75.DE.65.1–2

PROVENANCE

Duveen Brothers, New York.

J. Pierpont Morgan, New York.

J. Pierpont Morgan, Jr., New York. Sold, Parke Bernet, New York, March 25, 1944, lot 647.

Paula de Koenigsberg, Buenos Aires, 1945.

Claus de Koenigsberg, Buenos Aires.

Rosenberg and Stiebel, New York, 1975.

Purchased by J. Paul Getty, 1975.

EXHIBITIONS

New York. The Metropolitan Museum of Art, on loan, 1914–1915, from J. Pierpont Morgan.

Buenos Aires. Museo Nacional de Bellas Artes, *Exposición de obras maestras: Colección Paula de Koenigsberg*, October 1945, ex. cat. no. 206, illus.

Buenos Aires. Museo Nacional de Arte Decorativo, *El arte de vivir en Francia del siglo XVIII*, September–November 1968, ex. cat., no. 427, illus. pl. CCXI.

BIBLIOGRAPHY

Comte Xavier de Chavagnac, *Catalogue des porcelaines françaises de M. J. Pierpont Morgan*, 1910, no. 107, illus. pl. XXXII.

Wilson, "Sèvres," pp. 5–24, illus.

167a

167b

167 LIDDED POTPOURRI VASE *(vase vaisseau à mât)*
Sèvres Manufactory, circa 1760
Painting attributed to Charles-Nicolas Dodin
Soft paste porcelain; pink and green ground colors; colored enamel decoration; gilding
Painted underneath with the blue crossed L's (partially abraided) of the Sèvres Manufactory.
Height: 1'2¾" (37.5 cm); Width: 1'1 11/16" (34.8 cm); Depth: 6 13/16" (17.4 cm)
Accession number 75.DE.11

PROVENANCE

George William, 7th Earl of Coventry, Croome Court, Worcestershire. Part of a *garniture* with a pair of *vases hollandais nouveaux.* Sold, Christie's, London, June 12, 1874, lot 150 (part), for £ 10,500.

William Humble, 1st Earl of Dudley, Dudley House, London. Sold privately 1885/86.

William J. Goode, London. Offered for sale, Christie's, London, July 17, 1895, lot 147 (part), bought in for £ 8,400. Sold, Christie's, London, May 20, 1898, lot 94b (part), to Pilkington, for £ 6,450.

Asher Wertheimer, London, 1898.

Duveen Brothers, New York.

J. Pierpont Morgan, New York.

J. Pierpont Morgan, Jr., New York, by descent, 1913. Sold, Parke Bernet, New York, January 8, 1944, lot 486.

Paula de Koenigsberg, Buenos Aires, 1945.

Claus de Koenigsberg, Buenos Aires.

Rosenberg and Stiebel, New York, 1975.

Purchased by J. Paul Getty, 1975.

EXHIBITIONS

New York. The Metropolitan Museum of Art, on loan, 1914–1915, from J. Pierpont Morgan.

Buenos Aires. Museo Nacional de Bellas Artes, *Exposición de obras maestras: Colección Paula de Koenigsberg*, October 1945, ex. cat., no. 205, illus.

Buenos Aires. Museo Nacional de Arte Decorativo, *El arte de vivir en Francia del siglo XVIII*, September–November 1968, ex. cat.

BIBLIOGRAPHY

Comte Xavier de Chavagnac, *Catalogue des porcelaines françaises de M. J. Pierpont Morgan*, 1910, no. 109, illus pl. XXXIII.

Frederick Litchfield, "Imitations and Reproductions: Part I—Sèvres Porcelain," *Connoisseur*, September 1917, p. 6.

Wilson, "Sèvres," pp. 5–24, illus.

Wilson, *Selections*, no. 29, pp. 58–59, illus.

COMMENTARY

The figure scene painted on the front of this vase appears to be based on engravings after paintings by David Teniers *le jeune.* A Minton reproduction of this vase was made in the 1880's for Georgina, Countess of Dudley (wife of the 1st Earl, married 1865, died 1929).

168a

168b

168c

168 PAIR OF VASES *(pot-pourri fontaine* or *pot-pourri à dauphins)*
Sèvres Manufactory, circa 1760
Painting attributed to Charles-Nicolas Dodin
Enameled and gilded soft paste porcelain; pink, green, and *bleu lapis* ground colors
Painted underneath the central section of one vase with the blue crossed L's of the Sèvres Manufactory.
Height: 11¾″ (29.8 cm); Width: 6½″ (16.5 cm); Depth: 5¾″ (14.6 cm)
Accession number 78.DE.358.1–2

PROVENANCE

Marquise de Pompadour, Hôtel Pompadour, Paris, 1760–1764.

(?) Grace Caroline, Duchess of Cleveland (wife of the 6th Duke, married 1815, died 1883).

William Goding, before 1862. Sold, Christie's, London, March 19, 1874, lot 100, to E. Rutter, Paris (for the Earl of Dudley), for £6,825.

William Humble, 1st Earl of Dudley. Offered for sale, Christie's, London, May 21, 1886, lot 194, bought in for £2,625. Returned to Dudley House, London.

Sir Joseph C. Robinson, Bt., Dudley House, London. Purchased circa 1920 with the contents of Dudley House.

Dr. Joseph Labia (son-in-law of Sir Joseph C. Robinson, Bt.), London. Sold, Sotheby's, London, February 26, 1963, lot 23.

The Antique Porcelain Company, London and New York, 1963.

Nelson Rockefeller, New York, 1976/77.

The Sloan-Kettering Institute for Cancer Research, New York, 1976/77.

Purchased by the J. Paul Getty Museum, 1978.

EXHIBITIONS

London. The South Kensington Museum, *Special Loan Exhibition of Works of Art*, June 1862, ex. cat., nos. 1281 and 1282.

BIBLIOGRAPHY

Jean Cordey, *Inventaire des biens de Madame de Pompadour rédigé après son décès*, 1939, p. 39.

Ronald Freyberger, "Chinese Genre Painting at Sèvres," *American Ceramic Circle Bulletin*, 1970–1971, pp. 29–44, illus.

Marcelle Brunet and Tamara Préaud, *Sèvres, des origines à nos jours*, 1978, p. 68, illus. (one) pl. XXII.

Wilson, "Acquisitions 1977 to mid 1979," no. 8, pp. 44–45, illus.

Rosalind Savill, "Two Pairs of Sèvres Vases at Boughton House," *Apollo*, August 1979, pp. 128–133, illus.

Madelaine Jarry, *Chinoiserie*, 1981, p. 120, illus. (detail of one).

Wilson, *Selections*, no. 28, pp. 56–57.

COMMENTARY

These vases are listed in the Sèvres sales registers as being sold for 960 *livres* cash, as part of a *garniture* of five vases and two wall lights, to an unnamed purchaser on May 30, 1760. They are listed as being in the marquise de Pompadour's *chambre du lit* in her Parisian home in 1764, after her death. They formed a set, which consisted of a *vase vaisseau à mât* and a pair of wall lights, now in the Musée du Louvre, Paris, together with a pair of *vases pot-pourri à bobèches*, present whereabouts unknown.

169

169 PAIR OF LIDDED CHESTNUT BOWLS *(marronnières)*

Sèvres Manufactory, circa 1760
One bowl marked by the *répareur* François-Firmin Dufresne or Fresne
Soft paste porcelain; *bleu céleste* ground color; colored enamel decoration; gilding
Bowl 1 incised underneath with the mark *J* and with *FR* for Dufresne.

1: Height: 5$\frac{1}{4}$" (13.4 cm); Width: 10$\frac{9}{16}$" (27.0 cm); Depth: 8$\frac{5}{16}$" (21.1 cm)
2: Height: 5$\frac{1}{4}$" (13.4 cm); Width: 10$\frac{1}{2}$" (26.7 cm); Depth: 8$\frac{3}{16}$" (20.8 cm)
Accession number 82.DE.171.1–2

PROVENANCE

(?) The Antique Porcelain Company, London and New York.

(?) Private collection, Switzerland.

Swiss art market, 1980.

Armin B. Allen, New York, 1980.

Purchased by the J. Paul Getty Museum, 1982.

BIBLIOGRAPHY

Sassoon, "Acquisitions 1982," no. 9, pp. 48–52, illus.

170

170 PLAQUES ON A *JARDINIERE*

Paris and Sèvres Manufactory, circa 1760
Maker unknown
Soft paste porcelain; green ground color; colored enamel decoration; gilding; gilt-bronze frame
No marks
Height: 6$\frac{9}{16}$" (16.6 cm); Width: 11$\frac{1}{2}$" (29.2 cm); Depth: 5$\frac{5}{8}$" (14.3 cm)
Accession number 73.DI.62

PROVENANCE

Private collection, Paris.

Gaston Bensimon, Paris.

Purchased by J. Paul Getty, 1973.

COMMENTARY

The scene of the *Marriage Contract* painted on the front of this piece is also found on other Sèvres porcelains including a *cuvette Courteille* of 1760 painted by Charles-Nicolas Dodin, which is now in the Metropolitan Museum of Art, New York.

171

171 VASE *(cuvette Mahon, troisième grandeur)*
Sèvres Manufactory, 1761
Painted by Jean-Louis Morin
Soft paste porcelain; pink ground color overlaid with blue enamel; colored enamel decoration; gilding
Painted under one foot with the blue crossed L's of the Sèvres Manufactory enclosing the date letter I for 1761, and with Morin's mark M.

Height: $5\frac{7}{8}$" (15.0 cm); Width: $9\frac{1}{16}$" (23.0 cm); Depth: $4\frac{11}{16}$" (11.9 cm)
Accession number 72.DE.65

PROVENANCE

Probably sold on March 30, 1763, by the Sèvres Manufactory to Lemaître as part of a *garniture* with another *cuvette Mahon* for 264 *livres* each, and with a more expensive *cuvette à masques.*

De Bargigli. Offered for sale, Christie's, Geneva, April 22, 1970, lot 18, bought in.

Sold, Christie's, London, October 4, 1971, lot 42.

Olivier Lévy, Paris, 1971.

French and Company, New York, 1971.

Purchased by J. Paul Getty, 1972.

BIBLIOGRAPHY

Wilson, "Sèvres," pp. 19–24, illus.

COMMENTARY

The painted scene of figures on the front panel is based on a detail of an engraving by J.-P. Le Bas of a *kermesse* by David Teniers *le jeune*, then in the collection of the comtesse de Verrouë in Paris and now in the State Hermitage, Leningrad.

172

172 CUP AND SAUCER *(tasse enfoncée et soucoupe)*
Sèvres Manufactory, 1761
Maker unknown
Soft paste porcelain; pink ground color overlaid with blue enamel; colored enamel decoration; gilding
Saucer painted underneath with the blue crossed L's of the Sèvres Manufactory enclosing the date letter I for 1761, and with a dot. Saucer incised *oo* underneath. Cup incised *DU* underneath in two places.

Cup: Height: $3\frac{9}{16}$" (9.1 cm); Width: $4\frac{3}{16}$" (10.7 cm); Depth: $3\frac{3}{8}$" (8.6 cm)
Saucer: Height: $1\frac{1}{2}$" (3.8 cm); Diameter: $6\frac{1}{8}$" (15.6 cm)
Accession number 79.DE.62

PROVENANCE

Olivier Lévy, Paris.

French and Company, New York, early 1970's.

Mrs. John W. Christner, Dallas. Sold, Christie's, New York, June 9, 1979, lot 241.

Purchased at that sale by the J. Paul Getty Museum.

BIBLIOGRAPHY

Wilson, "Acquisitions 1979 to mid 1980," item A, p. 19, illus.

173a

173b

173 LIDDED BOWL ON STAND

(écuelle et plateau ronde)

Sèvres Manufactory, 1764
Painted by Pierre-Antoine Méreaud *l'aîné*
Soft paste porcelain; colored enamel decoration; gilding
Bowl and stand both painted underneath with the blue crossed L's of the Sèvres Manufactory enclosing the date letter L for 1764, and with Méreaud's mark *S*. Bowl incised *DU* and O, and the stand, *I*.

Bowl: Height: 4 7/8″ (12.4 cm); Width: 7 3/4″ (19.7 cm); Depth: 6″ (15.2 cm)
Stand: Height: 1 9/16″ (3.9 cm); Diameter: 8 5/16″ (21.1 cm)
Accession number 78.DE.65

PROVENANCE

Madame Louise of France (youngest daughter of Louis XV).

(?) Mrs. Lyne Stephens, Norfolk, London, and Paris. Sold, Christie's, London, May 9ff., 1895, lot 733, to William Boore, for £ 130.

Mortimer L. Schiff, New York. Sold by his heir, John L. Schiff, Christie's, London, June 22, 1938, lot 25.

Purchased at that sale by J. Paul Getty.

BIBLIOGRAPHY

Barry Shifman, "A Newly Discovered Piece of Royal Sèvres Porcelain," *The J. Paul Getty Museum Journal* 6–7, 1978–1979, pp. 53–56, illus.

Wilson, *Selections*, no. 33, pp. 66–67, illus.

COMMENTARY

The lid and the stand bear the arms of Madame Louise, an unmarried daughter of Louis XV, and the monogram *ML*. The Sèvres sales register of February 24, 1764, shows that Madame Louise paid 240 *livres* for an "ecuelle et plateau frize armoriée," which is almost certainly this piece.

174

174 CHOCOLATE POT

Sèvres Manufactory, circa 1765
Maker unknown
Soft paste porcelain; carmine red enamel; gilding
Painted underneath with the blue crossed L's of the Sèvres Manufactory. Incised 26 and 48.

Height: 3 7/16″ (8.8 cm); Width: 4 11/16″ (11.9 cm); Depth: 2 11/16″ (6.8 cm)
Accession number 79.DE.63

PROVENANCE

Mrs. John W. Christner, Dallas. Sold, Christie's, New York, June 9, 1979, lot 204.

Purchased at that sale by the J. Paul Getty Museum.

BIBLIOGRAPHY

Wilson, "Acquisitions 1979 to mid 1980," item D, p. 19, illus.

175

175 PAIR OF LIDDED VASES

(vases à têtes de bouc)

Sèvres Manufactory, circa 1767–1770
Possibly molded by Michel-Dorothée Coudray; possibly finished by the *répareur* Nantier
Soft paste porcelain; *bleu nouveau* ground color; gilding
Each vase incised *c.d.* underneath for the *mouleur*. Vase 1 incised *N 1* and vase 2 incised *N 2* underneath for the *répareur*.

Height: 1′1 7/16″ (34.2 cm); Width: 8 5/8″ (21.9 cm); Depth: 6 5/8″ (16.8 cm)
Accession number 82.DE.36.1–2

PROVENANCE

J. Rochelle Thomas, London.

Private collection, New York. Sold, Parke Bernet, New York, January 12, 1957, lot 247.

Christian Humann, New York. Sold, Sotheby's, New York, April 22, 1982, lot 41.

Armin B. Allen, New York, 1982.

Purchased by the J. Paul Getty Museum, 1982.

BIBLIOGRAPHY

Sassoon, "Acquisitions 1982," no. 11, pp. 54–56, illus.

176 CUP AND SAUCER (*gobelet Bouillard et soucoupe*)

Sèvres Manufactory, 1770
Painted by Jacques Fontaine
Soft paste porcelain; *bleu céleste* ground color; *grisaille* enamel decoration; gilding
Cup painted underneath with the blue crossed L's of the Sèvres Manufactory enclosing the date letter *r* for 1770, and with Fontaine's mark of five dots. Cup incised C; saucer incised 6.

Cup: Height: 2½" (6.3 cm); Width: 3⅝" (9.2 cm); Depth: 2$^{13}/_{16}$" (7.1 cm)
Saucer: Height: 1¼" (3.2 cm); Diameter: 5$^{5}/_{16}$" (13.5 cm)
Accession number 79.DE.65

PROVENANCE

Private collection. Sold, Christie's, London, June 21, 1976, lot 151.

Mrs. John W. Christner, Dallas. Sold, Christie's, New York, June 9, 1979, lot 227.

Purchased at that sale by the J. Paul Getty Museum.

BIBLIOGRAPHY

Wilson, "Acquisitions 1979 to mid 1980," item B, p. 19, illus.

176a

176b

176c

COMMENTARY

For an illustration of the shape of the handle of this cup see the catalogue for the exhibition *Porcelaines de Vincennes: Les Origines de Sèvres*, Grand Palais, Paris, 1977, nos. 319–322.

177 CUP AND SAUCER (*gobelet litron et soucoupe, deuxième grandeur*)

Sèvres Manufactory, 1773
Painted by Etienne-Jean Chabry *fils*; gilded by Michel-Barnabé Chauveaux *l'aîné*
Soft paste porcelain; *bleu céleste* ground color; colored enamel decoration; gilding.
Cup and saucer painted underneath with the blue crossed L's of the Sèvres Manufactory enclosing the date letter U for 1773, and with Chabry's mark *ch* in blue; also painted with Chauveaux's mark # in gold. Saucer incised *da* underneath.

Cup: Height: 2⅝" (6.7 cm); Width: 3½" (8.9 cm); Depth: 2$^{9}/_{16}$" (6.6 cm)
Saucer: Height: 1$^{9}/_{16}$" (3.9 cm); Diameter: 5$^{7}/_{16}$" (13.9 cm)
Accession number 79.DE.64

PROVENANCE

Mrs. John W. Christner, Dallas. Sold, Christie's, New York, June 9, 1979, lot 226.

Purchased at that sale by the J. Paul Getty Museum.

BIBLIOGRAPHY

Wilson, "Acquisitions 1979 to mid 1980," item C, p. 19, illus.

COMMENTARY

For an illustration of the shape of the handle of this cup see the catalogue for the exhibition *Porcelaines de Vincennes: Les Origines de Sèvres*, Grand Palais, Paris, 1977, no. 361.

177a

177b

177c

178

178 PAIR OF VASES *(vases bouc du Barry B)*
Sèvres Manufactory, 1778
(?) Painted by Fallot; gilded by Jean Chauveaux *le jeune*
Hard paste porcelain; colored enamel decoration; gilding
Each vase painted underneath with the gold crossed L's of the Sèvres Manufactory flanked by the date letters AA in gold for 1778, all under a crown for hard paste; each vase also painted underneath with Chauveaux's mark IN in gold and with an abraided F for Fallot (?).

Height: 11⅝″ (29.5 cm); Width: 7″ (17.9 cm); Depth: 4¾″ (12.0 cm)
Accession number 70.DE.99.1–2

PROVENANCE

Sir Richard Wallace, Paris.

Lady Wallace, Paris, by inheritance, 1890.

Sir John Murray Scott, Paris, by inheritance, 1897.

Victoria, Lady Sackville, Paris, by inheritance, 1912.

Jacques Seligmann, Paris.

Mortimer L. Schiff, New York. Sold by his heir, John L. Schiff, Christie's, London, June 22, 1938, lot 26.

Purchased at that sale by J. Paul Getty.

COMMENTARY

These vases were previously mounted on nineteenth-century marble plinths, each of which has a paper label inked *29 R. Wallace.*

---

179 CUP AND SAUCER *(gobelet litron et soucoupe, deuxième grandeur)*
Sèvres Manufactory, 1781
Painted by Capelle; gilded by Etienne-Henry Le Guay *père*
Soft paste porcelain; brown ground color (? *merde d'oie*); colored enamel decoration; enamels in imitation of jewels; gilding and gold foils
Cup and saucer both painted underneath with the blue crossed L's of the Sèvres Manufactory enclosing the date letters DD for 1781, and with Capelle's blue triangular mark. Saucer also painted with Le Guay's mark LG. Saucer incised *44*; cup incised *36a* over *6*. Saucer bears a paper label under the base inked *Coll^{n}. of the Marchioness of Conyngham 1908. R.M. Wood Esq.*

Cup: Height: 2¾″ (6.9 cm); Depth: 3¹¹⁄₁₆″ (9.4 cm)
Saucer: Height: 1⅜″ (3.6 cm); Diameter: 5⁵⁄₁₆″ (13.5 cm)
Accession number 81.DE.28

PROVENANCE

Jane, Marchioness of Conyngham (wife of the 3rd Marquess, married 1854, died 1907), London and Ascot. Sold, Christie's, London, May 4, 1908, lot 289, to Harding.

R. M. Wood, London. Sold, Christie's, London, May 27, 1919, lot 96, to Mallett's, London.

Henry Walters, New York. Sold by his widow, Parke Bernet, New York, November 30, 1943, lot 1009.

Private collection, New York. Sold, Christie's, New York, December 3, 1977, lot 166.

Armin B. Allen, New York, 1977.

Purchased by the J. Paul Getty Museum, 1981.

BIBLIOGRAPHY

Adrian Sassoon, "Two Acquisitions of Sèvres Porcelain," *The J. Paul Getty Museum Journal* 10, 1982, pp. 87–90, illus.

Wilson, *Selections,* no. 40, pp. 80–81, illus.

COMMENTARY

The scene *L'Offrande à l'amour* painted on the cup is based on an engraving by C. L. Jubier after a painting by Jean-Baptiste Huet.
In the records of work carried out by Capelle in January 1781 and for kiln firings in February of that year, two *gobelets litrons* of this size with jeweled decoration by Le Guay are noted as having *merde d'oie* ground color.

179a

179b

180 PAIR OF VASES *(vases hollandais nouveaux, deuxième* [?] *grandeur)*
Sèvres Manufactory, 1785
Painted by Jacques-François-Louis de Laroche
Soft paste porcelain; *bleu céleste* ground color; colored enamel decoration; gilding
Each vase painted underneath with the crossed L's of the Sèvres Manufactory and Laroche's mark *h*. Base of each central section incised *25*; one base section incised O.

  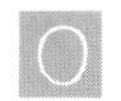

Height: 10" (25.3 cm); Width: 8⅞" (22.5 cm); Depth: 6¼" (15.9 cm)
Accession number 83.DE.341.1–2

PROVENANCE

Baroness Alexis de Goldschmidt-Rothschild, Switzerland.

Lovice Reviczky A.G., Zurich, 1983.

Purchased by the J. Paul Getty Museum, 1983.

BIBLIOGRAPHY

Wilson, "Acquisitions 1983," no. 12, pp. 209–211, 214, illus.

COMMENTARY

These vases are listed in the painters' records at Sèvres as having been painted by Laroche on October 7, 1785.

180

181

181 PAIR OF LIDDED BOWLS *(vases cassolettes)*
Paris and Sèvres Manufactory, circa 1785
Mounts attributed to Pierre-Philippe Thomire
Hard paste porcelain; *bleu nouveau* ground color; *rouge griotte* marble; gilt-bronze mounts
No marks
Height: 1'2¾" (37.5 cm); Width: 1'1½" (34.3 cm); Depth: 10¼" (26.1 cm)
Accession number 73.DI.77.1–2

PROVENANCE

Mrs. H. Dupuy, New York. Sold, Parke Bernet, New York, April 3, 1948, lot 404.

P. Cei and E. Lugli.

French and Company, New York, 1973.

Purchased by J. Paul Getty, 1973.

COMMENTARY

A drawing for this model of vase is in the Sèvres Archives. It is inscribed with the information that the vase was to be mounted by "M Thomire," with the date 1784.

182a

182b

182 WINE BOTTLE COOLER *(seau à bouteille ordinaire)*
Sèvres Manufactory, circa 1790
Painted decoration attributed to Charles-Eloi Asselin after engraved designs by Charles Monnet and Jean-Baptiste-Marie Pierre; model designed by Jean-Claude Duplessis
Soft paste porcelain; *bleu nouveau* ground color; colored enamel decoration; gilding
Bowl incised *38* underneath; foot ring incised *5*. Monogram *WJG* for the owner William J. Goode scratched on the underside in two places.

Height: 7 7/16″ (18.9 cm); Width: 10 3/16″ (25.8 cm)
Accession number 82.DE.5

PROVENANCE

Made for Louis XVI. Ordered in 1783 for the Château de Versailles, delivered in 1790.

Robert Napier, Glasgow, the Shandon collection, by 1862. Sold, Christie's, London, April 11, 1877, lot 347.

William J. Goode, London. Sold, Christie's, London, July 17, 1895, lot 136.

Sold, Sotheby's, Belgravia, 1979, described as being of nineteenth-century date.

Private collection, London. Sold, Sotheby's, London, October 21, 1980, lot 207.

Winifred Williams Ltd., London, 1980.

Purchased by the J. Paul Getty Museum, 1982.

EXHIBITIONS

London. The South Kensington Museum, *Special Loan Exhibition of Works of Art*, June 1862, ex. cat., no. 1323, p. 122.

BIBLIOGRAPHY

J. C. Robinson, *Catalogue of the Works of Art Forming the Collection of Robert Napier*, 1865, no. 3501 or 3502, p. 260.

Adrian Sassoon, "Two Acquisitions of Sèvres Porcelain," *The J. Paul Getty Museum Journal* 10, 1982, pp. 91–94, illus.

Wilson, *Selections*, no. 48, pp. 96–97, illus.

183 PAIR OF WINE BOTTLE COOLERS *(seaux à bouteilles ordinaires)*
Sèvres Manufactory, 1792
Decorated by Jean-Jacques Dieu; model designed by Jean-Claude Duplessis
Hard paste porcelain; black ground color; platinum and gold decoration
Each cooler painted underneath with a gold crown for hard paste over the gold crossed L's of the Sèvres Manufactory enclosing the date letters OO for 1792; each cooler also painted with Dieu's triangular mark (abraided on one). *Répareur's* mark *AB* incised on one cooler; *BS* incised on the other.

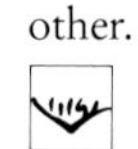  

Height: 6 7/16″ (16.3 cm); Width: 9 3/16″ (23.4 cm); Depth: 7 5/16″ (18.6 cm)
Accession number 72.DE.53.1–2

PROVENANCE

Dalva Brothers, New York, 1972.

Purchased by J. Paul Getty, 1972.

BIBLIOGRAPHY

Wilson, *Selections*, no. 49, pp. 98–99, illus.

183

184

MOUNTED ORIENTAL PORCELAIN

184 EWER
Porcelain: Chinese, Kangxi (1662–1722)
Mounts: Paris, circa 1700–1710
Makers unknown
Hard paste porcelain; colored enamel decoration; gilt-bronze mounts
No marks
Height: 1′6⅛″ (46.1 cm); Width: 1′1⅞″ (35.2 cm); Depth: 5⅜″ (13.8 cm)
Accession number 82.DI.3

PROVENANCE

Edward R. Bacon, New York, by 1919.

Gaston Bensimon, Paris. Sold, Hôtel Drouot, Paris, November 18–19, 1981, lot 103.

Purchased after that sale by the J. Paul Getty Museum, 1982.

BIBLIOGRAPHY

John Getz, *Catalogue of Chinese Art Objects, Including Porcelains, Potteries, Jades, Bronzes, and Cloisonné Enamels, Collected by Edward R. Bacon,* 1919, no. 65, p. 31, illus. pl. XII.

Wilson, "Acquisitions 1981," no. 6, pp. 85–86, illus.

Wilson et al., *Mounted Oriental Porcelain,* no. 1, pp. 21–23, illus.

185

185 PAIR OF LIDDED VASES
Porcelain: Chinese, Kangxi (1662–1722)
Mounts: Paris, circa 1710–1715
Makers unknown
Hard paste porcelain; colored enamel decoration; gilt-bronze mounts
No marks
Height: 1′3¾″ (40.0 cm); Diameter: 11″ (27.9 cm)
Accession number 72.DI.50.1–2

PROVENANCE

M. and Mme Louis Guiraud, Paris. Sold, Palais Galliera, Paris, December 10, 1971, lot 11.

Alexander and Berendt, Ltd., London, 1971.

Purchased by J. Paul Getty, 1972.

EXHIBITIONS

New York. The China Institute in America, *Chinese Porcelains in European Mounts,* October 1980–January 1981, ex. cat., no. 14, illus.

BIBLIOGRAPHY

Wilson et al., *Mounted Oriental Porcelain,* no. 2, pp. 24–27, illus.

186

186 PAIR OF LIDDED VASES
Porcelain: Chinese, Kangxi (1662–1722)
Mounts: Paris, circa 1715–1720
Makers unknown
Hard paste porcelain; colored enamel decoration; gilt-bronze mounts
Mounts stamped in nine places on each vase with the crowned C for 1745–1749.
Height: 1′1½″ (34.2 cm); Width: 1′¾″ (32.5 cm); Depth: 1′1″ (33.0 cm)
Accession number 75.DI.5.1–2

PROVENANCE

Mrs. Landon K. Thorne, New York.

Matthew Schutz Ltd., New York, 1975.

Purchased by J. Paul Getty, 1975.

EXHIBITIONS

New York. The China Institute in America, *Chinese Porcelains in European Mounts*, October 1980–January 1981, ex. cat., no. 3, illus.

BIBLIOGRAPHY

Scheurleer, *Porzellan*, no. 151, p. 280, illus.

Wilson et al., *Mounted Oriental Porcelain*, no. 4, pp. 32–35, illus.

187

187 LIDDED BOWL
Porcelain: Japanese (Imari), circa 1700
Mounts: Paris, circa 1717–1722
Makers unknown
Hard paste porcelain; colored enamel decoration; gilding; silver mounts
No marks
Height: 11″ (27.9 cm); Width: 1′1⅜″ (34.0 cm); Depth: 10⅞″ (27.5 cm)
Accession number 79.DI.123.a–b

PROVENANCE

Mrs. Walter Hayes Burns, North Mymms Park, Hertfordshire, by 1933.

Major General Sir George Burns (son of Mrs. Walter Hayes Burns), North Mymms Park. Sold, Christie's, North Mymms Park, September 24–26, 1979, lot 45.

Purchased at that sale by the J. Paul Getty Museum.

EXHIBITIONS

London. 25 Park Lane, *Three French Reigns*, February–April 1933, ex. cat., no. 226.

BIBLIOGRAPHY

Wilson, "Acquisitions 1979 to mid 1980," no. 5, pp. 8–9, illus.

Wilson et al., *Mounted Oriental Porcelain*, no. 3, pp. 28–31, illus.

COMMENTARY

An Imari porcelain bowl with silver mounts of the same design is in the Bayerisches Nationalmuseum, Munich. The mounts bear the Paris mark of the *Maison Commune*, which can variously be read for the years 1697–1704 or 1717–1722.

188

188 LIDDED BOWL
Porcelain: Japanese (Imari), circa 1680
Mounts: Paris, circa 1717–1727
Makers unknown
Hard paste porcelain; colored enamel decoration; gilding; silver mounts
Silver elements marked variously with a fleur-de-lys (the Paris *décharge* mark for small objects of 1717–1722); a dragonfly (the Paris date mark for 1722–1727); a salmon's head (the Paris *décharge* mark for small silver objects of 1744–1750); and a dog's head (the Paris *décharge* mark for small silver objects of 1732–1738).
Height: 8¾″ (22.3 cm); Width: 10⅝″ (27.1 cm); Depth: 8⅜″ (21.2 cm)
Accession number 74.DI.27

PROVENANCE

Consuelo Vanderbilt (Mme Jacques Balsan).

Matthew Schutz Ltd., New York, 1974.

Purchased by J. Paul Getty, 1974.

BIBLIOGRAPHY

Scheurleer, *Porzellan*, no. 439, illus.

Wilson et al., *Mounted Oriental Porcelain*, no. 5, pp. 36–38, illus.

189

189 FIGURE OF GUANYIN
Porcelain: Chinese, Kangxi, circa 1700
Mounts: Paris, circa 1735–1740
Makers unknown
Hard paste porcelain; gilt-bronze mounts
No marks
Height: 1′1¼″ (33.6 cm); Width: 5¾″ (14.6 cm); Depth: 4″ (10.2 cm)
Accession number 78.DE.64

PROVENANCE

Mortimer L. Schiff, New York. Sold by his heir, John L. Schiff, Christie's, London, June 22, 1938, lot 15.

Purchased at that sale by J. Paul Getty.

190

190 BOWL AND STAND
Bowl: Chinese, Kangxi (1662–1722)
Stand: Japanese (Imari), late seventeenth century
Mounts: French or German, circa 1740
Makers unknown
Hard paste porcelain; colored enamel decoration; gilding; gilt-bronze mounts
No marks
Height: 7⅛″ (18.7 cm); Diameter: 713/16″ (19.9 cm)
Accession number 74.DI.28

PROVENANCE

Anne Beddard. Sold, Sotheby's, London, June 15, 1973, lot 36.

Frank Partridge Ltd., London, 1973.

Purchased by J. Paul Getty, 1974.

EXHIBITIONS

New York. The China Institute in America, *Chinese Porcelains in European Mounts*, October 1980–January 1981, ex. cat., no. 9, illus.

BIBLIOGRAPHY

Scheurleer, *Porzellan*, no. 451, illus.

Wilson et al., *Mounted Oriental Porcelain*, no. 6, pp. 39–41, illus.

191a

191b

191 PAIR OF DECORATIVE GROUPS
Figures, rockwork, and lions: Chinese, Kangxi (1662–1722)
Spheres: Chinese, Qianlong (1736–1795)
Flowers: Chantilly Manufactory, circa 1740
Mounts: Paris, circa 1740–1745
Makers unknown
Hard and soft paste porcelain; colored enamel decoration; gilt-bronze mounts
No marks
Height: 1′ (30.4 cm); Width: 9″ (22.8 cm); Depth: 5″ (12.7 cm)
Accession number 78.DI.4.1–2

PROVENANCE

H. J. King. Sold, Christie's, London, February 17, 1921, lot 13, to Duveen.

Edgar Worsch, New York, 1928.

Robert Ellsworth, New York, 1975.

Alan Hartman, New York.

Matthew Schutz Ltd., New York, 1977.

Purchased by the J. Paul Getty Museum, 1978.

BIBLIOGRAPHY

Wilson, "Acquisitions 1977 to mid 1979," no. 5, pp. 40–41, illus.

Wilson et al., *Mounted Oriental Porcelain*, no. 7, pp. 42–44, illus.

192

192 PAIR OF LIDDED VASES
Porcelain: Chinese, Kangxi (1662–1722)
Mounts: Paris, circa 1745–1749
Makers unknown
Hard paste porcelain; colored enamel decoration; gilding; gilt-bronze mounts
Mounts on vases stamped in a total of fifteen places with the crowned C for 1745–1749.
Height: 1′½″ (31.8 cm); Width: 1′¼″ (31.2 cm); Depth: 8½″ (21.6 cm)
Accession number 72.DI.41.1–2

PROVENANCE

Baroness van Zuylen, Paris. Sold, Palais Galliera, Paris, June 8, 1971, lot 42.

Rosenberg and Stiebel, New York, 1971.

Purchased by J. Paul Getty, 1972.

EXHIBITIONS

New York. The China Institute in America, *Chinese Porcelains in European Mounts*, October 1980-January 1981, ex. cat., no. 16, illus.

BIBLIOGRAPHY

Wilson et al., *Mounted Oriental Porcelain*, no. 8, pp. 45–47, illus.

193 PAIR OF EWERS
Porcelain: Chinese, Kangxi (1662–1722)
Mounts: Paris, circa 1745–1749
Makers unknown
Hard paste porcelain; colored enamel decoration; gilt-bronze mounts
Ewer 1 stamped on the foot mount with the crowned C for 1745–1749, and with No and No 16; painted B-27-a in red under the base.
Ewer 2 stamped on the foot mount with two crowned C marks and with No. 16; painted B-27-b in red under the base.
Height: 1′11⅝″ (60.0 cm); Width: 1′1″ (33.0 cm); Depth: 8½″ (21.5 cm)
Accession number 78.DI.9.1–2

PROVENANCE

(?) Ives, comte de Cambacérès, Paris.

François-Gérard Seligmann, Paris.

Jacques Helft, Paris.

Hans Stiebel, Paris.

Henry Ford II, Grosse Pointe Farms, Michigan. Sold, Sotheby Parke Bernet, New York, February 25, 1978, lot 56.

Purchased at that sale by the J. Paul Getty Museum.

EXHIBITIONS

New York. The China Institute in America, *Chinese Porcelains in European Mounts*, October 1980-January 1981, ex. cat., no. 28, illus.

BIBLIOGRAPHY

Wilson, "Acquisitions 1977 to mid 1979," no. 6, pp. 41–42, illus.

Wilson et al., *Mounted Oriental Porcelain*, no. 9, pp. 48–52, illus.

193

194

194 LIDDED BOWL

Porcelain: Chinese, Kangxi (1662–1722)
Mounts: Paris, circa 1745–1749
Makers unknown
Hard paste porcelain; colored enamel decoration; gilt-bronze mounts
Mounts stamped in five places with the crowned C for 1745–1749. Inside of bowl incised with a six-character Chinese reign mark of the Ming emperor Xuande. Base painted with the two characters *zen you* (precious jade).
Height: 1′3¾″ (40.0 cm); Width: 1′3½″ (39.3 cm); Depth: 11″ (27.8 cm)
Accession number 74.DI.19

PROVENANCE

Sold, Galerie Jean Charpentier, Paris, December 14, 1933, lot 107.

Mme Henry Farman, Paris. Sold, Palais Galliera, Paris, March 15, 1973, lot 25.

Frank Partridge Ltd., London, 1973.

Purchased by J. Paul Getty, 1974.

EXHIBITIONS

New York. The China Institute in America, *Chinese Porcelains in European Mounts,* October 1980–January 1981, ex. cat., no. 19, illus.

BIBLIOGRAPHY

Wilson et al., *Mounted Oriental Porcelain,* no. 10, pp. 53–57, illus.

195

195 PAIR OF VASES

Porcelain: Chinese, Kangxi (1662–1722)
Mounts: Paris, circa 1745–1749
Makers unknown
Hard paste porcelain; colored enamel decoration; gilt-bronze mounts
Mounts of each vase stamped with four crowned C marks for 1745–1749.
Height: 1′½″ (31.7 cm); Width: 1′2″ (35.5 cm); Depth: 10½″ (26.7 cm)
Accession number 79.DI.121.1–2

PROVENANCE

Masurel family, France. Sold late 1970's.

Bernard Barouch Steinitz, Paris.

Alexander and Berendt, Ltd., London, 1979.

Purchased by the J. Paul Getty Museum, 1979.

EXHIBITIONS

New York. The China Institute in America, *Chinese Porcelains in European Mounts*, October 1980–January 1981, ex. cat., no. 20, illus.

BIBLIOGRAPHY

Wilson, "Acquisitions 1979 to mid 1980," no. 6, pp. 9–10, illus.

Wilson et al., *Mounted Oriental Porcelain*, no. 11, pp. 58–61, illus.

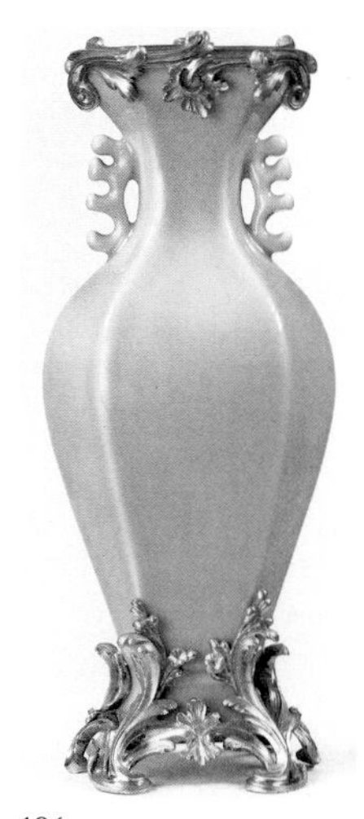

196

196 VASE

Porcelain: Chinese, Yongzheng, circa 1730
Mounts: Paris, circa 1745–1750
Makers unknown
Hard paste porcelain; colored enamel decoration; gilt-bronze mounts
No marks
Height: 1′ 2½″ (36.8 cm); Width: 6″ (15.2 cm); Depth: 4½″ (11.5 cm)
Accession number 75.DI.69

PROVENANCE

Trustees of Swinton Settled Estates. Sold, Christie's, London, December 4, 1975, lot 46.

Purchased at that sale by J. Paul Getty.

EXHIBITIONS

New York. The China Institute in America, *Chinese Porcelains in European Mounts*, October 1980–January 1981, ex. cat., no. 18, illus.

BIBLIOGRAPHY

Wilson et al., *Mounted Oriental Porcelain*, no. 12, pp. 62–64, illus.

197

197 PAIR OF POTPOURRI VASES

Porcelain: Japanese (Arita or early Hirado kilns), circa 1700
Mounts: Paris, circa 1750
Makers unknown
Hard paste porcelain; colored enamel decoration; gilt-bronze mounts
No marks
Height: 6″ (15.2 cm); Width: 7⅜″ (18.7 cm); Depth: 6½″ (16.5 cm)
Accession number 77.DI.90.1–2

PROVENANCE

Didier Aaron and Claude Lévy, Paris.

Etienne Lévy, Paris, 1977.

Purchased by the J. Paul Getty Museum, 1977.

BIBLIOGRAPHY

Wilson, "Acquisitions 1977 to mid 1979," no. 2, p. 37, illus.

Wilson et al., *Mounted Oriental Porcelain*, no. 13, pp. 65–67, illus.

198

198 VASE

Porcelain: Chinese, Qianlong (1736–1795)
Mounts: Paris, circa 1750–1755
Makers unknown
Hard paste porcelain; colored enamel decoration; gilt-bronze mounts
One mount marked on inside with a double T.
Height: 1′ 2½″ (36.9 cm); Width: 1′ 4¼″ (41.2 cm); Depth: 11″ (27.9 cm)
Accession number 72.DI.42

PROVENANCE

Rosenberg and Stiebel, New York, 1972.

Purchased by J. Paul Getty, 1972.

EXHIBITIONS

New York. The China Institute in America, *Chinese Porcelains in European Mounts*, October 1980–January 1981, ex. cat., no. 8, illus.

BIBLIOGRAPHY

Scheurleer, *Porzellan*, no. 326, illus.

Wilson et al., *Mounted Oriental Porcelain*, no. 15, pp. 70–73, illus.

199 LIDDED POT
Porcelain: Chinese (Dehua), Kangxi, circa 1670–1700
Mounts: Paris, circa 1765–1770
Makers unknown
Hard paste porcelain; gilt-bronze mounts
Porcelain lid impressed with a seal mark.
Height: 9⅞" (25.1 cm); Width: 7⅜" (18.7 cm); Depth: 6¼" (15.9 cm)
Accession number 78.DI.359

PROVENANCE

Kraemer et Cie, Paris, 1930's.

Henry Ford II, Grosse Pointe Farms, Michigan. Sold, Sotheby Parke Bernet, New York, February 25, 1978, lot 61.

Partridge (Fine Arts) Ltd., London, 1978.

Purchased by the J. Paul Getty Museum, 1978.

EXHIBITIONS

New York. The China Institute in America, *Chinese Porcelains in European Mounts*, October 1980–January 1981, ex. cat., no. 11, illus.

BIBLIOGRAPHY

Wilson, "Acquisitions 1977 to mid 1979," no. 9, pp. 44, illus.

Wilson et al., *Mounted Oriental Porcelain*, no. 16, pp. 74–76, illus.

199

200

200 STANDING VASE
Porcelain: Chinese, Qianlong, mid-eighteenth century
Mounts: Paris, circa 1785
Mounts attributed to Pierre-Philippe Thomire
Hard paste porcelain; colored enamel decoration; gilt-bronze mounts; *rouge griotte* marble
Underside of bowl painted with an indistinct date 1781 (?).
Height: 2′7¾" (80.7 cm); Diameter: 1′10¼" (56.5 cm)
Accession number 70.DI.115

PROVENANCE

(?) Princess Isabella Lubormirska, Castle Lancut, Poland.

Count Alfred Potocki (great-grandson of Princess Isabella Lubormirska), Castle Lancut, removed 1944.

Rosenberg and Stiebel, New York, 1953.

Purchased by J. Paul Getty, 1953.

BIBLIOGRAPHY

Geoffrey de Bellaigue, *Sèvres Porcelain from the Royal Collection*, The Queen's Gallery, London, 1979–1980, ex. cat., no. 11, pp. 31–32.

Michel Beurdeley, *La France à l'encan 1789–1799*, 1981, p. 117, illus.

Wilson et al., *Mounted Oriental Porcelain*, no. 17, pp. 77–81, illus.

Wilson, *Selections*, no. 45, pp. 90–91, illus.

201

201 PAIR OF VASES
Porcelain: Chinese, Kangxi (1662–1722)
Mounts: French (possibly German), circa 1860–1870
Makers unknown
Hard paste porcelain; colored enamel decoration; gilt-bronze mounts
No marks
Height: 1′11½″ (59.7 cm); Width: 12″ (30.6 cm); Depth: 11⅛″ (28.2 cm)
Accession number 78.DI.240.1–2

PROVENANCE

Mrs. Evelyn St. George, Cam House, London. Sold, Sotheby's, London, July 24–25, 1939, lot 81.

Purchased at that sale by J. Paul Getty.

EXHIBITIONS

Woodside, California. Filoli, on loan, 1979–present.

BIBLIOGRAPHY

Wilson et al., *Mounted Oriental Porcelain*, no. 18, pp. 82–84, illus.

202

202 PAIR OF VASES
Porcelain: Chinese, Kangxi (1662–1722)
Mounts: Paris, circa 1870–1900
Makers unknown
Hard paste porcelain; colored enamel decoration; gilding; gilt-bronze mounts
No marks
Height: 1′10½″ (57.2 cm); Diameter: 8¼″ (21.2 cm)
Accession number 78.DI.239.1–2

PROVENANCE

Mme Louis Burat, Paris. Sold, Galerie Jean Charpentier, Paris, June 17–18, 1937, lot 55.

Sold anonymously, Sotheby's, London, July 1, 1966, lot 38.

Frank Partridge Ltd., London, 1966.

Purchased by J. Paul Getty, 1967.

BIBLIOGRAPHY

Wilson et al., *Mounted Oriental Porcelain*, no. 19, pp. 85–87, illus.

203

MOUNTED HARDSTONES

203 VASE
Paris (possibly Italian), circa 1760
Maker unknown
Nero antico marble; gilt-bronze mounts
No marks
Height: 1′½″ (31.7 cm); Width: 1′7¾″ (50.2 cm); Depth: 11⅛″ (28.3 cm)
Accession number 79.DJ.183

PROVENANCE

Sold, "Property of a Lady," Christie's, London, December 6, 1979, lot 4.

Purchased at that sale by the J. Paul Getty Museum.

BIBLIOGRAPHY

Wilson, "Acquisitions 1979 to mid 1980," no. 2, pp. 4–5, illus.

COMMENTARY

The Sèvres Manufactory produced vases of this model from 1761. Some were painted to simulate marble and fitted with gilt-bronze mounts similar to those on this piece. These are listed as *vases Choiseul* in the Sèvres Archives. Three such porcelain examples are in the Victoria and Albert Museum, London.

204

204 PAIR OF VASES

Paris (possibly Italian), circa 1765–1770
Maker unknown
Porphyry; gilt-bronze mounts
No marks
Height: 1′3¼″ (38.7 cm); Width: 1′4⅛″ (41.0 cm); Depth: 10⅞″ (27.7 cm)
Accession number 83.DJ.16.1–2

PROVENANCE

Sir Everard Radcliffe, Bt., Rudding Park, Yorkshire.

Lovice Reviczky A.G., Zurich, 1982.

Purchased by the J. Paul Getty Museum, 1983.

EXHIBITIONS

Barnard Castle, County Durham. The Bowes Museum, *French Art of the 17th and 18th Centuries from Northern Collections*, July–August 1965, ex. cat., no. 37.

BIBLIOGRAPHY

Wilson, "Acquisitions 1983," no. 9, pp. 199–201, illus.

COMMENTARY

These vases are based on an engraved design executed in Parma by Ennemond-Alexandre Petitot and dated 1764.

205

205 LIDDED BOWL

Paris, circa 1770
Maker unknown
Porphyry; gilt-bronze mounts
No marks
Height: 1′4″ (40.6 cm); Width: 1′4½″ (41.9 cm); Depth: 9½″ (24.1 cm)
Accession number 73.DJ.88

PROVENANCE

I. Rosenbaum, Frankfurt. Sold, Parke Bernet, New York, December 5–6, 1946, lot 309.

Dalva Brothers, New York, 1973.

Purchased by J. Paul Getty, 1973.

206

206 PAIR OF URNS

Paris, circa 1780
Maker unknown
Porphyry; gilt-bronze mounts
No marks
Height: 1′2″ (35.6 cm); Diameter: 9″ (22.9 cm)
Accession number 74.DJ.24.1–2

PROVENANCE

Matthew Schutz Ltd., New York, 1974.

Purchased by J. Paul Getty, 1974.

207

207 PAIR OF STANDING TAZZAS

Paris, circa 1785
Maker unknown
Jaune foncé marble and *brèche violette* (?); gilt-bronze mounts
One mount, a replacement, stamped *BY* for the *bronzier* Louis-Auguste-Alfred Beurdeley.
Height: 1′2⅞″ (37.8 cm); Width: 9⅝″ (24.3 cm); Depth: 9⅞″ (25.2 cm)
Accession number 74.DJ.4.1–2

PROVENANCE

Napoléon Lannes, 2e duc de Montebello.

Louis-Auguste-Alfred Beurdeley, Paris, by 1882.

Alfred-Emanuel-Louis Beurdeley (son of Louis-Auguste-Alfred Beurdeley), Paris. Sold, May 19–20, 1899, lot 178.

Lindon collection. Sold, Sotheby's, London, June 26, 1964, lot 87.

R. L. Harrington Ltd., London, 1967.

Dalva Brothers, New York.

Purchased by J. Paul Getty, 1974.

208

TEXTILES

208 PANEL OF FABRIC

Lyons, circa 1710
Maker unknown
Silk; gold and silver thread
No marks
Length: 11′1″ (337.8 cm); Width: 1′8″ (50.8 cm)
Accession number 79.DD.67

PROVENANCE

Loewi-Robertson Inc., Los Angeles, 1979.

Purchased by the J. Paul Getty Museum, 1979.

209 HANGINGS FOR A BED

French, circa 1718
Maker unknown
Silk satin; cording; velour; silk embroidery; damask and linen panels
No marks
Height: 13′7⅜″ (415.0 cm); Width: 5′11½″ (182.0 cm); Depth: 6′ (183.0 cm)
Accession number 79.DD.3

PROVENANCE

(?) Château de Montbrillon, Aix-en-Provence.

P. Bertrand, Paris (?), by 1933.

Gerald C. Paget, London and New York, 1970's.

Purchased by the J. Paul Getty Museum, 1979.

EXHIBITIONS

Paris. Musée des Arts Décoratifs, *L'Exposition rétrospective de la chambre à coucher*, January–February 1933, ex. cat., no. 129, illus.

Versailles. Château de Versailles, Salon de la Guerre, June 1936.

BIBLIOGRAPHY

Wilson, "Acquisitions 1977 to mid 1979," no. 12, pp. 48–49, illus.

209

210

210 PANEL OF FABRIC
Lyons, circa 1770
Maker unknown
Silk; gold and silver thread
No marks
Length: 3′5″ (104.1 cm); Width: 1′9″ (53.2 cm)
Accession number 79.DD.122

PROVENANCE

Loewi-Robertson Inc., Los Angeles, 1979.

Purchased by the J. Paul Getty Museum, 1979.

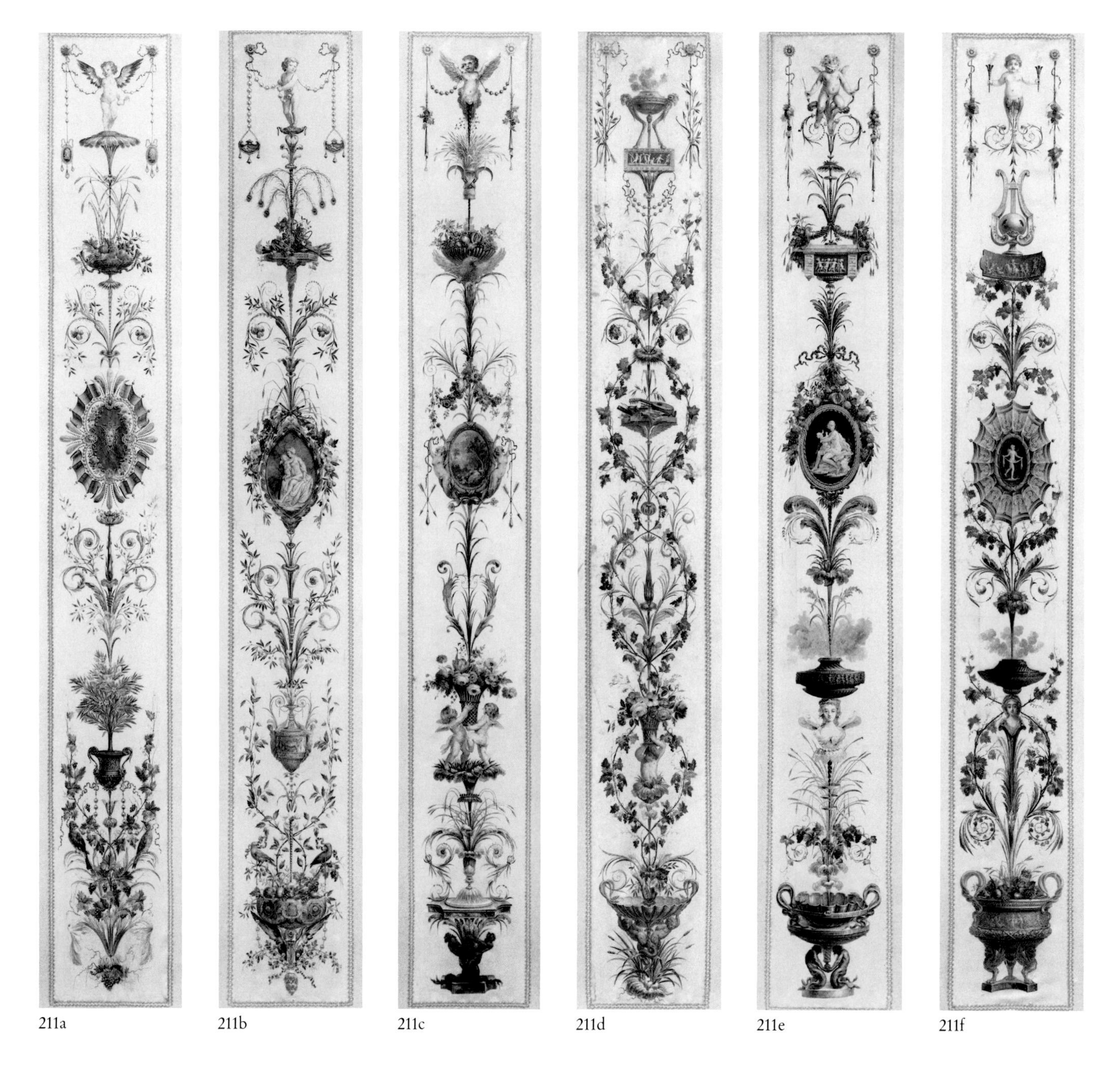

211a 211b 211c 211d 211e 211f

211 SIX PAINTED PANELS
Paris, circa 1780
Maker unknown
Gouache on silk with gold paint
One panel painted with the monograms MJL and LSX of the comte and comtesse de Provence.
Height: 4′9″ (144.8 cm); Width: 7″ (17.8 cm)
Accession number 73.DH.89.1–6

PROVENANCE

Made for Louis-Stanislas-Xavier and Marie-Josephine-Louise, comte and comtesse de Provence.

Baron Louis de Rothschild. Sold, Parke Bernet, New York, May 13, 1955, lot 165.

Dalva Brothers, New York, 1973.

Purchased by J. Paul Getty, 1973.

BIBLIOGRAPHY

Wilson, *Selections*, no. 43, pp. 86–87, illus.

212

TAPESTRIES

212 VERDURE TAPESTRY
French, circa 1630
Maker unknown
Wool
No marks
Height: 10′10″ (330.5 cm); Width: 7′11½″ (242.5 cm)
Accession number 69.DD.37

PROVENANCE

Gift of Dr. Albert Best, Los Angeles, 1969.

213 FIVE TAPESTRIES FROM *THE STORY OF THE EMPEROR OF CHINA*
Beauvais Manufactory, circa 1690–1705
Woven after designs by Guy-Louis Vernansal, Jean-Baptiste Monnoyer, and Jean-Baptiste Belin de Fontenay
Wool and silk
Each tapestry woven with the arms and monogram of the comte de Toulouse.

The Collation
Woven *VERNANSAL.INT.ET.PU.*
Height: 13′10½″ (423.0 cm); Width: 10′2″ (310.0 cm)
Accession number 83.DD.336

The Harvesting of Pineapples
Woven *BEHAGLE.*
Height: 13′7½″ (415.0 cm); Width: 8′5½″ (258.0 cm)
Accession number 83.DD.337

The Astronomers
No marks
Height: 13′9″ (419.0 cm); Width: 10′5½″ (319.0 cm)
Accession number 83.DD.338

The Emperor on a Journey
No marks
Height: 13′7½″ (415.0 cm); Width: 8′4″ (254.0 cm)
Accession number 83.DD.339

The Return from the Hunt
Woven *BEHAGLE.*
Height: 13′8½″ (418.0 cm); Width: 9′6″ (290.0 cm)
Accession number 83.DD.340

PROVENANCE

Made for Louis-Alexandre de Bourbon, comte de Toulouse. Part of a set of nine tapestries in the *Chambre du Roi* and the *Antichambre du Roi* of the Château de Rambouillet by 1718.

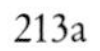

213a

213b

213c

213d

213e

Louis-Philippe, King of the French, by inheritance through his mother. Six tapestries from the set sold, Paris, January 25–27, 1852, lot 8.

Duchesse d'Uzès, France. Sold in America, 1926.

Private collection, Newport, Rhode Island.

Rosenberg and Stiebel, New York, 1983.

Purchased by the J. Paul Getty Museum, 1983.

BIBLIOGRAPHY

Moutié and de Dion, "Quelques Documents sur le Duchépairie de Rambouillet," *Mémoires et documents publiés par la Société archéologique de Rambouillet* 7, 1886, pp. 208, 227.

Badin, *Beauvais*, p. 13.

Edith Standen, "The Story of the Emperor of China: A Beauvais Tapestry Series," *Metropolitan Museum of Art Journal* 2, 1976, pp. 103–117.

Bremer-David, "Acquisitions 1983," no. 1, pp. 173–180, illus.

214 *CHAR DE TRIOMPHE*
Gobelins Manufactory, 1715/16
Woven from a cartoon by Baudrain Yvart *père* after a design by Charles Le Brun
Wool and silk
Part of original backing bears the inscription *N.º 194 Port.s Du Char,/ 6: Sur 3: au[ne]. de haut/ 2: au[ne] 1/2 de Cours* over *10 - 6 six pieces/ 8 520.* Woven with the arms of France and Navarre.
Height: 11′4½″ (347.0 cm); Width: 8′9¼″ (267.0 cm)
Accession number 83.DD.20

PROVENANCE

Made for Louis XIV. Delivered posthumously to the Garde-Meuble de la Couronne on October 27, 1717.

Mme Fulco de Bourbon, Patterson, New York.

Michael de Bourbon (son of Mme Fulco de Bourbon), Pikeville, Kentucky.

Purchased by the J. Paul Getty Museum, 1983.

BIBLIOGRAPHY

Fenaille, *Gobelins*, vol. 2, pp. 16–22.

Wilson, *Selections*, no. 8, pp. 16–17, illus.

Bremer-David, "Acquisitions 1983," no. 3, pp. 183–185, 187, illus.

COMMENTARY

Charles Le Brun designed this tapestry in 1659 for the minister Nicolas Fouquet's tapestry works at Maincy. After Fouquet's disgrace in 1659 the design was woven at the Gobelins Manufactory with the arms of France and Navarre in place of those of Fouquet.

214

215

215 *CHANCELLERIE*
Gobelins Manufactory, circa 1728–1730
Woven by Etienne-Claude Le Blond after designs by Guy-Louis Vernansal and Claude Audran
Wool and silk
Signature G. LE. BLOND and a fleur-de-lys woven at lower right corner.
Height: 11′1″ (338.0 cm); Width: 8′10¼″ (270.0 cm)
Accession number 65.DD.5

PROVENANCE

Woven for Germain-Louis de Chauvelin, marquis de Grosbois.

(?) French and Company, New York.

Mortimer L. Schiff, New York. Sold by his heir, John L. Schiff, Christie's, London, June 22, 1938, lot 74.

Purchased at that sale by J. Paul Getty.

BIBLIOGRAPHY

Fenaille, *Gobelins*, vol. 3, p. 139.

Göbel, *Wandteppiche*, pp. 172–173.

216 *THE LOVES OF THE GODS*
Beauvais Manufactory, circa 1722–1749
Woven after paintings by François Boucher
Wool and silk
No marks
Height: 12′ (366.0 cm); Width: 24′9″ (754.0 cm)
Accession number 63.DD.6

PROVENANCE

(?) Royal family of Portugal.

Jules Paul Porges, Portugal and later Paris.

C. Ledyard Blair.

French and Company, New York, 1937.

Purchased by J. Paul Getty, 1937.

BIBLIOGRAPHY

M. Vaucaire, "Les Tapisseries de Beauvais," *Les Arts*, August 1902, p. 16, illus.

Badin, *Beauvais*, p. 61, illus.

George L. Hunter, "Beauvais-Boucher Tapestries," *Arts and Decoration*, March 1919, p. 246.

Hunter, *Tapestries*, p. 173.

George L. Hunter, "America's Beauvais–Boucher Tapestries," *International Studio*, November 1926, pp. 26–28, illus.

Göbel, *Wandteppiche*, p. 227.

Erik Zahle, "François Boucher's dobbelte billedavaening," *Det Danske Kunstindustrimuseum: Virksomhed* 3, 1959–1964, p. 68.

Jarry, "Boucher Tapestries," p. 224, illus. fig. 2.

216

217

217 *TOILET OF PSYCHE*
Beauvais Manufactory, circa 1741–1753
Woven after a painting by François Boucher, under the administration of Nicolas Besnier and the direction of Jean-Baptiste Oudry
Wool and silk
Signature BESNIER & OVDRY–A BEAVVAIS woven at lower left.
Height: 11′ (335.0 cm); Width: 8′9″ (267.0 cm)
Accession number 63.DD.2

PROVENANCE

Sir Anthony de Rothschild, Bt., London.

Henry Walters, New York. Sold by his widow, Parke Bernet, New York, April 26, 1941, lot 739, to French and Company, New York.

Purchased by J. Paul Getty, 1963.

BIBLIOGRAPHY

Jarry, "Boucher Tapestries," p. 224.

218 *TOILET OF PSYCHE*
Beauvais Manufactory, circa 1741–1770
Woven after a painting by François Boucher, under the administration of Nicolas Besnier and the direction of Jean-Baptiste Oudry
Wool and silk
Signature *BESNIER & OUDRY A BEAUVAIS* woven at lower right.
Height: 9′4″ (284.5 cm); Width: 13′5″ (409.0 cm)
Accession number 68.DD.23

PROVENANCE

Rupert, 2nd Earl of Iveagh, Pyrford Court, Surrey. Sold, Christie's, Pyrford Court, June 4, 1968, lot 206.

Purchased at that sale by J. Paul Getty.

COMMENTARY

This panel is of the same design as No. 217 in this handbook.

219 *TOILET OF PSYCHE*
Beauvais Manufactory, circa 1741–1770
Woven after a painting by François Boucher, under the administration of Nicolas Besnier and the direction of Jean-Baptiste Oudry
Wool and silk
No marks
Height: 10′ (305.0 cm); Width: 15′6″ (472.5 cm)
Accession number 71.DD.470

PROVENANCE

Duc de Gramont, Paris. Sold, Galerie Georges Petit, Paris, May 22, 1925, lot 73.

Duveen Brothers, London, 1933.

Anna Thomson Dodge, Rose Terrace, Grosse Pointe Farms, Michigan. Sold, Christie's, London, June 24, 1971, lot 137.

Purchased at that sale by J. Paul Getty.

EXHIBITIONS

London. 25 Park Lane, *Three French Reigns*, February–April 1933, ex. cat., no. 528.

BIBLIOGRAPHY

Badin, *Beauvais*, p. 60.

219

220

220 *THE ABANDONMENT OF PSYCHE*
Beauvais Manufactory, circa 1750
Woven after a painting by François Boucher
Silk and wool
Signature *f. Boucher* woven at lower left.
Height: 11′11½″ (364.5 cm); Width: 9′2″ (280.0 cm)
Accession number 63.DD.3

PROVENANCE

Sir Anthony de Rothschild, Bt., London.

E. M. Hodgkins, Paris.

French and Company, New York.

Purchased by J. Paul Getty, 1939.

BIBLIOGRAPHY

Badin, *Beauvais*, p. 60.

Jarry, "Boucher Tapestries," p. 224.

221

221 *PSYCHE AT THE BASKET-MAKER'S*

Beauvais Manufactory, circa 1750
Woven after a painting by François Boucher
Wool and silk
Signature *f. Boucher* woven at lower left.
Also woven with the arms of France and Navarre.
Height: 11′4″ (345.5 cm); Width: 8′3″ (251.5 cm)
Accession number 63.DD.4

PROVENANCE

Edward, 1st Earl of Iveagh, London.

Walter Guiness, London.

Jacques Seligmann, Paris.

Purchased by J. Paul Getty, 1938.

BIBLIOGRAPHY

Badin, *Beauvais*, p. 60.

Hunter, *Tapestries*, p. 144.

Jarry, "Boucher Tapestries," p. 224.

222

222 *PSYCHE AT CUPID'S PALACE*

Beauvais Manufactory, circa 1750
Woven after a painting by François Boucher
Wool and silk
No marks
Height: 10′11″ (332.7 cm); Width: 17′8″ (538.5 cm)
Accession number 63.DD.5

PROVENANCE

Sir Anthony de Rothschild, Bt., London.

E. M. Hodgkins, Paris.

French and Company, New York.

Purchased by J. Paul Getty, 1938.

BIBLIOGRAPHY

Badin, *Beauvais*, p. 60.

Jarry, "Boucher Tapestries," p. 224.

223 FOUR TAPESTRIES FROM *THE STORY OF DON QUIXOTE*

Gobelins Manufactory, 1772–1773
Woven after paintings by Charles-Antoine Coypel; *alentours* after designs by Michel Audran
Wool and silk

DON QUIXOTTE GUERI DE SA FOLIE, PAR LA SAGES (as woven)
Signature *AUDRAN* woven at bottom right corner and, with the date 1773, in the *galon.*
Height: 12′2″ (371.0 cm); Width: 12′10″ (391.0 cm)
Accession number 82.DD.66

LE REPAS DE SANCHO, DANS L'ILE DE BARATARIA (as woven)
Signature *AUDRAN* and date *1772* woven in the *galon* and the border at the bottom right corner.
Height: 12′2″ (371.0 cm); Width: 16′5½″ (502.0 cm)
Accession number 82.DD.67

ENTREE DE SANCHO DANS L'ILE DE BARATARIA (as woven)
Signature *AUDRAN* woven at the bottom right corner and, with the date 1772, in the *galon.*
Height: 12′2″ (371.0 cm); Width: 13′9¾″ (421.0 cm)
Accession number 82.DD.68

POLTRONERIE DE SANCHO A LA CHASSE (as woven)
Signature *AUDRAN* woven in the bottom right corner and, with the date 1772, in the *galon.*
Height: 12′2″ (371.0 cm); Width: 13′6″ (411.0 cm)
Accession number 82.DD.69

PROVENANCE

Given by Louis XVI on August 20, 1786, to Albert and Marie-Christine (sister of Marie-Antoinette), Duke and Duchess of Saxe-Teschen, joint governors of the Austrian Netherlands.

223a

Archduke Karl of Austria, 1822.

Archduke Albrecht of Austria, 1847.

Archduke Friederich of Austria, 1895. Removed to London by 1936.

Alice Bucher, Lucerne, Switzerland. Offered for sale, Sotheby's, London, December 8, 1967, lot 1, bought in.

Galerie Römer, Zurich, 1981. Sold, Sotheby's, Monaco, June 14, 1981, lot 571.

Purchased at that sale by the J. Paul Getty Museum.

BIBLIOGRAPHY

Fenaille, *Gobelins*, vol. 3, pp. 237ff.

Göbel, *Wandteppiche*, p. 163.

Bremer-David, *"Acquisitions 1982,"* no. 13, pp. 60–66, illus.

Wilson, *Selections*, no. 36, pp. 72–73, illus.

COMMENTARY

These tapestries were part of the eighth weaving of this series, carried out between 1763 and 1787. The paintings by Coypel for the figure scenes are all now in the Château de Compiègne.

223b (Reproduced at slightly larger scale than others of the set.)

223c

223d

224a

224b

224c

224d

224 FOUR OF THE *TENTURES DE BOUCHER*

Gobelins Manufactory, circa 1776–1778
Central scenes after paintings by François Boucher; *alentours* after designs by Louis Tessier and Maurice Jacques; woven under the direction of Jacques Neilson
Wool and silk

Diana and Callisto, Vertumnus and Pomona
Signature *NEILSON. ex.* woven at lower right, and *F.Boucher* woven in the medallion.
Height: 12′7″ (383.5 cm); Width: 20′6″ (624.8 cm)
Accession number 71.DD.466

COMMENTARY

The Boucher painting of *Diana and Callisto* (left side), dated 1769, is now in the Wallace Collection, London. The painting of *Vertumnus and Pomona* (right side), dated 1763, is now in the Musée du Louvre, Paris.

Venus on the Waters
Signature *NEILSON, ex.* woven at lower right.
Height: 12′7″ (383.5 cm); Width: 10′5″ (317.5 cm)
Accession number 71.DD.467

COMMENTARY

The Boucher painting of *Venus on the Waters*, dated 1763 or 1764, was still at the Gobelins Manufactory as late as 1870; it is now lost.

Venus and Vulcan
Signature *NEILSON, ex.* woven at lower right.
Height: 12′6″ (381.0 cm); Width: 16′ (487.7 cm)
Accession number 71.DD.468

COMMENTARY

The Boucher painting of *Venus and Vulcan*, 1764, is now in the Grand Trianon, Versailles.

Aurora and Cephalus
Signature *NEILSON, ex.* woven at lower right.
Height: 12′6″ (381.0 cm); Width: 10′7″ (322.5 cm)
Accession number 71.DD.469

COMMENTARY

The Boucher painting of *Aurora and Cephalus*, dated 1763, is now in the Musée du Louvre, Paris.

PROVENANCE

Given by Louis XVI in 1782 to Grand Duke Paul Petrovitch (later Czar Paul I) and Duchess Maria Feodorovna of Russia. Hung at the Palace of Pavlovsk (near Saint Petersburg) until after 1925. Sold by the Soviet Government.

Duveen Brothers, New York.

Norton Simon. Sold, Parke Bernet, New York, May 8, 1971, lot 233.

Purchased at that sale by J. Paul Getty.

EXHIBITIONS

Allentown, Pennsylvania. Allentown Art Museum, *Great Periods of Tapestry*, February 1961.

BIBLIOGRAPHY

Duchess Maria Feodorovna, "Description of Pavlovsk," 1795, in Alexandre Benois, *Les Trésors d'art en Russie*, 1907, vol. 3, pp. 375, 379, illus.

Fenaille, *Gobelins*, vol. 4, pp. 285–287, illus.

Sir Martin Conway, *Art Treasures in Soviet Russia*, 1925, p. 125.

Jarry, "Boucher Tapestries," pp. 222–231.

Wilson, *Selections*, no. 38, pp. 76–77, illus.

225

225 *NEPTUNE AND AMYMONE*

Gobelins Manufactory, circa 1780
Woven after a design by François Boucher, under the direction of Jacques Neilson and the supervision of Maurice Jacques
Wool and silk
F. BOUCHER PIX woven in central oval panel.
Height: 15′6″ (472.0 cm); Width: 12′¾″ (368.0 cm)
Accession number 73.DD.90

PROVENANCE

Conte Francesco Castelbarco Albani, Italy. Sold, Sotheby's, Florence, May 22, 1973, lot 79.

Purchased at that sale by J. Paul Getty.

COMMENTARY

The painting for this scene, dated 1765, is now in the Grand Trianon, Versailles.

CARPETS

226 CARPET

Savonnerie Manufactory, 1665/66
Probably made in the workshops of
Philippe Lourdet
Wool and linen
No marks
Length: 21′11⅜″ (669.0 cm); Width: 14′5″
(440.0 cm)
Accession number 70.DC.63

PROVENANCE

Louis XIV, Palais du Louvre, Paris, 1667.

Church of Saint-André-des-Arts, Paris, 1769.

(?) Parguez-Perdreau, Paris March 1914.

Arnold Seligmann, Paris, March–June 1914.

George A. Kessler, June 1914.

Mortimer L. Schiff, New York. Sold by his heir, John L. Schiff, Christie's, London, June 22, 1938, lot 77.

Purchased at that sale by J. Paul Getty.

BIBLIOGRAPHY

Jules Guiffrey, *Inventaire général du mobilier de la couronne sous Louis XIV: Tapis*, 1885–1886, no. 18, p. 378.

Verlet, *Waddesdon,* pp. 174, 421, nn. 5, 11.

Wilson, *Selections*, no. 1, pp. 2–3, illus.

COMMENTARY

This carpet is almost certainly no. 18 in the inventory of Louis XIV and was therefore delivered by 1667 for the Galerie d'Apollon in the Louvre, Paris. It was cut down in length, probably in the late nineteenth century, and the short borders were reknotted. In 1769 it was recorded as measuring 7 1/2 *aunes* in length (approximately 922.0 cm) and 3 2/3 *aunes* in width (approximately 436.0 cm), as in the original inventory.

226 (detail, half of carpet)

227

227 PAIR OF THREE-PANEL SCREENS

Savonnerie Manufactory, between 1714 and 1740
Woven after designs by Jean-Baptiste Belin de Fontenay and Alexandre-François Desportes
Wool and linen
No marks
Height: 8′11¾″ (273.6 cm); Width: 6′4⅛″ (193.2 cm)
Accession number 83.DD.260.1–2

PROVENANCE

(?) Mme d'Yvon, Paris. Sold, Galerie Georges Petit, Paris, May 30–June 4, 1892, lot 673.

Jacques Seligmann, Paris. Sold, Galerie Georges Petit, Paris, March 9–12, 1914, lot 343.

Germain Seligman, Paris, 1927.

François-Gérard Seligmann, Paris, by 1960. Sold, Sotheby's, Monaco, June 14–15, 1981, lot 54.

Dalva Brothers, New York, 1981.

Purchased by the J. Paul Getty Museum, 1983.

EXHIBITIONS

Paris. Manufacture Nationale des Gobelins, *Tapis de la Savonnerie*, December 1926–January 1927, no. 96.

Paris. Bibliothèque Nationale, *Le Siècle de Louis XIV*, February–April, 1927, no. 1268.

Paris. Musée des Arts Décoratifs, *Louis XIV: Faste et décors*, May–October 1960, ex. cat., no. 774, illus. pl. CII.

Richmond, Virginia. *CINOA*, April 1983.

BIBLIOGRAPHY

Verlet, *Waddesdon*, pp. 301, 457–458, n. 82.

Wilson, "Acquisitions 1983," no. 2, pp. 180–183, illus.

228

228 FOUR-PANEL SCREEN

Savonnerie Manufactory, woven between 1719 and 1769
Woven after designs by Alexandre-François Desportes
Wool and linen
No marks
Each panel: Height: 6′⅞″ (185.1 cm); Width: 2′1″ (63.5 cm)
Accession number 75.DD.1

PROVENANCE

The Earl of Caledon, Tyttenhanger Park, Hertfordshire.

Alexander and Berendt, Ltd., London, 1973.

Sold to an Australian collector.

Alexander and Berendt, Ltd., London, 1975.

Purchased by J. Paul Getty, 1975.

BIBLIOGRAPHY

Verlet, *Waddesdon*, p. 467, n. 20, and see no. 15.

Wilson, *Selections*, no. 12, pp. 24–25, illus.

229a (detail)

229b (detail, center)

229 CARPET

Aubusson Manufactory, circa 1830
Maker unknown
Wool and linen
No marks
Length: 25′ (762.0 cm); Width: 20′ (609.6 cm)
Accession number 79.DC.163

PROVENANCE

J. Paul Getty.

230

DECORATIVE CARVINGS

230 STILL LIFE
Paris, 1789
By Aubert-Henri-Joseph Parent
Lindenwood
Incised AUBERT PARENT FECIT AN. 1789 under the base.
Height: 2′3⅜″ (69.4 cm); Width: 1′6⅞″ (47.9 cm); Depth: 2⅜″ (6.2 cm)
Accession number 84.SD.76

PROVENANCE

David Peel, London.

Paul Mellon. Sold, Christie's, New York, November 22, 1983, lot 275.

Dalva Brothers, New York, 1983.

Purchased by the J. Paul Getty Museum, 1984.

BIBLIOGRAPHY

Colin Streeter, "Two Carved Reliefs by Aubert Parent," *The J. Paul Getty Museum Journal* 13, 1985, pp. 53–66, illus.

231

231 STILL LIFE
Paris, 1791
By Aubert-Henri-Joseph Parent
Lindenwood
Incised AUBERT PARENT. 1791 under the base. An inventory number, 172n, is stenciled in black on back.
Height: 1′11⅛″ (58.7 cm); Width: 1′3⅝″ (39.7 cm); Depth: 2¼″ (5.7 cm)
Accession number 84.SD.194

PROVENANCE

Jacques Kugel, Paris, 1984.

Purchased by the J. Paul Getty Museum, 1984.

BIBLIOGRAPHY

Colin Streeter, "Two Carved Reliefs by Aubert Parent," *The J. Paul Getty Museum Journal* 13, 1985, pp. 53–66, illus.

232

DECORATIVE DRAWINGS

232 DRAWING FOR A WALL LIGHT
Paris, circa 1775
Attributed to Richard de Lalonde
Pen and ink with wash on paper
No marks
Height: 11¾″ (29.9 cm); Width: 8¼″ (20.7 cm)
Accession number 79.GA.179

PROVENANCE

Maison Odiot, Paris. Sold, Sotheby's, Monaco, November 26, 1979, lot 609.

Purchased at that sale by the J. Paul Getty Museum.

BIBLIOGRAPHY

Wilson, "Acquisitions 1979 to mid 1980," item B, p. 12, illus.

COMMENTARY

Entry No. 134 in this handbook shows six wall lights that are based on this design. The design is for a two-branch wall light, those in the Museum's collection have three branches.

233

234

233 DRAWING FOR A EWER

Paris, circa 1775–1780
Attributed to Robert-Joseph Auguste
Brown ink with brown and gray washes on paper
No marks
Height: 1′3 13/16″ (40.2 cm); Width: 10 1/16″ (25.6 cm)
Accession number 79.GA.180

PROVENANCE

Maison Odiot, Paris. Sold, Sotheby's, Monaco, November 26, 1979, lot 610.

Purchased at that sale by the J. Paul Getty Museum.

BIBLIOGRAPHY

Claude Frégnac et al., *Les Grands Orfèvres de Louis XVIII à Charles X*, Collection connaissance des arts, 1965, p. 194, illus.

Wilson, "Acquisitions 1979 to mid 1980," item C, p. 13, illus.

---

234 DRAWING FOR URNS AND VASES

Paris, circa 1780
Artist unknown
Pen and ink with gray and black washes on paper
Penciled *Salembier*, perhaps a later attribution to Henri Salembier.
Height: 1′8 7/8″ (53.1 cm); Width: 3′7 1/8″ (109.5 cm)
Accession number 79.GA.178

PROVENANCE

Maison Odiot, Paris. Sold, Sotheby's, Monaco, November 26, 1979, lot 584.

Purchased at that sale by the J. Paul Getty Museum.

BIBLIOGRAPHY

Wilson, "Acquisitions 1979 to mid 1980," item A, p. 11, illus.

235

236

235 DRAWING FOR AN INKSTAND
Paris, circa 1780
Attributed to Robert-Joseph Auguste
Black ink with watercolor washes in blue, yellow, and pink on paper
No marks
Height: 1′5 5/16″ (44.0 cm); Width: 1′3 5/16″ (38.9 cm)
Accession number 79.GA.181

PROVENANCE

Maison Odiot, Paris. Sold, Sotheby's, Monaco, November 26, 1979, lot 612.

Purchased at that sale by the J. Paul Getty Museum.

BIBLIOGRAPHY

Wilson, "Acquisitions 1979 to mid 1980," item E, p. 16, illus.

236 DRAWING FOR A WINE COOLER
Paris, circa 1785–1790
Attributed to Jean-Guillaume Moitte
Black ink with gray washes on paper
Stamped *J.B.C. Odiot N.°* at lower right and inked *228*.
Height: 1′2 7/16″ (36.6 cm); Width: 1′½″ (31.8 cm)
Accession number 79.GA.182

PROVENANCE

Maison Odiot, Paris. Sold, Sotheby's, Monaco, November 26, 1979, lot 627.

Purchased at that sale by the J. Paul Getty Museum.

BIBLIOGRAPHY

Wilson, "Acquisitions 1979 to mid 1980," item D, pp. 14–15, illus.

COMMENTARY

This drawing is for a silver-gilt wine cooler made by Henry Auguste. The cooler was part of a large service presented by the city of Paris to Napoleon at his coronation in 1804, and it is now at the Château de Malmaison.

GERMAN
Decorative Arts

237

CABINET

237 TRAVELING DESK
Augsburg (?), circa 1560
Maker unknown
Pine carcass veneered with holly, apple, sycamore, thuya, and stained fruitwoods; oak drawers
No marks
Height: 1′3½″ (39.4 cm); Width: 1′9½″ (54.6 cm); Depth: 1′4″ (40.6 cm)
Accession number 78.DA.111

PROVENANCE

Katherine Schratt.

Julius Bohler, Munich, 1960.

Purchased by J. Paul Getty, 1960.

EXHIBITIONS

San Francisco. California Palace of the Legion of Honor, *The Triumph of Humanism*, September 1977–January, 1978, ex. cat., no. 221.

BIBLIOGRAPHY

L. Müller, *Der Wrangelschrank und die verwandten süddeutschen Intarsienmöbel des 16. Jahrhunderts*, 1956, no. 74, illus. pls. 185, 186.

238

COMMODES

238 PAIR OF COMMODES
Munich, circa 1745
Carving attributed to Joachim Dietrich; side panels after engraved designs by François de Cuvilliés
Carved, painted, and gilded pine; gilt-bronze mounts; *jaune rosé de Brignolles* marble tops
No marks
Height: 2′8¾″ (83.2 cm); Width: 4′1¾″ (126.4 cm); Depth: 2′⅜″ (61.9 cm)
Accession number 72.DA.63.1–2

PROVENANCE

Jacques Helft, New York.

Georges Lurcy, New York. Sold, Parke Bernet, New York, November 9, 1957, lot 383.

Frank Partridge Ltd., London.

Maharanee of Baroda, Paris.

Frank Partridge Ltd., London, 1972.

Purchased by J. Paul Getty, 1972.

239

DESK

239 ROLLTOP DESK
Neuwied, circa 1785
Attributed to David Roentgen; gilt-bronze plaque attributed to Pierre Gouthière
Oak veneered with mahogany and burl amboyna; gilt-bronze mounts
No marks
Height: 5′6¼″ (168.3 cm); Width: 5′1⅜″ (155.9 cm); Depth: (open) 4′1⅞″ (126.7 cm), (closed) 2′11⅛″ (89.3 cm)
Accession number 72.DA.47

PROVENANCE

Count János Pálffy, Palais Pálffy, Vienna. Sold, Glückselig und Warndorfer, Vienna, March 7, 1921, lot 209, to Castiglione.

Baroness Marie de Reitz, Vienna.

French and Company, New York.

Purchased by J. Paul Getty, 1972.

EXHIBITIONS

Washington, D.C. The State Department, on loan, 1960's.

BIBLIOGRAPHY

Heinrich Kreisel, *Die Kunst des deutschen Möbels*, 1973, vol. 3, illus. fig. 17.

Hans Huth, *Roentgen Furniture*, 1974, illus. 64–68.

Josef Maria Greber, *Abraham und David Roentgen: Möbel für Europa*, 1980, vol. 2., illus. figs. 683, 684.

Dietrich Fabian, *Die Entwicklung der Roentgen-Schreibmöbel*, 1982, p. 45, illus. figs. 66–67.

Wilson, *Selections*, no. 44, pp. 88–89, illus.

240

SECRETAIRE

240 *SECRETAIRE*
Berlin, circa 1794
Attributed to David Hacker; clock movement by Christian Mollinger
Pine and oak veneered with mahogany, satinwood, bloodwood, and kingwood; white marble; gilt-bronze mounts
Clock face painted *Mollinger à Berlin.*
Height: 8′ (243.8 cm); Width: 3′8″ (111.8 cm); Depth: 2′ (60.9 cm)
Accession number 84.DA.87

PROVENANCE

Reputedly made for Frederick William III, King of Prussia, Berlin.

Prussian Royal Collection, Schloss on the Pfaueninsel, Berlin.

Private collection, Berlin.

Herr Ragaller, Berlin.

Sold, Weinmüller, Munich, May 2–5, 1956, lot 111.

Sold, Weinmüller, Munich, October 23–24, 1974, lot 861.

Private collection, Munich.

Juan Portela, New York.

Purchased by the J. Paul Getty Museum, 1984.

EXHIBITIONS

(?) Berlin. Berlin Academy Exhibition, 1794, ex. cat., no. 325, p. 61.

BIBLIOGRAPHY

(?) Carl Christian Horvath, *Potsdams Merkwürdigkeiten beschrieben und durch Plans und Prospekte erläutert*, 1798, p. 22.

Dietrich Fabian, *Die Entwicklung der Roentgen-Schreibmöbel*, 1982, pp. 53–55, figs. 77d–g.

Stürmer, *Möbelkunst*, pl. 102.

Heinrich Kreisel, *Die Kunst des deutschen Möbels*, 1973, vol. 3, illus. 264.

Wilson, "Acquisitions 1984," no. 5, pp. 83–88, illus.

241

TORCHERES

241 PAIR OF *TORCHERES*
Potsdam (?), circa 1740
Maker unknown
Carved, painted, and gilded wood; crushed glass
No marks
Height: 7′¼″ (214.0 cm)
Accession number 79.DA.5.1–2

PROVENANCE

Neues Palais, Potsdam, 1895. Purchased in Amsterdam, 1895. Displayed in the Japis Gallerie, 1926.

Sold, Palais Galliera, Paris, December 9, 1963, lot 93.

Fabius Frères, Paris, 1970's.

Purchased by the J. Paul Getty Museum, 1979.

BIBLIOGRAPHY

Burkhard Meier, *Potsdam Schlösser und Gärten aufgenommen von der Staatliche Bildstelle,* 1926, illus. fig. 46.

Wilson, "Acquisitions 1977 to mid 1979," no. 13, p. 49, illus.

COMMENTARY

Six other *torchères* of this model are known, four in the Rijksmuseum, Amsterdam, and two in a private collection in Paris.

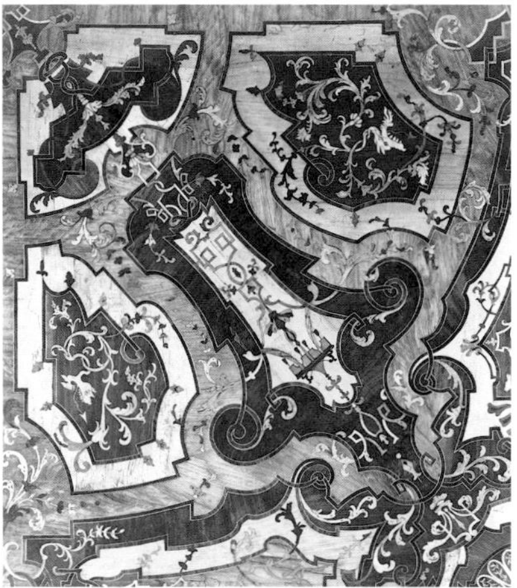
242
This photograph shows only one of the four panels of this floor.

FLOOR

242 FLOOR
German (?), circa 1725
Maker unknown
Pine veneered with kingwood, *bois satiné*, sycamore, tulipwood, and olive
No marks
Length: 9′11″ (302.2 cm); Width: 10′11″ (332.7 cm)
Accession number 78.DH.360.1–4

PROVENANCE

The Metropolitan Museum of Art, New York. Source unknown, deaccessioned, 1970.

Dalva Brothers, New York, 1970.

Purchased by the J. Paul Getty Museum, 1978.

BIBLIOGRAPHY

Wilson, "Acquisitions 1977 to mid 1979," no. 10, p. 46, illus.

243

CERAMICS: MEISSEN MANUFACTORY

243 SET OF FIVE VASES
Meissen Manufactory, circa 1730
Painting attributed to Johann Gregor Höroldt; largest vase molded by Schiefer
Hard paste porcelain; colored enamel decoration; gilding
Each vase painted under its base with the blue *AR* monogram of Augustus the Strong, Elector of Saxony. Larger lidded vase (1) incised with Schiefer's mark of a cross with four dots.

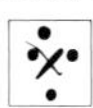

Lidded vase (1): Height: 1′2¹¹⁄16″ (37.3 cm); Width: 9½″ (24.1 cm)
Lidded vases (2 and 3): Height: 1′¹¹⁄16″ (32.2 cm); Width: 7⅝″ (19.4 cm)
Open vases (4 and 5): Height: 10⅞″ (27.6 cm); Width: 7″ (17.8 cm)

Accession number 83.DE.334.1–5

PROVENANCE

Private collection. Sold, Sotheby's, London, March 5, 1957, lot 123.

The Antique Porcelain Company, London, 1957.

Alamagna family, Milan, 1961–1982.

The Antique Porcelain Company, London, 1982.

Purchased by the J. Paul Getty Museum, 1983.

BIBLIOGRAPHY

Sassoon, "Acquisitions 1983," no. 16, pp. 217–222, illus.

COMMENTARY

Several of the scenes of oriental figures can be identified in a book of drawings attributed to Johann Gregor Höroldt. Known as the Schulz Codex, the book is now in the Museum des Kunsthandwerks, Leipzig.

244 PAIR OF LIDDED VASES
Vases: Meissen Manufactory, circa 1735–1740
Lids: Possibly Meissen porcelain replacements, circa 1760
Decoration: Dresden (?), possibly nineteenth century
One vase probably molded by Rehschuck
Hard paste porcelain; colored enamel decoration; gilding
Each vase painted under its base with the blue *AR* monogram of Augustus the Strong, Elector of Saxony. Each incised with a cross under the base; on one vase the cross is plain (probably the mark of the molder Rehschuck), and on the other it takes the form of a running cross.

Height: 1′ 2″ (35.5 cm); Diameter: 7 7/8″ (20.1 cm)
Accession number 73.DE.65.1–2

PROVENANCE

Private collection, Zurich.

French and Company, New York, 1973. Sold, Sotheby's, London, March 27, 1973, lot 39.

Purchased at that sale by J. Paul Getty.

244

245

245 GROUP OF JAPANESE FIGURES
Meissen Manufactory, circa 1745
Model by Johann Joachim Kändler
Hard paste porcelain; colored enamel decoration; gilt bronze
Any marks that might be under the base are concealed by the gilt-bronze mount.
Height: 1′ 5 3/4″ (45.1 cm); Width: 11 5/8″ (29.5 cm); Depth: 8 9/16″ (21.7 cm)
Accession number 83.DE.271

PROVENANCE

Figure group:

Private European collection. Sold, Sotheby's, London, March 2, 1982, lot 168.

Winifred Williams Ltd., London, 1982.

Parasol:

Paul Schnyder von Wartensee, Switzerland.

Winifred Williams Ltd., London, 1982.

Entire group purchased by the J. Paul Getty Museum, 1983.

BIBLIOGRAPHY

M. A. Pfeiffer, "Ein Beitrag zur Quellengeschichte des europäischen Porzellans," *Werden und Wirken: Ein Festgruss für Karl W. Hiersemann*, 1924, p. 285.

Sassoon, "Acquisitions 1983," no. 17, pp. 222–224, illus.

COMMENTARY

Kändler was paid twenty-four *Reichstallers* for creating the model for this group in 1745.

246a

246b

246 PAIR OF VASES MOUNTED WITH FLOWERS

Bowls: Meissen Manufactory, circa 1740
Flowers: French (Vincennes Manufactory), circa 1745–1750
Mounts: French (Paris), circa 1745–1749
Makers unknown
Hard paste porcelain bowls; colored enamel decoration; soft paste porcelain flowers; gilt-bronze mounts
Each bowl painted on the base with the blue *AR* monogram of Augustus the Strong, Elector of Saxony. Mounts struck with the crowned C for 1745–1749.
Height: 1′3⅝″ (39.7 cm); Width: 1′3⅛″ (38.3 cm); Depth: 1′1⅜″ (34.0 cm)
Accession number 79.DI.59.1–2

PROVENANCE

Consuelo Vanderbilt (Mme Jacques Balsan).

Matthew Schutz Ltd., New York, 1979.

Purchased by the J. Paul Getty Museum, 1979.

COMMENTARY

These bowls have been cut down from Meissen vases that originally had sharply incurving shoulders with trumpet-shaped necks.

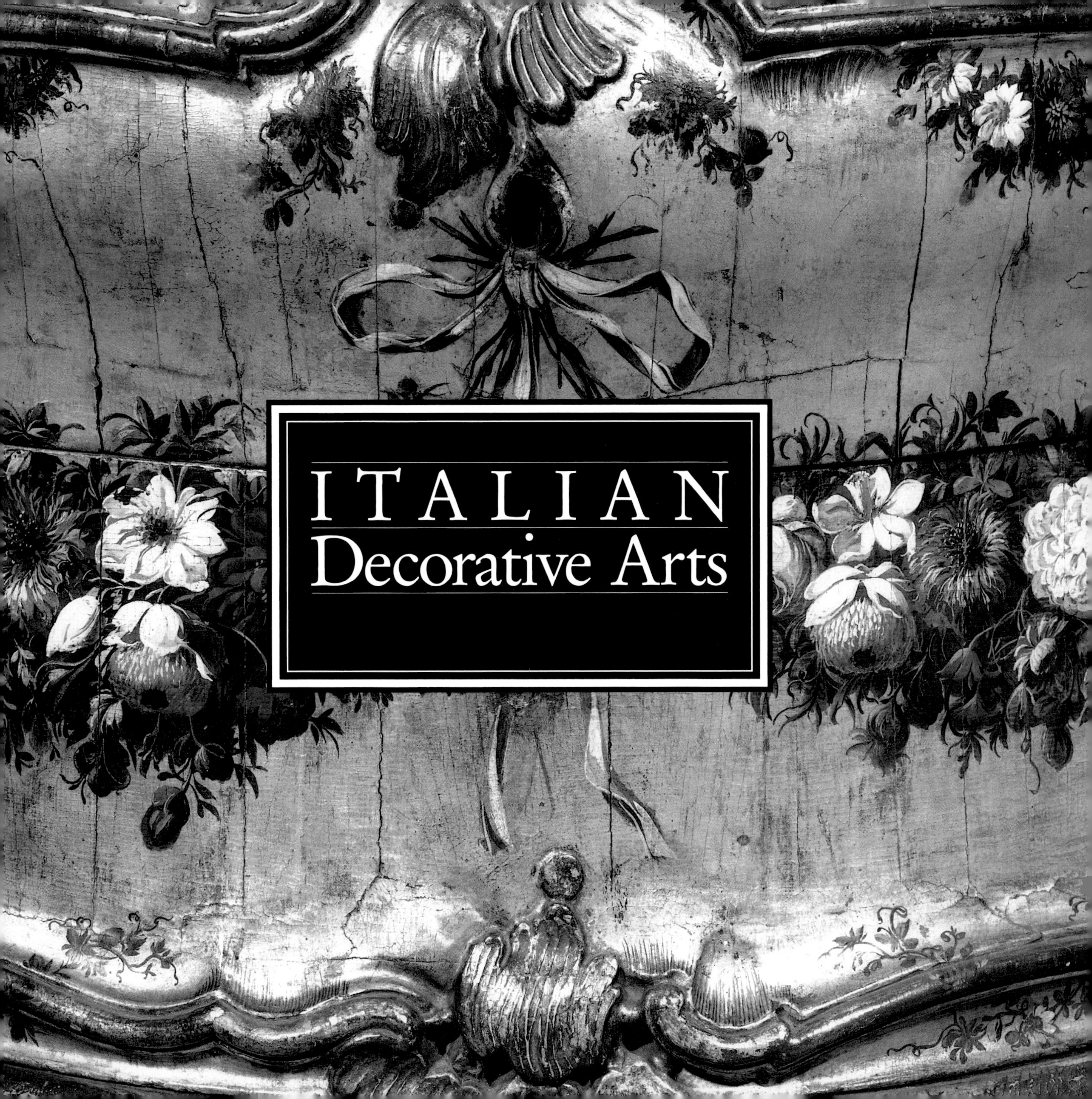
ITALIAN
Decorative Arts

247

248

249

CABINETS

247 *CASSONE*
Milan, circa 1550–1600
Maker unknown
Walnut; parcel-gilt
No marks
Height: 2′5⅛″ (73.9 cm); Width: 5′5¾″ (167.0 cm); Depth: 2′⅛″ (61.3 cm)
Accession number 68.DA.8

PROVENANCE

Earls of Warwick, Warwick Castle, Warwickshire.

Frank Partridge Ltd., London, 1968.

Purchased by J. Paul Getty, 1968.

EXHIBITIONS

San Francisco. California Palace of the Legion of Honor, *The Triumph of Humanism*, September 1977–January 1978, ex. cat., no. 205, illus.

Tulsa, Oklahoma. The Philbrook Art Center, *Gloria dell'Arte: A Renaissance Perspective,* October 1979–January 1980, ex. cat., no. 85, illus.

---

248 *CASSONE*
Rome, circa 1550–1600
Maker unknown
Carved walnut; parcel-gilt
No marks
Height: 2′5⅛″ (74.0 cm); Width: 5′5 9/16″ (166.6 cm); Depth: 2′¼″ (61.8 cm)
Accession number 78.DA.120

PROVENANCE

H. Blairman and Sons, London, 1963.

Purchased by J. Paul Getty, 1963.

EXHIBITIONS

Tulsa, Oklahoma. The Philbrook Art Center, *Gloria dell'Arte: A Renaissance Perspective*, October 1979–January 1980, ex. cat., no. 86.

COMMENTARY

One of a set of at least eight *cassoni*. Four are in the Frick Collection, New York, two are in the State Hermitage, Leningrad, and one is in the Philadelphia Museum of Art.

---

249 CABINET
Florence, circa 1600–1650
Maker unknown
Carved walnut
No marks
Height: 3′9¼″ (114.9 cm); Width: 6′7¾″ (202.5 cm); Depth: 1′9½″ (54.6 cm)
Accession number 78.DA.107

PROVENANCE

Ugo Bardini, Florence, 1960.

Purchased by J. Paul Getty, 1960.

---

250 CABINET
Umbria (?), late seventeenth century; remodeled later
Maker unknown
Carved walnut
No marks
Height: 3′10¾″ (118.7 cm); Width: 4′1¼″ (125.0 cm); Depth: 1′10½″ (57.1 cm)
Accession number 78.DA.109

PROVENANCE

Ugo Bardini, Florence, 1960.

Purchased by J. Paul Getty, 1960.

250

COMMODE

251 COMMODE
Venice, circa 1745–1750
Maker unknown
Gilded, painted, and silvered oak
No marks
Height: 2′8⅛″ (81.5 cm); Width: 4′9⅞″ (147.0 cm); Depth: 2′⅝″ (62.5 cm)
Accession number 83.DA.282

PROVENANCE

Private collection, Saint-Malo, France. Sold at auction in Saint-Malo, 1982.

Didier Aaron, Paris. Sold, Sotheby's, London, July 15, 1983, lot 114.

Purchased at that sale by the J. Paul Getty Museum.

BIBLIOGRAPHY

Wilson, "Acquisitions 1983," no. 15, pp. 216–217, illus.

TABLES

252 SIDE TABLE
Rome, circa 1720–1730
Maker unknown
Carved and gilded pine; modern marble top
No marks
Height: 3′1″ (93.9 cm); Width: 6′3″ (190.5 cm); Depth: 3′2″ (96.5 cm)
Accession number 82.DA.8

PROVENANCE

Private collection, England.

Jacques Kugel, Paris, 1981.

Purchased by the J. Paul Getty Museum, 1982.

251

252

253

253 CONSOLE TABLE
Piedmont (?), circa 1730
Maker unknown
Carved and gilded oak; *sarrancolin* marble top
No marks
Height: 2′10¼″ (86.9 cm); Width: 6′5¼″ (196.2 cm); Depth: 2′6¾″ (78.1 cm)
Accession number 78.DA.118

PROVENANCE

Elsie de Wolfe (Lady Mendl).

Purchased by J. Paul Getty, 1949.

254

254 CONSOLE TABLE
Northern Italy, circa 1740
Maker unknown
Gilded oak
No marks
Height: 2′10″ (86.3 cm); Width: 5′1¾″ (156.8 cm); Depth: 1′3¾″ (40.0 cm)
Accession number 69.DA.34

PROVENANCE

Sold, Palais Galliera, Paris, March 25, 1969, lot 125.

Claude Sère, Paris.

Purchased by J. Paul Getty, 1969.

255

255 WRITING TABLE
Naples (?), 1799
By Francesco Abbiati
Oak, walnut, and poplar veneered with purple wood, satinwood, ebony, and various fruitwoods
Inscribed FRAN^{CO} ABBIATI 1799 in the central roundel of marquetry on the top.
Height: 2′6⅝″ (77.8 cm); Width: 2′10$\frac{7}{16}$″ (87.5 cm); Depth: 2′10$\frac{7}{16}$″ (87.5 cm)
Accession number 84.DA.77

PROVENANCE

Private collection, Cleveland.

Dalva Brothers, New York, 1970's.

Purchased by the J. Paul Getty Museum, 1984.

256

SEAT FURNITURE

256 SIDE CHAIR
Turin, circa 1710–1715
Maker unknown
Gilded wood; modern silk upholstery copying the original
No marks
Height: 4′2⅝″ (128.5 cm); Width: 1′9⅞″ (55.6 cm); Depth: 2′3⅜″ (69.5 cm)
Accession number 83.DA.281

PROVENANCE

(?) Royal House of Savoy, Racconigi, Turin.

Mrs. Walter Hayes Burns, North Mymms Park, Hertfordshire.

Major General Sir George Burns (son of Mrs. Walter Hayes Burns), North Mymms Park. Sold, Christie's, North Mymms Park, September 24–26, 1979, lot 215, one of five.

Partridge (Fine Arts) Ltd., London, 1979.

Purchased by the J. Paul Getty Museum, 1983.

BIBLIOGRAPHY

Wilson, "Acquisitions 1983," no. 14, pp. 214–216, illus.

COMMENTARY

Eight chairs from this set in the Palazzo Racconigi (near Turin) and a pair in the Toledo Museum of Art are still covered with their original upholstery. Another pair, with replaced upholstery, is in a private collection, New York.

257

257 FOLDING STOOL

Turin (?), circa 1735
Maker unknown
Carved and gilded walnut; modern velvet upholstery
Stamped twice on the seat rail with three fleur-de-lys, and the letters FON for the Château de Fontainebleau.
Height: 1′4¼″ (41.1 cm); Width: 2′3⅛″ (68.9 cm); Depth: 1′5⅛″ (43.5 cm)
Accession number 74.DA.26

PROVENANCE

Château de Fontainebleau, probably during the nineteenth century.

Matthew Schutz Ltd., New York, 1974.

Purchased by J. Paul Getty, 1974.

COMMENTARY

Twelve examples of this model are in the Palazzo Reale, Turin, two were in the Béraudière collection (sold 1918), and one is in a private collection, Paris.

CHINESE
Decorative Arts

258a

258b

259

CERAMICS

258 GARNITURE OF THREE LIDDED VASES AND TWO OPEN VASES
Chinese, Kangxi (1662–1722)
Maker unknown
Hard paste porcelain; blue enamel decoration
No marks
Lidded vases: Height: 1′½″ (31.8 cm); Diameter: 10¾″ (27.3 cm)
Open vases: Height: 11⅛″ (28.3 cm); Diameter: 5″ (12.7 cm)
Accession number 72.DE.72.1–5

PROVENANCE

Dukes of Northumberland. Probably sold circa 1910.

Ralph Chait, New York and London, 1970's.

Neil Sellin, New York, 1972.

Purchased by J. Paul Getty, 1972

259 PAIR OF LIDDED VASES
Chinese, Kangxi (1662–1722)
Maker unknown
Hard paste porcelain; blue enamel decoration
No marks
Height: 1′5″ (43.2 cm); Diameter: 10″ (25.4 cm)
Accession number 72.DE.73.1–2

PROVENANCE

Dukes of Northumberland. Probably sold circa 1910.

Ralph Chait, New York and London, 1970's.

Neil Sellin, New York, 1972.

Purchased by J. Paul Getty, 1972.

260

261

260 PAIR OF LIDDED VASES
Chinese, Yongzheng, circa 1730
Maker unknown
Hard paste porcelain; colored enamel decoration
Each vase bears a label, pasted within the lip, printed with FONTHILL HEIRLOOMS and with the inventory number $\frac{670}{3}$.
Height: 2′¾″ (62.9 cm); Diameter: 1′1″ (33.0 cm)
Accession number 72.DE.62.1–2

PROVENANCE

Possibly taken from the Summer Palace, Beijing, when it was sacked in 1860, and brought to England by Lord Lock of Drylaw.

Alfred Morrison, Fonthill House, Wiltshire.

John Greville Morrison, Lord Margadale of Islay, Fonthill House, by descent. Sold, Christie's, London, June 5, 1972, lot 29.

Purchased at that sale by J. Paul Getty.

261 FIGURE OF AN ELEPHANT
Chinese, Qianlong (1736–1795)
Maker unknown
Hard paste porcelain; colored enamel decoration; gilding
No marks
Height: 1′9¾″ (55.2 cm); Width: 1′1½″ (34.2 cm); Depth: 10″ (25.4 cm)
Accession number 72.DE.61

PROVENANCE

George Christie. Sold, Christie's, London, June 5, 1972, lot 24.

Purchased at that sale by J. Paul Getty.

ENGLISH
Decorative Arts

262

CABINETS

262 CABINET ON STAND

Cabinet: Dutch, late seventeenth century
Stand: English, late seventeenth century
Makers unknown
Painted and silvered wood; brass mounts
No marks
Cabinet: Height: 2′8¼″ (82.0 cm); Width: 3′3 5/16″ (99.8 cm); Depth: 1′6½″ (46.9 cm)
Stand: Height: 2′7¾″ (80.6 cm); Width: 3′10½″ (118.1 cm); Depth: 1′10″ (55.8 cm)
Accession number 78.DA.113

PROVENANCE

A. Cook, London, 1961.

Purchased by J. Paul Getty, 1961.

BIBLIOGRAPHY

R. W. P. Luff, "Oriental Lacquer and English Japan. Some Cabinets from the Collection of Mr. J. Paul Getty at Sutton Place, Surrey," *Antique Collector*, December 1962, p. 257, illus.

263

263 CABINET ON STAND

Cabinet: Japanese, mid-seventeenth century
Stand: English, late seventeenth century
Makers unknown
Lacquered and silvered wood; brass mounts
No marks
Cabinet: Height: 1′11½″ (59.6 cm); Width: 2′6″ (76.2 cm); Depth: 1′5⅞″ (45.4 cm)
Stand: Height: 2′8¼″ (81.9 cm); Width: 2′7½″ (80.0 cm); Depth: 1′9½″ (54.6 cm)
Accession number 78.DA.116

PROVENANCE

Lord Plender of Sunridge, England.

R. W. Symonds, London.

Lady Hague. Sold, Sotheby's, London, June 23, 1961, lot 114.

Purchased at that sale by J. Paul Getty.

BIBLIOGRAPHY

R. W. Symonds, *Old English Walnut and Lacquer Furniture*, 1921, illus. opposite frontispiece.

R. W. Symonds, "English Lacquer Cabinets," *Old Furniture Magazine*, vol. 3, no. 34, 1928, illus. p. 139.

R. W. Symonds, "Englische Möbel der Sammlung von Plender," *Pantheon*, July 1930, pp. 332–337.

R. W. Symonds, "Furniture in the Collection of Lord Plender," *Apollo*, December 1934, pp. 305–311, illus. p. 309.

R. W. Symonds, "Furniture from the Indies," *Connoisseur*, May 1934, illus. p. 282.

R. W. Symonds, "The Age of Charles II," *Connoisseur*, June 1943, illus. p. 117.

R. W. Symonds, "An English Japan Cabinet," *Country Life*, June 1956, illus. p. 1280.

264 PAIR OF CABINETS ON STANDS

English, circa 1690–1700
Maker unknown
Painted and silvered wood; brass mounts
No marks
Cabinets: Height: 2′8½″ (82.5 cm); Width: 3′1″ (93.9 cm); Depth: 1′7½″ (49.5 cm)
Stands: Height: 2′7¼″ (79.3 cm); Width: 3′5¼″ (104.7 cm); Depth: 1′11½″ (59.6 cm)
Accession number 78.DA.117

PROVENANCE

Mrs. Geoffrey Hart, London.

Purchased by J. Paul Getty, 1961.

EXHIBITIONS

London. Victoria and Albert Museum, *The Orange and the Rose*, October 1964–January 1965, no. 220 (one of the pair).

BIBLIOGRAPHY

R. W. Symonds, "The City of Westminster and Its Furniture Makers," *Connoisseur*, July 1937, pp. 3–9, illus. pp. 2, 9.

R. W. Symonds, "The Age of Charles II," *Connoisseur*, June 1943, illus. p. 125.

Horace Shipp, "At Home and Its Treasures–Mrs. Geoffrey Hart's Collection at Hyde Park Gardens," *Apollo*, December 1955, illus. p. 181.

264a

264b

265

SEAT FURNITURE

265 PAIR OF ARMCHAIRS
London, circa 1740–1745
In the style of William Bradshaw
Carved pine; parcel-gilt; modern silk upholstery
No marks
Height: 3′2½″ (97.9 cm); Width: 2′3¼″ (69.3 cm); Depth: 2′7⅜″ (79.7 cm)
Accession number 78.DA.96.1–2

PROVENANCE

R. W. Miller. Sold, Christie's, London, January 21, 1960, lot 43, to Pallott.

A. Cook, London.

Purchased by J. Paul Getty, 1960.

COMMENTARY

Another pair of armchairs from this set was sold at auction in London in 1960 and again in New York in 1983.

266

MIRROR

266 MIRROR
London, circa 1745
Attributed to Matthias Lock
Carved and gilded pine details on oak support
No marks
Height: 7′ (213.3 cm); Width: 4′2″ (127.0 cm)
Accession number 78.DH.243

PROVENANCE

Dukes of Westminster.

Frank Partridge Ltd., London, 1967.

Purchased by J. Paul Getty, 1967.

267

268

269

SILVER
All objects in this section are from the estate of J. Paul Getty.

267 PAIR OF CANDLESTICKS
London, 1703
By John Barnard
Silver
Each candlestick marked with leopard's head erased, Britannia standard mark, date letter G for 1703, and maker's mark BA. Engraved with initials M.B.
Height: 6¼" (15.8 cm); Width: 4⅜" (11.2 cm)
Accession number 78.DG.134.1–2

---

268 MONTEITH
London, 1705
By John Rand
Silver
Marked with lion's head erased, Britannia standard mark, date letter J for 1705, and maker's mark Ra. Engraved with an unidentified coat of arms.
Height: 10" (25.5 cm); Diameter: 1′2½″ (36.8 cm)
Accession number 78.DG.149

EXHIBITIONS

Los Angeles. Los Angeles County Museum of Art, on loan, 1982–present.

---

269 PAIR OF SUGAR CASTORS
London, 1730
By Paul de Lamerie
Silver gilt
Bodies and lids marked with lion's head erased, Britannia standard mark, date letter P for 1730, and maker's mark LA. Engraved *1730, VIº2=27–12*, and Vº1–27; also engraved with Garter coat of arms and Howard crest.
Height: 9⅜" (23.8 cm); Diameter: 3⅞" (9.9 cm)
Accession number 78.DG.180.1–2

PROVENANCE

Dukes of Northumberland.

S. J. Phillips, London.

EXHIBITIONS

Minneapolis. The Minneapolis Institute of Arts, on loan, 1980–1981.

Los Angeles. Los Angeles County Museum of Art, on loan, 1982–present.

270

270 SALT

London, 1734
By Paul de Lamerie
Silver
Marked with lion passant, leopard's head crowned, date letter T for 1734, and maker's mark PL under a crown. Engraved with a crest of a bull under a crown.
Height: 2⅜″ (5.9 cm); Width: 4¼″ (10.7 cm)
Accession number 78.DG.179

COMMENTARY

This salt is en suite with No. 280 in this handbook, which is by Thomas Pitts.

271

271 CAKE BASKET

London, 1741
By Peter Archambo
Silver
Marked with lion passant, leopard's head crowned, date letter F for 1741, and maker's mark PA. Engraved with the arms of Gordon.
Height: 9¼″ (23.5 cm); Width: 1′2¼″ (36.2 cm); Depth: 1′¼″ (31.2 cm)
Accession number 78.DG.136

PROVENANCE

(?) Made for Charles, 2nd Duke of Richmond and Lennox.

Dukes of Richmond and Gordon, Goodwood House, Sussex, by descent. Sold, circa 1938.

EXHIBITIONS

Minneapolis. The Minneapolis Institute of Arts, on loan, 1980–1981.

272

272 TWO-HANDLED CUP AND COVER

London, 1749
By Peter Archambo and Peter Meure
Silver gilt
Body and lid marked with lion passant, leopard's head crowned, date letter O for 1749, and makers' marks PA and PM. Engraved on body with an unidentified coat of arms.
Height: 5⅛″ (13.1 cm); Width: 1′ (30.5 cm); Depth: 6½″ (16.6 cm)
Accession number 78.DG.156

EXHIBITIONS

Minneapolis. The Minneapolis Institute of Arts, on loan, 1980–1981.

273

273 PAIR OF SAUCEBOATS
London, 1749
Attributed to John Swift
Silver
Each sauceboat marked with lion passant, leopard's head crowned, date letter O for 1749, and rubbed maker's mark, probably for John Swift. Engraved with an unidentified emblem.
Height: 5½″ (13.9 cm); Width: 7¾″ (19.6 cm); Depth: 4⅛″ (10.5 cm)
Accession number 78.DG.131.1–2

274

274 PAIR OF SALTS
London, 1756
By David Hennell
Silver
Each salt marked with date letter A for 1756 and maker's mark D.H.
Height: 2⅛″ (5.4 cm); Width: 3⅞″ (9.8 cm); Depth: 3¾″ (9.5 cm)
Accession number 78.DG.162.1–2

275

275 TWO PAIRS OF SALTS WITH FOUR SALT SPOONS
London, 1760–1761
By David Hennell
Silver
Each salt marked with lion passant, leopard's head crowned, and maker's mark DH. One pair marked with the date letter E for 1760, the other pair with F for 1761. Spoons engraved with an unidentified crest.
Height: 2″ (5.1 cm); Width: 3⅞″ (9.8 cm); Depth: 3½″ (8.9 cm)
Accession number 81.DG.14.1–8

276

276 PAIR OF SAUCEBOATS
London, 1767
By George Hunter
Silver
Each sauceboat marked with lion passant, leopard's head crowned, date letter M for 1767, and maker's mark GH. The three feet engraved W, L, and A, respectively.
Height: 3⅛″ (8.1 cm); Width: 4⅞″ (12.3 cm); Depth: 2¾″ (7.0 cm)
Accession number 78.DG.137.1–2

277

278

277 MUSTARD POT
London, 1767
By John Langford and John Sibelle
Silver
Body marked with lion passant, leopard's head crowned, date letter M for 1767, and makers' marks IL and IS in a quatrefoil. Engraved with a crest. Lid marked with lion passant.
Height: 2 11/16" (6.8 cm); Width: 3" (7.8 cm); Depth: 2" (5.0 cm)
Accession number 78.DG.133

278 SUGAR CASTOR
London, 1769
Maker unknown
Silver
Body and lid marked with lion passant and maker's mark I D . IM. Body also marked with leopard's head crowned and date letter O for 1769.
Height: 6 1/2" (16.4 cm); Diameter: 2 1/4" (5.8 cm)
Accession number 78.DG.166

279 PAIR OF SAUCEBOATS
London, 1778
By Thomas Smith
Silver
Each sauceboat marked with lion passant, leopard's head crowned, date letter C for 1778, and maker's mark TS.
Height: 5 3/4" (14.5 cm); Width: 7 1/2" (19.1 cm); Depth: 3 7/8" (9.9 cm)
Accession number 78.DG.174.1–2

279

280

280 SALT
London, 1787
By Thomas Pitts
Silver
Marked with lion passant, leopard's head crowned, sovereign's head, date letter M for 1787, and maker's mark TP. Engraved with a crest of a bull under a crown.
Height: 2 3/8" (6.2 cm); Diameter: 4 1/4" (10.8 cm)
Accession number 78.DG.178

COMMENTARY

This salt is en suite with No. 270 in this handbook, which is by Paul de Lamerie.

281

281 SUGAR CASTOR
London, 1789 (possibly 1809)
By Samuel Davenport
Silver
Body and lid marked with lion passant and maker's mark SD. Body also marked with leopard's head crowned and date letter O for 1789 or possibly 1809.
Height: 5⅝″ (14.2 cm); Diameter: 2⅜″ (6.1 cm)
Accession number 78.DG.167

282

282 SALVER
London, 1801
By John Wakelin and Robert Garrard
Silver
Marked with lion passant, leopard's head crowned, sovereign's head, date letter F for 1801, and makers' marks IW over RG. Engraved with the coat of arms of the Marquess of Exeter and *COR UNUM VIA UNA* on front.
Height: 1¾″ (4.6 cm); Diameter: 1′7¼″ (48.9 cm)
Accession number 78.DG.175

PROVENANCE

Henry, 1st Marquess of Exeter. Sold by his eventual heirs, Christie's, London, July 17, 1959, lot 47.

283

283 SUGAR CASTOR
London, 1803
Maker unknown
Silver
Body marked with lion passant, leopard's head crowned, sovereign's head, date letter H for 1803, and a rubbed maker's mark. Lid marked with lion passant.
Height: 6″ (15.3 cm); Diameter: 2⅛″ (5.3 cm)
Accession number 78.DG.168

284

284 MUSTARD POT
London, 1804
By Robert and Samuel Hennell
Silver
Body and lid marked with lion passant and makers' marks RH over SH. Body also marked with leopard's head crowned, sovereign's head, date letter I for 1804, and W. Body engraved with an unidentified crest.
Height: 3½″ (8.9 cm); Width: 4½″ (11.5 cm); Depth: 2⅝″ (6.7 cm)
Accession number 78.DG.183

285

285 PAIR OF MEAT DISHES
London, 1804
By William Simmons
Silver
Each dish marked with lion passant, leopard's head crowned, sovereign's head, date letter I for 1804, and maker's mark W.S. Each engraved on borders with an unidentified crest and a coat of arms.
Height: 1 7/16″ (3.6 cm); Width: 1′9 5/16″ (54.2 cm); Depth: 1′3⅝″ (39.6 cm)
Accession number 78.DG.172.1–2

286

286 PAIR OF LIDDED TUREENS, LINERS, AND STANDS
London, 1807
By Paul Storr
Silver
Marked as follows:
78.DG.130.1—Body and stand: Lion passant, leopard's head crowned, sovereign's head, date letter M for 1807, and maker's mark PS. Lid: Lion passant, date letter M, maker's mark PS, and stamped numeral 23. Liner: Lion passant, sovereign's head, date letter M, and maker's mark PS.

78.DG.130.2—Body and stand: Lion passant, leopard's head crowned, sovereign's head, date letter M, maker's mark PS. Lid: Lion passant, date letter M, maker's mark PS, and stamped numeral 2. Liner: Lion passant, sovereign's head, date letter M, and maker's mark PS.

Each tureen engraved on body with the arms of the dukes of Richmond and Gordon, and with the motto *EN LA ROSE LE FLEURIE.*
Height: 11¼″ (28.6 cm); Width: 1′6″ (45.7 cm); Depth: 1′¾″ (32.4 cm)
Accession number 78.DG.130.1–2

PROVENANCE

Charles, 4th Duke of Richmond and Lennox (succeeded 1806; Lord Lieutenant of Ireland 1807–1813).

Dukes of Richmond and Gordon, Goodwood House, Sussex, by descent. Sold, circa 1938.

EXHIBITIONS

Minneapolis. The Minneapolis Institute of Arts, on loan, 1980–1981.

Williamstown, Massachusetts. Sterling and Francine Clark Art Institute, on loan, 1983–present.

287

287 MUSTARD POT
London, 1809
By Rebecca Emes and Edward Barnard
Silver
Body and lid marked with lion passant. Lid also marked with date letter O for 1809; body, with leopard's head crowned, sovereign's head, and makers' marks RE over EB.
Height: 3³⁄₈" (8.7 cm); Width: 3⁷⁄₈" (9.8 cm); Depth: 2⁷⁄₈" (7.3 cm)
Accession number 78.DG.184

288

288 PAIR OF SALVERS
London, 1811
By William Bennett
Silver
Each salver marked with lion passant, leopard's head crowned, sovereign's head, date letter Q for 1811, and maker's mark WB. Each engraved with an unidentified coat of arms.
Height: 1⁵⁄₁₆" (3.3 cm); Width: 11⁷⁄₁₆" (29.1 cm); Depth: 9¹⁄₈" (23.1 cm)
Accession number 78.DG.169.1–2

289

289 PAIR OF COVERED DISHES
London, 1811
By Thomas Robins
Silver
Marked variously on bodies, lids, and handle with lion passant, leopard's head crowned, sovereign's head, date letter Q for 1811, maker's mark *TR* in script, and stamped numeral 3. Lids engraved with cornucopias.
Height: 5⁷⁄₈" (14.9 cm); Width: 11³⁄₈" (28.8 cm); Depth: 9¼" (23.4 cm)
Accession number 78.DG.173.1–2

290

290 ROSEWATER DISH
London, 1812
By Robert Garrard
Silver gilt
Marked with lion passant, leopard's head crowned, sovereign's head, date letter R for 1812, and maker's mark RG.
Height: 1¾" (4.3 cm); Diameter: 1′10⁷⁄₈" (58.1 cm)
Accession number 78.DG.161

291

291 MUSTARD POT
London, 1813
By Richard Sibley
Silver
Body and lid marked with lion passant, date letter S for 1813, and maker's mark RS. Body also marked with leopard's head crowned and sovereign's head. Lid engraved with an unidentified crest of a dog.
Height: 2⁷⁄₁₆" (6.2 cm); Width: 4¹⁄₈" (10.4 cm); Depth: 2⁷⁄₈" (7.2 cm)
Accession number 78.DG.165

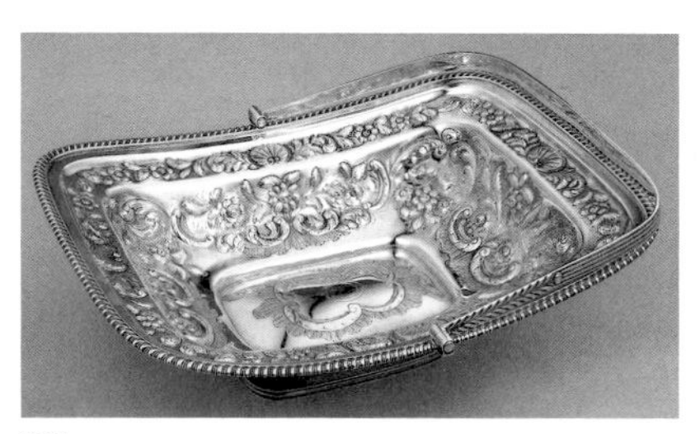

292

292 CAKE BASKET
London, 1815
By William Bateman
Silver
Body marked with lion passant, leopard's head crowned, sovereign's head, and date letter U for 1815. Body and handle marked with maker's mark WB.
Height: 10" (25.5 cm); Width: 1'1¼" (33.7 cm); Depth: 11¹⁄₁₆" (28.1 cm)
Accession number 78.DG.135

293

293 SALVER
London, 1821
By Rebecca Emes and Edward Barnard
Silver gilt
Marked with lion passant, leopard's head crowned, sovereign's head, date letter F for 1821, and makers' marks RE over EB. Engraved with Willmot-Horton coat of arms, showing Willmot-Horton impaling Boyce and the motto *QUOD VULT VALDE VULT.*
Height: 3⁵⁄₁₆" (8.4 cm); Diameter: 1'10⅝" (57.4 cm)
Accession number 78.DG.138

PROVENANCE

Sir George Lewis Willmot-Horton, 5th Bt., England.

294

294 PAIR OF MEAT DISHES
London, 1826
By Barak Mewburn
Silver
Each dish marked with lion passant, leopard's head, sovereign's head, date letter L for 1826, and maker's mark BM under a crown. Engraved on borders with an unidentified coat of arms.
Height: 1" (2.5 cm); Width: 1'3⁷⁄₁₆" (39.2 cm); Depth: 11¼" (28.5 cm)
Accession number 78.DG.171.1–2

295

295 MUSTARD POT
London, 1827
By Charles Fox
Silver
Body and lid marked with lion passant, date letter M for 1827, and maker's mark CF. Body also marked with a leopard's head erased and sovereign's head, and engraved with an unidentified crest of a bird.
Height: 2¾" (6.9 cm); Width: 3¾" (9.5 cm); Depth: 2¹⁵⁄₁₆" (7.5 cm)
Accession number 78.DG.164

296

296 EWER
London, 1827
By Charles Fox
Silver gilt
Marked with lion passant, leopard's head, sovereign's head, date letter M for 1827, and maker's mark CF. Engraved with an unidentified crest in two places.
Height: 10¾″ (27.5 cm); Width: 10½″ (26.5 cm); Depth: 5⅝″ (14.2 cm)
Accession number 78.DG.152

297

297 COFFEE POT
London, 1827
By Robert Garrard II
Silver; wooden handle
Body and lid marked with a lion passant, date letter M for 1827, and maker's mark RG under a crown. Body also marked with leopard's head crowned, sovereign's head, and *GARRARD ANTON STREET LONDON.*
Height: 11⅛″ (28.1 cm); Width: 8⅛″ (20.7 cm); Depth: 4¾″ (12.1 cm)
Accession number 78.DG.170

298

298 MUSTARD POT
London, 1828
By Richard Williams Atkins and William Nathaniel Somersall
Silver
Body and lid marked with lion passant, date letter N for 1828, and maker's mark RA. Body also marked with leopard's head crowned.
Height: 2⅞″ (7.3 cm); Width: 4¼″ (10.6 cm); Depth: 3″ (7.7 cm)
Accession number 78.DG.163

299

299 PAIR OF CANDELABRA
London, 1870
By Robert Garrard II
Silver gilt
Marked variously with lion passant, leopard's head crowned, sovereign's head, date letter P for 1870, and maker's mark RG.
Height: 1′10½″ (57.2 cm); Width: 1′4½″ (41.9 cm); Depth: 5 15/16″ (15.1 cm)
Accession number 78.DG.143.1–2

300

300 PAIR OF CANDELABRA
London, 1897
By Lambert
Silver gilt
Marked with lion passant, leopard's head erased, date letter B for 1897, maker's mark LG, and *LAMBERT COVENTRY STREET.*
Height: 2′½″ (62.3 cm); Width: 1′5¼″ (43.8 cm)
Accession number 78.DG.150.1–2

301

IRISH SILVER

301 COVERED CUP
Dublin, 1829
By James Fray
Silver
Body marked with a crowned harp, sovereign's head, figure of Hibernia, date letter I, and maker's mark IF. Lid marked with sovereign's head. Body engraved with an initial resembling a P within a crescent and a baron's coronet with the inscription *To the Earl & Countess of Erroll from Captain and Lady Agnes Byng. 7th September 1829.*
Height: 1′1″ (33.0 cm); Width: 9½″ (24.1 cm); Depth: 5⅜″ (13.6 cm)
Accession number 78.DG.139

PROVENANCE

William and Elizabeth, 1st Earl and Countess of Erroll.

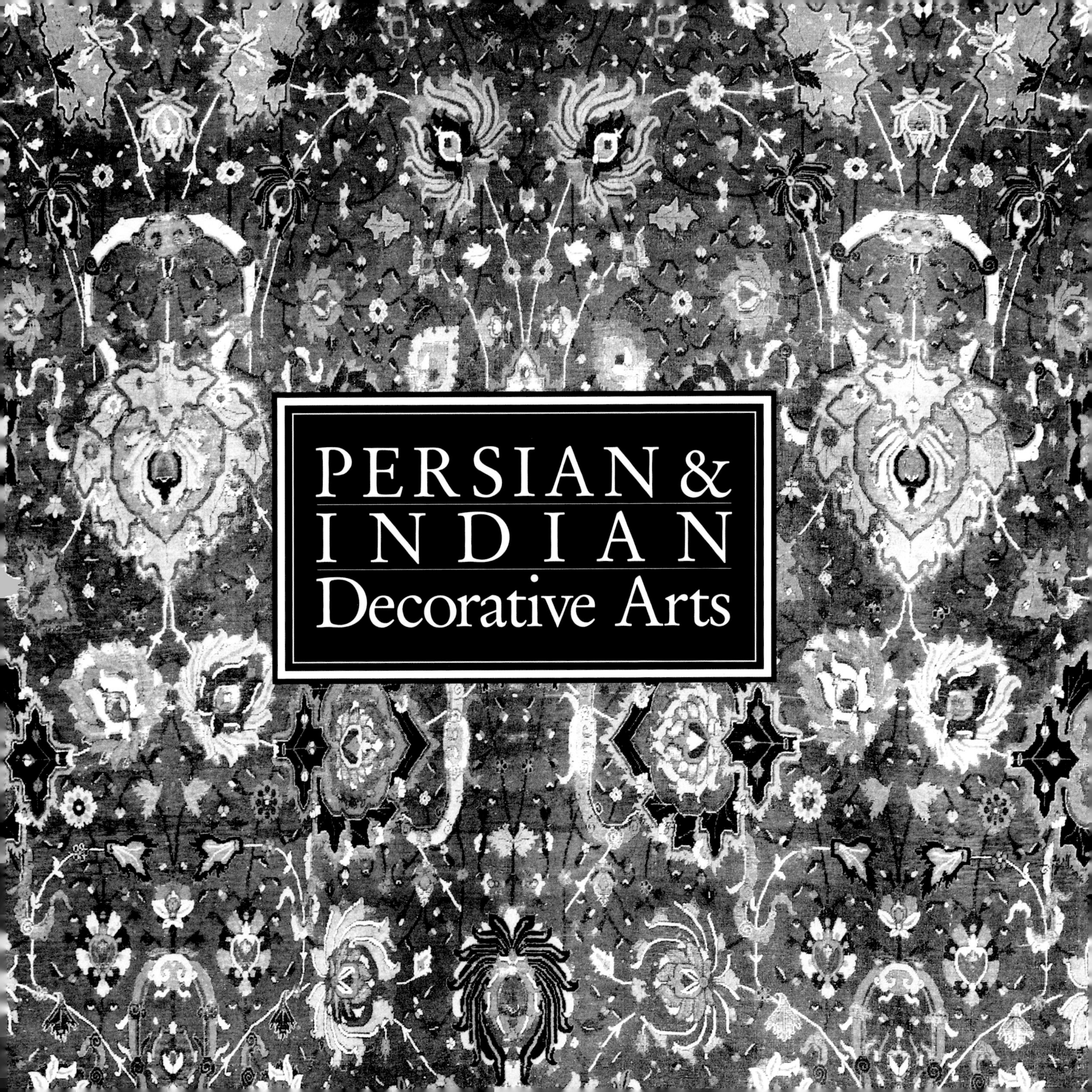
PERSIAN &
INDIAN
Decorative Arts

302

303
This photograph shows the full width of the carpet and over eleven feet of its length.

304

PERSIAN CARPETS

302 "POLONAISE" CARPET
Isfahan, circa 1600–1625
Silk with metallic thread
Length: 6′11″ (211 cm); Width: 4′10″ (147 cm)
Accession number 78.DC.83

PROVENANCE

Charles T. Yerkes, New York. Sold, American Art Association, New York, April 12, 1919, lot 212, to D. G. Kelekian.

Mortimer L. Schiff, New York. Sold, by his heir, John L. Schiff, Parke Bernet, New York, April 8, 1939, lot 69.

Purchased by J. Paul Getty.

303 CARPET
Herāt or Isfahan, late sixteenth century
Wool
Length: 25′10¼″ (788 cm); Width: 10′3¼″ (313 cm)
Accession number 78.DC.91

PROVENANCE

Hagop Kevorkian. Sold, Sotheby's, London, December 5, 1969, lot 20.

Purchased at that sale by J. Paul Getty.

EXHIBITIONS

New York. The Metropolitan Museum of Art, *Collection of Rare and Magnificent Oriental Carpets*, 1966, no. 5.

304 CARPET
Isfahan, circa 1600
Wool
Length: 26′6⅛″ (808 cm); Width: 11′5″ (348 cm)
Accession number 71.DC.75

PROVENANCE

Duveen Brothers, New York

Judge Elbert H. Gary, New York. Sold, American Art Association, New York, April 21, 1928, lot 304.

Martha Baird (Mrs. John D. Rockefeller, Jr.). Sold, Parke Bernet, New York, October 23, 1971, lot 728.

Purchased at that sale by J. Paul Getty.

305

305 "POLONAISE" CARPET

Isfahan, circa 1600–1625
Silk with metallic thread
Length: 6′7⅛″ (201 cm); Width: 4′7⅛″ (140 cm)
Accession number 70.DC.57

PROVENANCE

Rothschild collection, Paris.

Hagop Kevorkian, before 1947. Sold, Sotheby's, London, December 5, 1969, lot 6.

Purchased by J. Paul Getty.

EXHIBITIONS

Chicago. The Art Institute of Chicago, *An Exhibition of Antique Oriental Rugs*, February–March 1947, ex. cat., no. 44.

New York. The Metropolitan Museum of Art, *Collection of Rare and Magnificent Oriental Carpets*, 1966, no. 4.

BIBLIOGRAPHY

Maurice S. Dimand, "Persian Silk Carpets," *Connoisseur*, July 1975, p. 205, illus.

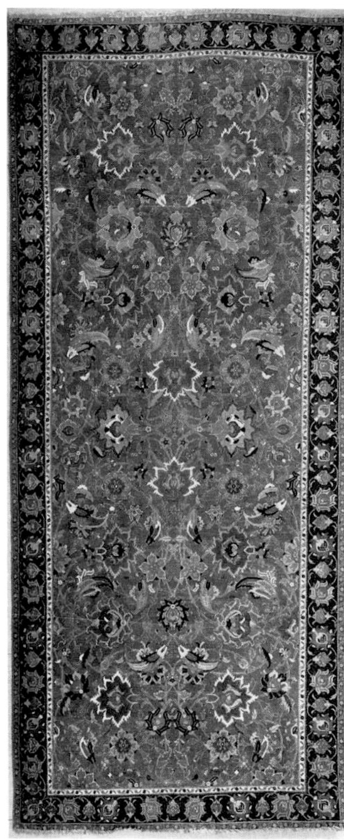

306

306 CARPET

Herāt or Isfahan, late sixteenth or early seventeenth century
Wool
Length: 13′8⅛″ (417 cm); Width: 5′9″ (175 cm)
Accession number 70.DC.65

PROVENANCE

J. Pierpont Morgan, New York.

Mortimer L. Schiff, New York. Sold by his heir, John L. Schiff, Christie's, London, June 22, 1938, lot 82.

Purchased at that sale by J. Paul Getty.

307

307 CARPET

Herāt or Isfahan, circa 1600
Wool
Length: 13′6 3⁄16″ (412 cm); Width: 5′9″ (175 cm)
Accession number 70.DC.66

PROVENANCE

Mortimer L. Schiff, New York. Sold by his heir, John L. Schiff, Christie's, London, June 22, 1938, lot 81.

Purchased at that sale by J. Paul Getty.

308

308 "POLONAISE" CARPET
Kāshān, circa 1620
Silk with metallic thread
Length: 9′1″ (277 cm); Width: 5′7″ (170 cm)
Accession number 68.DC.6

PROVENANCE

Baron Adolphe de Rothschild, Paris. Sold, Palais Galliera, Paris, March 18, 1968, lot 104.

Purchased at that sale by J. Paul Getty.

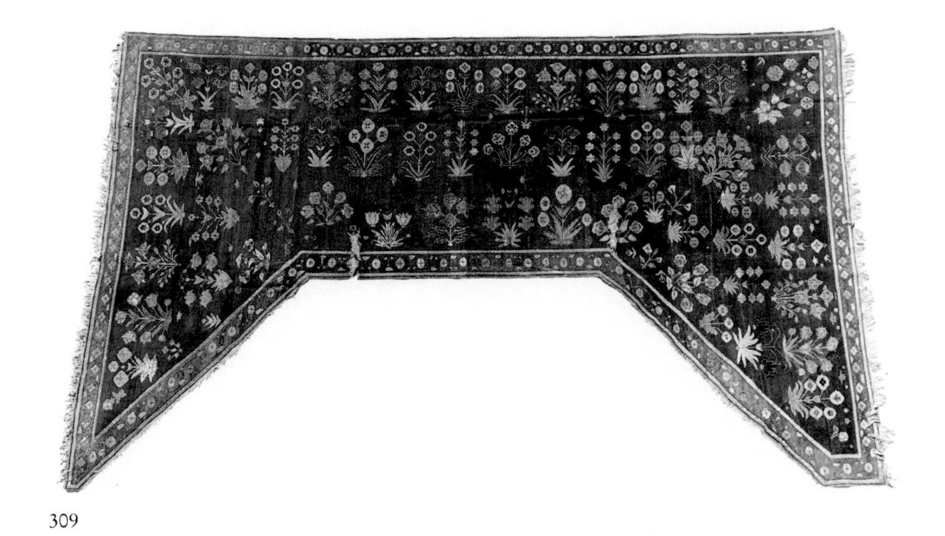

309

INDIAN CARPETS

309 PAIR OF SHAPED CARPETS
Mughal, circa 1628–1658
Wool
Length: 15′3″ (465 cm); Width: (max.) 10′4″ (315 cm), (min.) 5′1″ (155 cm)
Accession number 70.DC.58.1–2

PROVENANCE

Hagop Kevorkian. Sold, Sotheby's, London, December 5, 1969, lot 12.

Purchased at that sale by J. Paul Getty.

EXHIBITIONS

New York. The Metropolitan Museum of Art, *Collection of Rare and Magnificent Oriental Carpets*, 1966, nos. 26, 27.

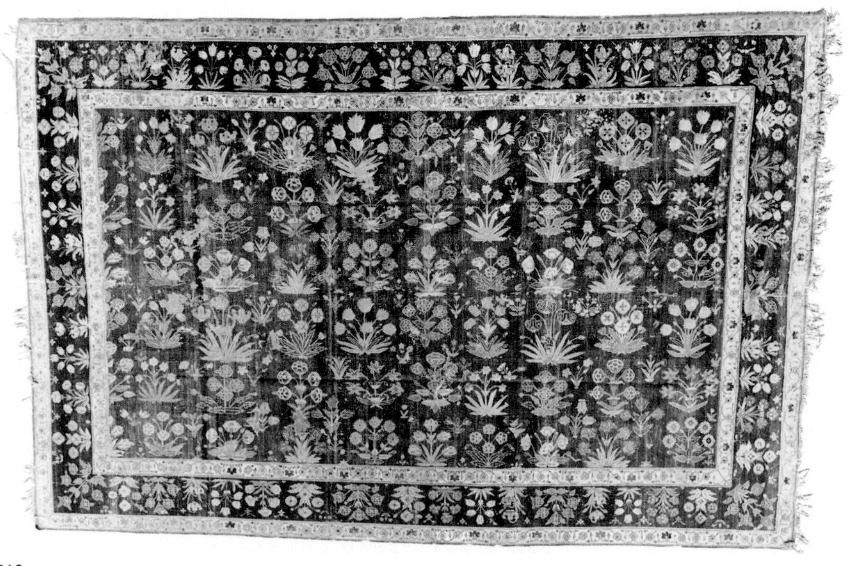

310

311

310 CARPET
Mughal, circa 1628–1658
Wool
Length: 15′ (457 cm); Width: 9′10″ (300 cm)
Accession number 70.DC.59

PROVENANCE

Hagop Kevorkian. Sold, Sotheby's, London, December 5, 1969, lot 13.

Purchased at that sale by J. Paul Getty.

EXHIBITIONS

New York. The Metropolitan Museum of Art, *Collection of Rare and Magnificent Oriental Carpets*, 1966, no. 25.

311 HUNTING CARPET
Lahore, circa 1625
Wool
Length: 6′6″ (198 cm); Width: 4′8″ (142 cm)
Accession number 70.DC.64

PROVENANCE

Guillaume, marquis de Biron, Paris, circa 1914.

William Salomon, Paris. Sold, American Art Association, New York, April 6, 1923, lot 543, to Duveen.

Duveen Brothers, New York.

C. J. Seibert, New York. Sold, Parke Bernet, New York, April 8, 1939, lot 67.

J. Paul Getty.

INDEXES

INDEX OF MAKERS

Please note: references are to entry numbers, not page numbers.

A

Abbiati, Francesco (cabinetmaker; active second half of the eighteenth century), 255

Archambo, Peter (silversmith; active from 1720, in partnership with Peter Meure [q.v.] 1749–1755, died 1767), 271, 272

Asselin, Charles-Eloi (Sèvres painter; active 1765–1798 and 1800–1804), 182

Atkins, Richard Williams (silversmith; active 1824–after 1830), 298

Aubusson Manufactory, 229

Aucoq, A. (silversmith; active late nineteenth century), 158

Audran, Claude, III (painter and designer; born 1658, died 1734), 215

Audran, Michel (Gobelins *entrepreneur;* born 1701, died 1771), 223

Auguste, Henry (silversmith; *maître* 1785, died 1816), 236

Auguste, Robert-Joseph (silversmith; born circa 1723, *maître* 1757, died 1805), 154, 233, 235

Avisse, Jean (*menuisier;* born 1723, *maître* 1745, died after 1796), 97

B

Bardet (Sèvres painter; active 1749 and 1751–1758), 160

Bardin (chaser; active last quarter of the eighteenth century), 16

Barnard, Edward (silversmith; born 1767, active 1808–1828, died circa 1853–1855), 287, 293

Barnard, John, I (silversmith; active 1685–1720), 267

Bateman, William, I (silversmith; born 1774, active 1799–circa 1840, died 1850), 292

Baudouin *père* (Sèvres gilder; active 1750–1800), 47

Baumhauer, Gaspard-Joseph (*ébéniste*; born 1747, active from 1760's), 13

Baumhauer, Joseph (*ébéniste; ébéniste privilégié du Roi* by 1767, died 1772), 13, 29, 60

Beauvais Manufactory, 213, 216–222

Belin de Fontenay, Jean-Baptiste (painter; born 1653, died 1715), 213, 227

Bellangé, Alexandre-Louis (*ébéniste*; born 1799, died 1863), 51

Bellanger, François-Joseph (architect; born 1744, *dessinateur des Menus Plaisirs* 1767, died 1818), 135

Beneman, Guillaume (*ébéniste*; worked as an *artisan libre*, employed by the Garde-Meuble de la Couronne from 1784, *maître* 1785, died after 1811), 16

Bennett, William (silversmith; active from 1796, died 1825), 288

Besnier, Nicolas (silversmith; *orfèvre du Roi* 1715; administrator of the Beauvais Manufactory 1734–1754), 217–219

Beurdeley, Louis-Auguste-Alfred (furniture maker and *bronzier;* born 1808, died 1882), 207

Boucault, Jean (*menuisier*; born circa 1705, *maître* 1728, died 1786), 100

Boucher, François (painter; born 1703, designer at the Beauvais Manufactory from 1734, supervisor at the Gobelins Manufactory from 1754, died 1770), 75, 158, 161, 162, 216–222, 224, 225

Boulle, André-Charles (*ébéniste*; born 1642, active by 1664, *ébéniste du Roi* 1672, died 1732), 5, 6, 20, 77–80, 125, 128

Boulle *fils:* either André-Charles Boulle II, known as Boulle de Sève (*ébéniste*; born 1685, died 1745), or Charles-Joseph Boulle (*ébéniste*; born 1688, died 1754), 58, 59

Bradshaw, William (chairmaker; active 1736–1745), 265

Buteux, Charles, *l'aîné* (Sèvres painter; born 1719, active 1756–1782, died 1782), 165

C

Caffiéri, Jacques (*bronzier;* born 1678, *maître* 1714, *fondeur-ciseleur des Bâtiments du Roi* 1736, died 1755), 87, 130

Caffiéri, Philippe (*bronzier;* born 1714, *maître* by 1743, *sculpteur-ciseleur ordinaire du Roi* 1755, died 1774), 133

Capelle (Sèvres painter; born circa 1722, active 1746–1800), 179

Capin (upholsterer to the court; active second half of the eighteenth century), 99, 103

Carlin, Martin (*ébéniste*; born circa 1730, *maître* 1766, died 1785), 46, 48, 68–70, 73

Cauvet, Gilles-Pierre (designer; born 1731, died 1788), 103

Chabry, Etienne-Jean, *fils* (Sèvres painter; born before 1749, active 1765–1787), 177

Chaillot (painter; active second half of the eighteenth century), 104

Chantilly Manufactory, 84, 191

Chatard (painter and gilder; active by 1785–after 1806), 103

Chaudron (gilder; active second half of the eighteenth century), 103

Chauveaux, Jean, *le jeune* (Sèvres gilder; active 1765–1802), 178

Chauveaux, Michel-Barnabé, *l'aîné* (Sèvres painter and gilder; born circa 1729, active 1753–1788), 177

Cheret, Jean-Baptiste-François (silversmith; *maître* 1759, died after 1791), 153

Clodion (sculptor; born 1738, died 1814), 50

Cochois, Charles-Michel (*ébéniste; maître* circa 1730, died 1764), 20

Coudray, Michel-Dorothé (Sèvres molder; born 1718, active 1753–1775, died 1775), 175

Coypel, Charles-Antoine (painter; born 1694, *premier peintre du Roi* 1747, died 1752), 223

Cressent, Charles (sculptor and *ébéniste*; born 1685, *ébéniste* to the duc d'Orléans 1719, died 1768), 22, 35, 81–83, 140

Cuvellier, E. J. (*ébéniste; maître* 1753), 10

Cuvilliés, François de (architect and designer; born circa 1695, died 1768), 238

D

Dardet, Claude-Gabriel (silversmith; *maître* 1715), 149

Davenport, Samuel (silversmith; active 1786–circa 1813), 281

Delafosse, Jean-Charles (architect and designer; born 1734, died 1789), 72, 124

Delorme, Adrien-Faizelot (*ébéniste; maître* 1748, died after 1783), 30, 65

Desforges, Jean (*ébéniste; maître* 1739), 25, 27

Desportes, Alexandre-François (painter; born 1661, died 1743), 227, 228

Dietrich, Joachim (sculptor; died 1753), 238

Dieu, Jean-Jacques (Sèvres painter and gilder; active 1777–1790, 1794–1798, and 1803–1810), 183

Digue (barometer maker; dates unknown), 81

Dodin, Charles-Nicolas (Sèvres painter; born 1734, active 1754–1803, died 1803), 75, 166–168, 170

Doirat, Etienne (*ébéniste*; born circa 1670, died 1732), 21

Dominicé, J.-F. (clockmaker; active first half of the eighteenth century), 80

Dubois, Jacques (*ébéniste*; born circa 1693, *maître* 1742, died 1763), 38, 39, 43

Dubois, René (*ébéniste*; born 1737, *maître* 1754, *ébéniste de la Reine* 1779, died 1799), 45

Dufresne, François-Firmin (Sèvres *tourneur* and *répareur;* born 1739, active 1756–1767, died 1769), 169

Dugourc, Jean-Démosthène (designer; born 1749, *dessinateur du Garde-Meuble de la Couronne* 1784, died 1825), 91

Duplessis, Jean-Claude (silversmith and designer; *directeur artistique* at Sèvres 1745–1774, *sculpteur-fondeur-doreur du Roi* 1747, *orfèvre du Roi* 1758, died 1774), 161, 163, 182, 183

Durand, F., *fils* (*ébéniste*; active late nineteenth and early twentieth centuries), 47

E

Emes, Rebecca (silversmith; active from 1808, died 1828), 287, 293

F

Fallot (Sèvres painter and gilder; active 1773–1790), 178

Feuchère, L.-F. (*bronzier;* died 1828), 122, 137

Feuchère, Pierre-François (*bronzier; maître* 1763), 132

Fieffé, Jean-Jacques, *père* (clockmaker; active 1747–1789), 83

Folin, Nicolas-Alexandre (clockmaker; *maître* 1784), 92

Foliot, Nicolas-Quinibert (*menuisier;* born 1706, *maître* circa 1730, died 1776), 99

Fontaine, Jacques (Sèvres painter; active 1752–1775 and 1778–1807), 176

Forestier, Etienne-Jean (*bronzier; maître* 1764), 16

Forestier, Pierre-Auguste (*bronzier;* born 1755, died 1835), 16

Fortier, Alexandre (clockmaker; active second half of the eighteenth century), 86

Foullet, Antoine (*ébéniste*; born circa 1710, *maître* 1749, died 1775), 89

Fox, Charles, II (silversmith; active 1822–after 1838), 295, 296

Fray, James (silversmith; active 1819–after 1829), 301

G

Gaillard, R.: either Robert (engraver; born 1722, died 1785), or René (engraver; born circa 1719, died 1790), 158

Galle, André (*bronzier;* active late eighteenth century–early nineteenth century), 16, 127

Garden, Phillips (silversmith; active 1738–1763), 146

Garnier, Pierre (*ébéniste; maître* 1742, died circa 1800), 40

Garrard, Robert (silversmith; active by 1735, in partnership with John Wakelin [q.v.] 1776–1802, died 1818), 282, 290

Garrard, Robert, II (silversmith; born 1793, active by 1818, royal goldsmith 1830, crown jeweler 1843, died 1881), 297, 299

Gaultier, Jacques (carver; active first half of the eighteenth century), 111

Germain, François-Thomas (silversmith; born 1726, *orfèvre du Roi* 1748–1764, died 1791), 132, 148, 151

Germain, Thomas (silversmith; born 1673, *maître* 1720, *orfèvre du Roi* 1723, died 1748), 148, 150

Gobelins Manufactory, 4, 55, 56, 214, 215, 223–225

Golle, Pierre (*ébéniste*; active second half of the seventeenth century, died 1683), 54

Gouthière, Pierre (*bronzier;* born 1732, *maître* 1758, died 1813 or 1814), 121, 135, 141, 239

Gudin, Jacques (clockmaker; born 1706, *maître* 1726, died circa 1744), 78

H

Hacker, David (cabinetmaker; active circa 1770–1820), 240

Hackwood, William (Wedgwood modeler; active 1769–1832, died 1839), 15

Hauré, Jean (sculptor; active as *entrepreneur des Meubles de la Couronne* 1780–1788, died after 1796), 16, 103, 132

Hennell, David (silversmith; born 1712, active from 1736, retired 1772, died 1785), 274, 275

Hennell, Robert (silversmith; born 1741, active from 1763, died 1811), 284

Hennell, Samuel (silversmith; born 1778, active before 1802, died 1837), 284

Heurtaut, Nicolas (*menuisier;* born 1720, *maître* 1755, died after 1771), 98

Höroldt, Johann Gregor (Meissen painter; born 1696, chief painter 1720–1756 and 1763–1765, died 1775), 243

Huet, Jean-Baptiste (painter; born 1745, died 1811), 179

Hunter, George, I (silversmith; active 1748–1772), 276

Huquier, Jacques-Gabriel (engraver and designer; born 1695, died 1772), 147

J

Jacob, Georges (*menuisier;* born 1739, *maître* 1765, retired 1796, died 1814), 102, 104

Jacob-Désmalter et Cie (firm of *menuisiers* formed by Georges Jacob's younger son François-Honoré-Georges [born 1770, retired 1824, died 1841]; after 1825 the business was run by François' son Georges-Alphonse Jacob-Désmalter [born 1799, active 1803–1847, died 1870]), 105

Jacques, Maurice (painter and designer; born circa 1712, died 1784), 224, 225

Joubert, Gilles (*ébéniste*; born 1689, *ébéniste ordinaire du Garde-Meuble de la Couronne* 1758, *ébéniste du Roi* 1763–1774, died 1775), 32

Jubier, C. L. (engraver; active from 1760), 179

K

Kändler, Johann Joachim (Meissen modeler; born 1706, active 1731, chief modeler 1733, died 1775), 245

L

Lacroix—Roger Vandercruse (*ébéniste*; born 1728, *maître* 1755, died 1799), 12

Lalonde, Richard de (designer; active last decades of the eighteenth century), 16, 232

Lambert (silversmith; active late nineteenth century), 300

Lamerie, Paul de (silversmith; born 1688, active from 1712, died 1751), 269, 270

Langford, John, II (silversmith; active until circa 1770), 277

Lapina (clockmaker; dates unknown), 89

Laroche, Jacques-François-Louis de (Sèvres painter; active 1758–1800), 180

Latz, Jean-Pierre (*ébéniste*; born circa 1691, *ébéniste privilégié du Roi* before May 1739, died 1754), 26, 36, 37, 86

Laurent, André (engraver; born 1708, died 1747), 75

Le Bas, J.-P. (engraver; born 1707, died 1783), 171

Le Blond, Etienne-Claude (tapestry maker; active 1727–1751), 215

Le Brun, Charles (painter and designer; born 1619, director of the Gobelins Manufactory 1663, died 1690), 214

Ledoux, Jean-Pierre (painter; born 1735, active at Sèvres 1758–1761, died after 1786), 159

Leeke, Ralph (silversmith; active 1679–after 1714), 146

Le Guay, Etienne-Henry, *père* (Sèvres gilder; born 1721, active 1749–1773, 1777–1778, and 1780–1796), 179

Leleu, Jean-François (*ébéniste;* born 1729, *maître* 1764, retired 1792, died 1807), 44, 52, 67

Le Noir, Etienne (clockmaker; born 1699, *maître* 1717, died after 1778), 10, 38, 88

Lepaute, Pierre-Henry (clockmaker; born 1745, died 1805), 80

Le Roy, Charles (clockmaker; born 1726, died 1779), 90

Le Roy, Julien (clockmaker; born 1686, *maître* 1713, died 1759), 79, 85, 87

Lock, Matthias (furniture designer and maker; active by 1740, died 1765), 266

Lourdet, Philippe (Savonnerie carpet maker; active circa 1630–1670), 226

M

Mariette, Jean (engraver, publisher, and author; born 1654, died 1742), 38, 128

Marot, Daniel (designer; born 1663, died 1752), 54

Martin, Gilles-François (sculptor and modeler; born circa 1713, died 1795), 16

Martincourt, Etienne (sculptor and *bronzier;* died after 1789), 90, 124

Martinière, Antoine-Nicolas (enameler; born 1706; *émailleur du Roi* 1742, died 1784), 85, 87

Meissen Manufactory, 120, 243–246

Meissonier, Juste-Aurèle (architect, designer, and silversmith; born circa 1693, *architecte-dessinateur de la Chambre et du Cabinet du Roi* 1725, died 1750), 147

Mennecy Manufactory, 157

Méreaud, Pierre-Antoine, *l'aîné* (Sèvres painter and gilder; born circa 1735, active 1754–1791, died 1791), 173

Merlet, G. (enameler; active late eighteenth–early nineteenth century), 92

Merz, Johann Georg (engraver; born 1694, died 1762), 38

Meunier, Etienne (*menuisier;* active first half of the eighteenth century), 94

Meure, Peter (silversmith; active 1749–1773, in partnership with Peter Archambo [q.v.] 1749–1755), 272

Mewburn, Barak (silversmith; active 1826–after 1831), 294

Moitte, Jean-Guillaume (designer; born 1746, died 1810), 236

Molitor, Bernard (*ébéniste*; born 1730, *maître* 1787, died after 1819), 42

Mollet, Armand-Claude (architect; born 1660, died 1742), 111

Mollinger, Christian (clockmaker; born 1754, died 1826), 240

Monnet, Charles (painter; born 1732, died after 1808), 182

Monnoyer, Jean-Baptiste (painter; born 1636, died 1699), 213

Montigny, Philippe-Claude (*ébéniste*; born 1734, *maître* 1766, died 1800), 14

Morin, Jean-Louis (Sèvres painter; born 1732, active 1754–1787), 161, 171

N

Nantier (Sèvres *répareur;* active 1767–1776), 175

Neilson, Jacques (tapestry maker; born circa 1718, director of the Gobelins Manufactory low-warp looms 1759, died 1788), 224, 225

O

Oeben, Jean-François (*ébéniste*; born circa 1720, *ébéniste du Roi* 1754, *maître* 1761, died 1763), 31, 36, 37, 62, 63, 66

Osmond, Robert (*bronzier; maître* 1746, died 1789), 88

Oudry, Jean-Baptiste (painter; born 1668, director of the Beauvais Manufactory 1734, died 1755), 217–219

P

Parent, Aubert-Henri-Joseph (sculptor, designer, and architect; born 1753, died 1835), 230, 231

Petit, Nicolas (*ébéniste*; born 1732, *maître* 1761, died 1791), 30

Petitot, Ennemond-Alexandre (architect and designer; born 1727, died 1801), 204

Pierre, Jean-Baptiste-Marie (painter and designer; born 1713, *premier peintre du Roi* 1770, died 1789), 182

Pierre, Jean-Jacques, *le jeune* (Sèvres painter; born before 1752, active 1763–1800), 46

Pineau, Nicolas (architect and designer; born 1684, died 1754), 38

Pitts, Thomas (silversmith; active circa 1787), 280

R

Rand, John (silversmith; active 1704–after 1713), 268

Raskin, Henry (restorer; dates unknown), 5

Rehschuck (Meissen molder; active first half of the eighteenth century), 244

Reinicke, Peter (Meissen modeler; born 1715, active from 1743, died 1768), 120

Riesener, Jean-Henri (*ébéniste*; born 1734, active from circa 1754, *maître* 1768, *ébéniste ordinaire du Roi* 1774–1784, retired 1801, died 1806), 33, 50, 71

Risenburgh, Bernard van, II (*ébéniste; maître* before 1730, died 1765 or 1766), 9, 10, 11, 23, 24, 28, 34, 41, 61, 64, 75

Robins, Thomas (silversmith; active from circa 1801, died 1859), 289

Rode (carver; active second half of the eighteenth century), 104

Roentgen, David (*ébéniste*; born 1743, *maître* of Paris guild 1780, died 1807), 239

Romilly, Jean (clockmaker; born 1714, *maître* 1752, died 1796), 82

S

Saint Germain, Jean-Joseph de (*bronzier;* active by 1747 and after 1772), 81, 82

Salembier, Henri (designer; active by circa 1770, died 1820), 234

Saunier, Claude-Charles (*ébéniste*; born 1735, *maître* 1765, died 1807), 47

Savonnerie Manufactory, 226–228

Schiefer (Meissen molder; active first half of the eighteenth century), 243

Sené, Jean-Baptiste-Claude (*menuisier;* born 1748, *maître* 1769, died 1803), 103

Sèvres Manufactory, 46–49, 52, 68, 69, 73, 75, 162–183, 203

Sibelle, John (silversmith; active by 1759), 277

Sibley, Richard, I (silversmith; active from 1803, died 1836), 291

Simmons, William (silversmith; active from circa 1773), 285

Sioux, Jean-Charles, *l'aîné* (Sèvres painter; born circa 1716, active 1752–1792), 48

Smith, Thomas, II (silversmith; active after 1771), 279

Solle, Karel (clockmaker; active mid-nineteenth century), 79

Somersall, William Nathaniel (silversmith; active after 1824), 298

Spohn, P. (restorer; dates unknown), 26

Storr, Paul (silversmith; born 1771, active by 1792, died 1844), 286

Swift, John (silversmith; active 1728–circa 1773), 273

T

Tandart, Jean-Baptiste (Sèvres painter; born 1731, active 1754–1803), 47

Tardieu, P.-F. (engraver; born 1711, died 1771), 72

Templetown, Elizabeth, Lady (designer; born 1747, died 1823), 15

Teniers, David, *le jeune* (painter; born 1610, died 1690), 167, 171

Tessier, Louis (painter; born circa 1719, died 1781), 36, 224

Thomire, Pierre-Philippe (*bronzier;* born 1751, active at Sèvres from 1783, retired 1823, died 1843), 16, 91, 136, 181, 200

Tilliard, Jean-Baptiste, *fils* (*menuisier; maître* 1752, died 1797), 101

Triquet (carver; active second half of the eighteenth century), 104

V

Vallois, Nicolas (sculptor; born 1738, active through the 1780's), 103

Vandé, Jean-Baptiste-Emmanuel (Sèvres gilder; active 1753–1779), 73

Vandercruse, Roger, known as Lacroix (*ébéniste*; born 1728, *maître* 1755, died 1799), 12

Varin, Jean, III (medalist, sculptor, and goldsmith; born circa 1604, died 1672), 4

Vernansal, Guy-Louis (painter; born 1648, died 1729), 213, 215

Villamarina, J. E. (clockmaker; dates unknown), 83

Vincennes Manufactory, 120, 158–161, 246

Vincent, Henry-François, *le jeune* (Sèvres gilder; born 1723, active 1753–1806), 49

Voisin, Charles (clockmaker; born 1686, *maître* 1710, died 1760), 84

W

Wakelin, John (silversmith; active by 1776, partner with Garrard family), 282

Weisweiler, Adam (*ébéniste*; born 1744, *maître* 1778, died 1820), 15, 17, 49

X

Xhrouet, Marie-Claude-Sophie (Sèvres painter and gilder; born 1757, active 1772–1788, died 1788), 69

Y

Yvart, Baudrain, *père* (painter; born 1611, died 1690), 214

INDEX OF OWNERS

The following index includes the names of private owners and dealers. Named residences are also listed. Please note: references are to entry numbers, not page numbers.

A

Aaron, Didier, 16, 40, 140, 147, 197, 251

Abamelek-Lazarev, Princess (Marie Demidov), 7

Abdy, Sir Robert, 41

Aguado, Mme Alexandre (marquise de Las Marismas del Guadalquivir), 111

Alamagna family, 243

Albani, conte Francesco Castelbarco, 225

Alexander and Berendt, Ltd., 13, 25, 54, 56, 57, 89, 96, 133, 134, 185, 195, 228

Allen, Armin B., 162, 169, 175, 179

Allnat, John, 16

Alvarez de Toledo family, 48

Anchier, Gauthiot d', 3

Antique Porcelain Company, The, 63, 157, 161, 168, 169, 243

Ardmore House (Middlesex), 54

Arenberg, ducs d', 19

Argyll, Duchess of (Elizabeth Gunning), 41

Argyll, dukes of, 41

Artois, comte d', 18

Atholl, 8th Duke of (John George Murray, Marquess of Tullibardine), 63

Augustus I, Elector of Saxony and King of Poland, 243, 244, 246

Austria, archdukes of, 223

Aveline et Cie, 9, 16, 17, 21

B

B . . . , vicomtesse de, 107

Backer, Hans, 152

Bacon, Edward R., 184

Baillie-Hamilton, Hon. Mrs. Robert (Mary Gavin), 63

Ball, C., 28

Ball, W., 51

Balsan, Mme Jacques (Consuelo Vanderbilt), 188, 246

Bardac, Jacques, 137

Bardini, Ugo, 1, 249, 250

Bargigli, de, 171

Barker, Alexander, 67

Baroda, Maharanee of, 17, 238

Baudoint family, 53

Beauharnais, Eugène (Duke of Leuchtenberg), 105

Beaumont, Château de (Côte d'Or), 138

Beckett-Denison, Christopher, 17

Beckford, Susan (Duchess of Hamilton), 17

Beckford, William, 17

Beddard, Anne, 190

Bensimon, Gaston, 5, 153, 170, 184

Béraudière, Jacques, comte de, 100

Bernheimer, 55

Bertrand, P., 209

Best, Dr. Albert, 212

Beurdeley, Alfred-Emanuel-Louis, 207

Beurdeley, Louis-Auguste-Alfred, 207

Biron, Guillaume, marquis de, 311

Blair, C. Ledyard, 216

Blairman, H., and Sons, 248

Block, Sidney J., 37

Blohm, Otto and Magdalena, 165

Bohler, Julius, 237

Boore, William, 173

Botibol, J. M., 12, 20, 30, 61, 64

Bourbon, Louis-Alexandre de (comte de Toulouse), 213

Bourbon, Louis-Henri, duc de (prince de Condé), 147

Bourbon, Michael de, 214

Branicka, Christine, 38

Branicki, Count Jan Klemens, 38

Brougham, lords, 20

Brunswick-Lüneberg, dukes of, 154

Bucher, Alice, 223

Buckingham and Chandos, dukes of, 56, 153

Burat, Mme Louis, 202

Burdett, Sir Francis, Bt., 10

Burdett-Coutts, Angela, Baroness, 10

Burdett-Coutts, Hon. William Bartlett, 10

Bureau Seraudey, Antoinette (Mme d'Inval), 111

Burns, Major General Sir George, 187, 256

Burns, Mrs. Walter Hayes, 187, 256

Burrell, Sir Peter (1st Lord Gwydir), 80

Burton-Jones, Hugh, 160

Burton-Jones, Kathleen (Mrs. Gifford-Scott), 160

C

Caledon, Earl of, 228

Cambacérès, ducs de, 51

Cambacérès, Ives, comte de, 105, 193

Cameron, 58, 62, 129

Cam House (London), 27, 201

Caradoc, John Hobart (2nd Lord Howden), 11

Carlhian, André, 111

Carlhian, R. and M., 115, 117

Carnarvon, Countess of (Almina Wombwell), 68, 69

Carrington, Robert, 1st Lord, 150

Cartier, A., Ltd, 154

Cartier family, 154

Cassel van Doorn, Baron and Baroness, 45

Castiglione, 239
Catherine II, Empress of Russia, 60
Cei, P., 181
Chait, Ralph, 258, 259
Chanteloup, Château de, 138
Chantilly, Château de, 147
Chappey, Edouard, 58
Chastellux, comte de, 33
Château-sur-Mer (Newport, Rhode Island), 104
Chauvelin, Germain-Louis de (marquis de Grosbois), 215
Chester Beatty, Sir Alfred, 29, 32, 59, 70
Chinese Palace (Oranienbaum, near Saint Petersburg), 60
Choiseul-Praslin, duc de, 138
Cholmondeley, Marchioness of (Sybil Sassoon), 6
Christie, George, 261
Christner, Mrs. John W., 172, 174, 176, 177
Clermont-Tonnerre, comtesse de, 141
Cleveland, Grace Caroline, Duchess of, 168
Clifden, Leopold George Frederick, 5th Viscount, 67
Clumber (Nottinghamshire), 12
Colbert family, 23
Colorno, Palazzo di (near Parma), 130
Colyear, Caroline (Baroness Scarsdale), 146
Compiègne, Château de, 103, 132
Condé, Louis-Henri, prince de (duc de Bourbon), 147
Consolo, Philip R., 36
Conyngham, Jane, Marchioness of, 179
Cook, A., 262, 265
Coope, Octavius E., 42
Cornbury Park (Oxfordshire), 2
Cornillion, Château de (Loire), 53
Cotterstock Hall (Northamptonshire), 57
Coty, François, 58
Coudira, Château de (Prégny, Switzerland), 26
Coventry, George William, 7th Earl of, 167
Crag Hall (Lancashire), 25
Cressart, Guillaume, 111
Cressart, Hôtel (Paris), 111
Cronier, E., 58
Croome Court (Worcestershire), 167
Cumberland, dukes of, 154
Currie, L., 36
Curzon, Sir Nathaniel (1st Baron Scarsdale), 146

D

Daguerre, Dominique, 73
Dalva Brothers, 76, 104, 183, 205, 207, 211, 227, 230, 242, 255
Damour family, 53
Darnault, François-Charles, 29
Daublay, M. and Mme Robert, 133
Daval, 9
David-Weill, A. M., 153
David-Weill, D., 147, 149, 151, 153
Davies, Charles, 80
Dawes, Sophie (baronne de Feuchères), 111
Demidov, Marie (Princess Abamelek-Lazarev), 6
Demidov, Prince Anatole, 5
Demidov, Prince Paul, 7
Dodge, Anna Thomson, 28, 60, 73, 81, 82, 94, 100, 102, 103, 110, 139, 145, 219
Donaldson, 17
Donjeux, Vincent, 17
Double, Léopold, 102
Doucet, Mme, 115
Douilla, Goupil de, 31
Dresden, Residenz, 28
Drey, David, 9
Duché family, 111
Dudley, earls of, 4, 56, 167, 168
Dundas, Henry (5th Viscount Melville), 57
Dupuy, Mrs. H., 181
Duras, Emmanuel-Felicité, duc de, 32
Durlacher, George, 21
Duselschon, Mme, 26
Dutasta, Paul, 137
Duvaux, Lazare, 159
Duveen Brothers, 3, 22, 60, 63, 73, 81, 82, 94, 100, 102, 110, 111, 139, 145, 166, 167, 191, 219, 224, 304, 311

E

Elizabeth, Empress of Russia, 60
Ellsworth, Robert, 191
Elst, Violet van der, 4
Ephrussi, Henri, 86
Erlestoke Mansion (Wiltshire), 50
Ernst Augustus, King of Hanover, 154
Erroll, William and Elizabeth, 1st Earl and Countess of, 301
Espirito Santo, José and Vera, 10, 150
Espirito Santo family, 40
Exeter, Henry, 1st Marquess of, 282
Exeter, Henry George Brownlow, 4th Marquess of, 80

F

Fabius Frères, 241
Fabre, B., et Fils, 58, 62, 143
Fane, Lady Grace Adelaide (Countess of Londesborough), 64
Fane, Lieutenant Colonel Hon. Henry, 57
Farman, Mme Henry, 194
Faunce, Maria Sophia (Hon. Mrs. Wilfred Brougham), 20
Ferrières, Château de (Tarn), 83
Feuchères, baronne de (Sophie Dawes), 111
Fielden family, 11
Fitzgerald, Mrs. Derek C. (Violet Sassoon), 67, 124
Fitzhenry, J. H., 153
Fogg, Samuel, 80
Foley, lords, 4
Fontainebleau, Château de, 32, 99, 103, 257
Fonthill Abbey (Wiltshire), 17
Fonthill House (Wiltshire), 260

Ford, Henry, II, 193, 199
Foster, Kate, 156
Founès, S., 26
Foz, marquis da, 5
France, government of, 132
Freda, Mrs. Rose, 97
Frederick Augustus III, Elector of Saxony and King of Poland, 28
Frederick William III, King of Prussia, 240
French and Company, 14, 19, 37, 57, 68, 69, 72, 77–79, 80, 87, 92, 121, 131, 138, 140, 171, 172, 181, 215–217, 220, 222, 239, 244
Friedel, de, 133
Fulco de Bourbon, Mme, 214

G
Gallet, 19
Galveias family, 148
Garenne, Charles-Claude de Taillepied, seigneur de la, 99
Gary, Judge Elbert H., 63, 304
Gavin, Mary (Hon. Mrs. Robert Baillie-Hamilton), 63
George III, King of England, 154
Georgian Court (Lakewood, New Jersey), 22, 81, 82
Gifford-Scott, Mrs. (Kathleen Burton-Jones), 160
Gignoux, A., 118
Godefroy, François-Ferdinand-Joseph, 40
Goding, William, 168
Goldschmidt-Rothschild, Baroness Alexis de, 180
Goldschmidt-Rothschild, Baron Maximilian von, 120
Gonzales, Manuel, 79
Goode, William J., 182
Goodwood House (Sussex), 271, 286
Gort, John, 6th Viscount, 4
Gould, Anna (duchesse de Talleyrand), 5
Gould, George Jay, 22, 81, 82
Goury de Rosland, 158
Gramont, duc de, 115, 219
Greenway, Lee, 133
Greffuhle, Henri, comte de, 9, 102
Grimston Park (Yorkshire), 11
Grimthorpe, Edmund, 1st Lord, 67
Grosbois, marquis de (Germain-Louis de Chauvelin), 215
Guiness, Walter, 221
Guiraud, M. and Mme Louis, 92, 185
Gunning, Elizabeth (Duchess of Argyll), 41
Gwydir, 1st Lord (Sir Peter Burrell), 80

H
Hague, Lady, 263
Hamilton, dukes of, 17, 50
Hamilton Palace (Lanarkshire, Scotland), 17, 50
Hamsterly Hall (Durham), 4
Harcourt, 40
Harding, 179
Harlaxton Manor (Lincolnshire), 4
Harrington, R. L., Ltd., 207
Harris, Moss, 17
Hart, Mrs. Geoffrey, 264
Hartman, Alan, 191
Harvey, Lady, 63
Heathfield Park (Sussex), 67, 124
Hébert, 60
Helft, Jacques, 121, 146, 150, 193, 238
Hertford, Richard, 4th Marquess of, 48
Hillingdon, lords, 66, 77
Hirsch, Henry, 61
Hodgkins, E. M., 45, 220, 222
Houghton Hall (Norfolk), 6
Howden, John Hobart Caradoc, 2nd Lord, 11
Humann, Christian, 175

I
Inval, Jean-Louis Milon d', 111
Inverary Castle (Argyll, Scotland), 41
Iveagh, Edward, 1st Earl of, 221
Iveagh, Rupert, 2nd Earl of, 218

J
Johnson, Deane and Anne, 113, 164, 165
Josse, H. H. A., 58
Julliot, C. F., 5

K
Kahn, Samuel, 128
Kedleston Hall (Derbyshire), 146
Kelekian, D. G., 302
Kessler, George A., 226
Kevorkian, Hagop, 303, 305, 309, 310
King, H. J., 191
Klaber and Klaber, 155
Koenigsberg, Claus de, 166, 167
Koenigsberg, Paula de, 166, 167
Kraemer et Cie, 11, 13, 34, 90, 119, 125–127, 135, 142, 199
Kugel, Jacques, 84, 85, 95, 126, 231, 252

L
Labia, Dr. Joseph, 56, 168
Lacroix, Léon, 18
Laird, Henry James, 54
Lamon, Sidney J., 131
Lancut (Poland), 200
Landau, Nicolas, 93
Le Despencer family, 56
Lee, Ronald, 56
Lefortier, Mme Annette, 99
Lemaître, 171
Leningrad, Museums and Palaces Collections, 105
Leslie collection, 36
Leuchtenberg, dukes of, 105
Levy, 56
Lévy, Claude, 197
Lévy, Etienne, 31, 78, 197
Lévy, Gilbert, 159
Lévy, Olivier, 171, 172
Lewis and Simmons, 63

Lindon collection, 207
Lion, Adolphe, 144
Lock of Drylaw, Lord, 260
Loewi-Robertson Inc., 208, 210
Londesborough, Countess of (Lady Grace Adelaide Fane), 64
Londesborough, Lords, 11
Louis XV, King of France, 60
Louis XVI, King of France, 16, 42, 71, 90, 132, 182, 223, 224
Louis, Dauphin of France (1729–1765), 28
Louis, Grand Dauphin of France (1661–1711), 5, 54
Louise-Elisabeth of France, Madame (Duchess of Parma), 130
Louise of France, Madame, 32, 173
Louis-Philippe, King of the French, 213
Louvre, Palais du, 226
Lowengard, Jules, 49
Lubormirska, Princess Isabella, 200
Lugli, E., 181
Lullier, 38
Lurcy, Georges, 238
Luxembourg, Palais du, 103, 132
Lydig, Rita, 131

M

Maclean, 17
Maisons, Château de, 18
Mallet family, 112
Mallett and Son Ltd., 144, 179
Marais, Château de (Seine-et-Oise), 5
Margadale of Islay, Lord (John Greville Morrison), 260
Maria Feodorovna, Czarina of Russia, 73, 224
Marie-Antoinette, Queen of France, 71, 102–104
M. Marin, 17
Marismas del Guadalquivir, marquise de Las (Mme Alexandre Aguado), 111
Marly-Le-Roi, Château de (Yvelines), 112
Marquis collection, 149
Masurel family, 195
Mazarin, duchesse de, 135, 141
Mecklenburg-Strelitz, Helen, Duchess of (Princess of Saxe-Altenburg), 60
Medinaceli, Duke of, 79
Medina-Sidonia, dukes of, 48
Melin, Mme Claude, 112
Mello, Château de (Oise), 3
Mello e Castro family, 148
Mellon, Paul, 230
Meloney, Mr. and Mrs. William Brown, 157
Melville, 5th Viscount (Henry Dundas), 57
Menars, marquis de, 151
Mendl, Lady (Elsie de Wolfe), 253
Mentmore Towers (Buckinghamshire), 44, 122, 132
Mereworth Castle (Kent), 56, 163
Metropolitan Museum of Art, The, 242
Michel, 103
Michel, Charles, 51
Miller, R. W., 265
Mills, Sir Charles, 66
Mobilier Royal, 132
Moltke, Count, 159
Montbrillon, Château de (Aix-en-Provence), 209
Montebello, 2e duc de (Napoléon Lannes), 207
Morgan, J. Pierpont, 166, 167, 306
Morgan, J. Pierpont, Jr., 166, 167
Morgan, Junius, 151
Moritzburg, Schloss (near Dresden), 28
Morrison, Alfred, 260
Mortemart Rochechouart, ducs de, 136
Moulinet family, 149
Murray Scott, Sir John, 45, 48, 178

N

Napier, Robert, 182
Narishkine, Prince, 47
Newcastle, 7th Duke of (Henry Pelham Archibald Douglas), 12
Northbrook, Florence, Countess of, 160
North Mymms Park (Hertfordshire), 187, 256
Northumberland, dukes of, 258, 259, 269
Norton, Martin, 152

O

Odiot, Maison, 232–236
Ojjeh, Akram, 38
Orléans, Louis-Philippe, duc d', 132
Orléans, Louis-Philippe-Joseph, duc d', 132

P

Paget, Gerald C., 209
Palais Rose (Paris), 5
Palais Royal (Paris), 132
Palewski, Mme Gaston (Violette de Talleyrand), 5
Pálffy, Count János, 78, 239
Pallott, 265
Parguez-Perdreau, 226
Parma, Duchess of (Madame Louise-Elisabeth of France), 130
Partridge, Frank, Ltd., 31, 36, 39, 45, 52, 66, 108, 122, 131, 190, 194, 202, 238, 247, 266
Partridge, John, 71
Partridge (Fine Arts) Ltd., 130, 199, 256
Patiño, Antenor, 9, 125
Paul, Prince, of Yugoslavia, 7
Paul I, Czar of Russia, 224
Pavlovsk, Palace of (near Saint Petersburg), 73, 145, 224
Peel, David, 230
Petit Trianon, 71, 102, 104
Pfaueninsel (Berlin), 239
Phillips, S. J., 150, 269
Pilkington, 167
Plender of Sunridge, Lord, 263
Polès, Mme, 155
Pompadour, Hôtel (Paris), 168
Pompadour, marquise de, 168
Pope's Manor (Berkshire), 67, 124, 150
Porges, Jules Paul, 216

Portela, Juan, 240
Portland, Duke and Duchess of, 163
Portugal, royal family of, 216
Potocka, Marianna (Szymanowska), 38
Potocki, Count Alfred, 200
Potsdam, Neues Palais, 241
Powis, earls of, 16
Provence, Louis-Stanislas-Xavier and Marie-Josephine-Louise, comte and comtesse de, 211
Prussian Royal Collection, 240
Puiforcat, 151
Pyrford Court (Surrey), 218

R

Radcliffe, Sir Everard, Bt., 204
Ragaller, Herr, 240
Rambouillet, Château de, 213
Redfern, 56
Redford, William, 96
Regainy, 156
Reitz, Baroness Marie de, 239
Reviczky A.G., Lovice, 180, 204
Richmond and Gordon, dukes of, 271, 286
Robert, Christie, 106
Roberts, Richard G., 74
Robinson, Eric, 163
Robinson, Sir Joseph C., Bt., 56, 168
Rochefoucauld, comte Philippe de La, 138
Rockefeller, Mrs. John D., Jr. (Martha Baird), 63, 304
Rockefeller, Nelson, 168
Römer, Galerie, 223
Rosebery, Countess of (Hannah de Rothschild), 44, 122, 132
Rosebery, earls of, 44, 122, 132
Rosenbaum, I., 205
Rosenberg and Stiebel, 23, 38, 41, 43, 46, 49, 65, 75, 80, 86, 106, 120, 123, 137, 156, 159, 166, 167, 192, 198, 200, 213
Rose Terrace (Grosse Pointe Farms, Michigan), 28, 60, 73, 81, 82, 94, 100, 102, 103, 110, 139, 145, 219
Rossignol, Jean, 148
Rothschild, Baron Adolphe de, 308
Rothschild, Alfred de, 52, 68, 69, 108
Rothschild, Baron Alphonse de, 38, 39, 46, 49, 123
Rothschild, Annie de (Hon. Mrs. Eliot Yorke), 26
Rothschild, Sir Anthony de, Bt., 26, 217, 220, 222
Rothschild, Baronne Cecilie de, 6
Rothschild, Baroness Clarice de, 38, 39, 46, 49, 123
Rothschild, Edmund de, 52, 108
Rothschild, Baron and Baronne Edouard de, 48
Rothschild, Baron Edouard de, 35, 83
Rothschild, Baron Gustave Salomon de, 6
Rothschild, Baron Guy de, 35, 83
Rothschild, Hannah de (Countess of Rosebery), 44, 122, 132
Rothschild, Baron Henri de, 121
Rothschild, Lionel de, 32, 108
Rothschild, Baron Louis de, 211
Rothschild, Baron Mayer Alphonse de, 35, 83
Rothschild, Baron Mayer Amschel de, 44, 122, 132
Rothschild, Baron Nathaniel de, 38, 39, 46, 49, 123
Rothschild collection, 10, 137, 305
Rouvière, Mme, 26
Rudding Park (Yorkshire), 204
Russian Imperial Collections, 73, 145

S

Sabet, Habib, 48, 73
Sackville, Victoria, Lady, 48, 178
Saget collection, 157
Sainsbury, Wilfred J., 156
Saint-André-des-Arts (Paris), 226
Saint-Cloud, Château de, 16, 42
Saint-Cloud, marquis de, 90
St. George, Mrs. Evelyn, 27, 201
Saint-Vrain, Château de (Seine-et-Oise), 136
Salomon, William, 311
San Donato Palace (Pratolino, near Florence), 5
Sassoon, Mr. and Mrs. Meyer, 67, 124, 150
Sassoon, Sir Philip, Bt., 6
Sassoon, Sybil (Marchioness of Cholmondeley), 6
Sassoon, Violet (Mrs. Derek C. Fitzgerald), 67, 124
Savedra, Carreras, 121
Savoy, royal house of, 256
Saxe-Altenburg, Helen, Princess of (Duchess of Mecklenburg-Strelitz), 60
Saxe-Teschen, Albert and Marie-Christine, Duke and Duchess of, 223
Scarsdale, barons, 146
Scépeaux de Beaupreau, Elisabeth-Louise-Adélaïde de, 111
Schiff, John L., 5, 42, 68, 69, 101, 141, 158, 173, 178, 189, 215, 226, 302, 306, 307
Schiff, Mortimer L., 5, 42, 68, 69, 101, 141, 158, 173, 178, 189, 215, 226, 302, 306, 307
Schnyder von Wartensee, Paul, 245
Schratt, Katherine, 237
Schutz, Matthew, Ltd., 97, 98, 109, 186, 188, 191, 206, 246, 257
Segoura, Maurice, 26, 136
Seibert, C. J., 311
Seillière, Baron Achille, 3
Seligmann, 67
Seligmann, Arnold, 9, 14, 226
Seligmann, Arnold, Rey and Co., 22, 33
Seligmann, François-Gérard, 14, 107, 116, 132, 193, 227
Seligman, Germain, 227
Seligmann, Jacques, 45, 48, 58, 116, 121, 178, 221, 227
Sellin, Neil, 114, 258, 259
Sère, Claude, 122, 254
Seymour, Henry, 131
Shandon collection, 182
Shrigley-Feigel, Mrs. S., 25

Simmons, H. J., 10
Simon, Norton, 3, 111, 224
Sloan-Kettering Institute for Cancer Research, The, 168
Smith, Sir Herbert, 4
Souza, Guedes de, 31, 45
Steinitz, Bernard Barouch, 53, 128, 195
Stephens, Mrs. Lyne, 173
Stern, Mrs. Benjamin, 144
Stiebel, Hans, 193
Stowe House (Buckinghamshire), 56
Summer Palace (Beijing), 260
Sutch, 21
Swinton Settled Estates, Trustees of, 196
Symonds, R. W., 263
Symons, Henry, and Co., 68, 69
Szechenyi, Countess Laszlo (Gladys Vanderbilt), 50, 80
Szymanowska, Marianna (Potocka), 38

T

Talleyrand, duchesse de (Anna Gould), 5
Talleyrand, Violette de (Mme Gaston Palewski), 5
Thomas, J. Rochelle, 175
Thorne, Mrs. Landon K., 186
Toulouse, comte de (Louis-Aléxandre de Bourbon), 213
Trévise, 5e duc de (Edouard Mortier), 105
Trevor and Co., 9
Tuileries, Palais des, 90, 103
Tullibardine, Marquess of (John George Murray, 8th Duke of Atholl), 63
Tyttenhanger Park (Hertfordshire), 228

U

Union Artistique, 111
Uthemann, F. F., 59
Uzès, duchesse d', 213

V

Vanderbilt, Consuelo (Mme Jacques Balsan), 188, 246
Vanderbilt, Cornelius, 50, 80
Vanderbilt, Gladys (Countess Laszlo Szechenyi), 50, 80
Vanderbilt, William K., 50, 80
Vandermeersch, 157
Vandyck, 42
Varenne, La Cour de, 8
Vernon House (London), 77
Versailles, Château de, 32, 99, 100, 182
Victoria, Frederick, Inc., 93, 144
Villa Demidov (Pratolino, near Florence), 7
Villafranca, Marquess of, 48
Vorontsov, Count, 60

W

Wallace, Sir Richard, 45, 48, 178
Walters, Henry, 33, 45, 47, 179, 217
Wartensee, Paul Schnyder von, 245
Warwick, earls of, 247
Watney, O. V., 2
Watson Taylor, George, 50
Weiller, René, 11
Wertheimer, Asher, 167
Wertheimer, Samuel, 50
Westminster, dukes of, 266
Westmorland, Jane, Countess of, 57
Wetmore, Edith M. K. and Maude A. K., 104
Wettin, Prince Ernst Heinrich von, 28
Wildenstein, Daniel, 38
Wildenstein, Georges, 38
Williams, Winifred, Ltd., 155, 160, 163, 182, 245
Willmot-Horton, 5th Bt. (Sir George Lewis), 293
Witley Court (Worcestershire), 4
Wolfe, Elsie de (Lady Mendl), 253
Wombwell, Almina (Countess of Carnarvon), 68, 69
Wood, R. M., 179
Worsch, Edgar, 191

Y

Yerkes, Charles T., 302
Yorke, Hon. Mrs. Eliot (Annie de Rothschild), 26
Yvon, Madame d', 227

Z

Zuylen, Baroness van, 106, 192